Better Stock Trading

Money and Risk Management

Better Stock Trading

Money and Risk Management

Daryl Guppy

John Wiley & Sons (Asia) Pte Ltd

Published in 2003 by John Wiley & Sons (Asia) Pte Ltd
2 Clementi Loop #02-01, Singapore 129809

This publication is designed to provide general information in regard to the subject matter and it is sold with the understanding that neither the Publisher, Editor or Author are engaged in providing legal, accounting or other professional advice or services and do not in any way warranty the accuracy or appropriateness of any of the formulae or instructions discussed in the Publication nor provide any warranty that use of any of the same may not cause injury, illness or damage to the user. Readers should seek appropriate advice from suitable qualified professionals or obtain independent advice or verification of the relevance and appropriateness of the use of any formula or instructions prior to use of these in relation to any of their activities.

All charts created by MetaStock®
© Daryl Guppy 2002
Email *100035.406@compuserve.com*   Internet *www.guppytraders.com*

Disclaimer
The material in this publication is of the nature of general comment only, and neither purports nor intends to be advice. Readers should not act on the basis of any matter in this publication without considering (and if appropriate, taking) professional advice with due regard to their own particular circumstances. The decision to trade and the method of trading is for the reader alone. The author and publisher expressly disclaim all and any liability to any person, whether a purchaser of this publication or not, in respect of anything and of the consequences of anything done or omitted to be done by any such person in reliance, whether whole or partial, upon the whole or any part of the contents of this publication.

■   Other Wiley Editorial Offices:
111 River Street, Hoboken, NJ, 07030, USA
The Atrium, Southern Gate, Chichester PO19 8SQ, England
John Wiley & Sons (Canada) Ltd, 22 Worcester Road, Rexdale, Ontario M9W 1L1,Canada
John Wiley & Sons Australia Ltd, 33 Park Road (PO Box 1226), Milton, Queensland 4064, Australia
Wiley – VCH, Pappelallee 3, 69469 Weinheim, Germany

■   Library of Congress Cataloging in Publication Data
ISBN 0-470-82101-9

Typeset in 12/14.4 point, Times New Roman by M. G. Dorett.
Printed in Singapore by Saik Wah Press Pte Ltd.
10 9 8 7 6 5 4 3 2

CONTENTS

FOREWORD

by Martin J. Pring

Author of *Getting Started in Technical Analysis*

There are many books available that make wild claims about the ease of making money in the financial markets. Others offer trading "secrets" revealed for the "first" time. The implication from all these texts is that it is a snap to trade your way to a financial nirvana. Just read the book and collect the profits. Unfortunately, as any professional will tell you, the reality of the marketplace is quite different. I won't deny that there are some situations where the neophyte will hit it rich with a lucky streak — but that's all it is: luck. It is surprising how good luck can unexpectedly reverse on a dime, as yesterday's financial genius is exposed for the inexperienced neophyte that he really is.

In *Better Stock Trading*, Daryl Guppy tells it the way it really is. No hype, no tripe — just cold, hard facts from someone who has been there and done it. It is really summed up in the closing paragraph of the preface: "How we manage risk determines how well we trade." I couldn't agree more. Those who give precedence to earning profits over managing risk are doomed to failure. In my seminars, I often make this point using the following example.

The importance of managing losses

	Capital ($)	Profit/Loss (%)	Profit/Loss amount ($)	Ending ($)
Trade 1	100.00	– 50	50.00	50.00
Trade 2	50.00	50	25.00	75.00
Trade 3	75.00	10	75.00	82.50
Trade 4	82.50	10	83.00	90.80
Trade 5	90.80	10	9.10	99.90

The starting amount of capital is $100. The first trade is a losing one that returns a loss of 50% and leaves an ending balance of $50 to begin the next trade. The next four trades are winners. The second trade increases by 50%, or $25, and leaves us with an ending balance of $75. The next three trades each make 10%. This gives us a total percentage gain in four trades of 80%. You would think that being down 50% and then up 80% would offer a great rate of return, yet when the calculation is made you are no further ahead. We are still a fraction under our starting capital. Concentrating on managing risk and cutting that initial loss would have returned a much higher rate of return.

This book is conveniently laid out in four parts. Part 1, "Performance Profiling," introduces us to the concept of risk and examines how different categories of traders deal with it. Traders apply a variety of trading strategies. This part of the book describes three important ones: trend, breakout, and support/resistance. Daryl Guppy tells us that there is a distinction between *timing the market* and *time in the market*. Charles Dow, the father of technical analysis, once said words to the effect that pride of opinion has been responsible for more losses than all other opinions combined. What he meant was that many traders, when they enter a position that subsequently goes against them, become converts to the "buy/hold" approach as they quickly decide that they are now in it for the "long term." Daryl Guppy explains that this is a cop-out and demonstrates that, in most situations, because of the time element, it leads to sub-par returns.

It is no coincidence that the subject of Part 2, protecting capital, precedes protecting profits, the subject of Part 3. That is because the number one objective of all professionals is to maintain principal. If you lose all your capital, you are out of business. By the same token, it is still necessary to protect profits as much as possible, because we are all subject to the temptations of greed and expect profitable positions to continue to grow. However, all trends eventually reverse, and unless profit protection strategies are put in place, it's likely that black ink will quickly dissolve into red.

The final part of the book, titled "Protect Portfolios," teaches us that portfolio risk overrides the risk management of individual trades. As a shopkeeper you can write off some of the inventory and survive, but you cannot write off the store and continue in business. The same is true for traders. Managing individual trades is fine, but you must also ensure that you keep an eye on the big picture by managing the portfolio. This part also explains the concept of diversification, along with how to judge performance against specific benchmarks.

Better Stock Trading won't make you rich overnight, or even over two or three nights! However, Daryl Guppy has laid out the rules, which, if faithfully followed, will enable you to achieve above-average returns, and that is all any serious market participant can ever hope to achieve.

Martin J. Pring
International Institute for Economic Research, Inc., Sarasota, Florida,
United States
December 2002
Martin J. Pring (www.pring.com) is the author of *Breaking the Black Box* and *Getting Started in Technical Analysis.*

PREFACE
CASH STACKS

Most of us dream of having a love affair with money. For many years I resisted this temptation. I subscribed to the view that money is made round to go around. No sooner did my pay check arrive than it was gone, spent on recreation and daily necessities.

It was a frugal farmer's wife who introduced me to the idea that money is made flat to stack. She believed that every spare dollar should be stacked away in a bank account. It took 10 years for this idea to sink in before I started banking spare cash instead of spending it.

It took a little longer for me to discover how money multiplies when it is stacked in just the right place. In the financial market it has a real opportunity to multiply. Correct stacking turns good trades into fabulous winners. Just cutting losses quickly is not enough to turn trading income into wealth. Money management techniques magnify returns, but most methods apply to institutions and funds.

Private traders who trade just their own account are most often undercapitalized. We simply do not have enough money in the market to achieve the diversity, the economy of scale, or the size of investment required to effectively apply many institutional money management techniques. Some private traders turn to derivatives, futures, options, and warrants markets to achieve the leverage they need to magnify returns. Often they also unwittingly magnify the risk in a trade.

This book examines a small selection of money management methods suitable for private traders. Some have been mentioned briefly in magazines, including *Stocks and Commodities*, *Active Trader*, and *Your Trading Edge*. They are examined in much greater detail here. The book is not written for those with millions of dollars invested in the stock market. It is written for those with $21,000, $60,000, $150,000 or so in the market.

Most of my income comes from trading Australian and some Asian markets. These are the methods I use, and many of the examples in the chapters that follow are personal trades. These methods are not perfect, although they are battle tested across many international markets. I offer them as possibilities you might like to consider for your own journey from Trader Average to Trader Success. You may disagree with some of the methods, but the general principle remains true for all markets: we grow capital by carefully managing losses. We do not grow capital by concentrating on profit.

This book is not intended to be a comprehensive guide to money management. Readers looking for more detailed analysis, and for a variety of methods, should turn to the other authors mentioned in the following chapters. Please remember that many of their methods require significant modification for use with small accounts.

FOUR TRADERS
We enlist the help of some typical traders throughout the book to demonstrate various techniques. They are Traders Novice, Average, Success, and Superstar. There is a little of each of them in every reader. We also have the occasional visit from Trader Lucky.

The differences between Trader Novice and Trader Superstar come from the way they understand and manage risk, The amount of money they have, their relative skill levels, and the number and size of their winning trades will also contribute to their performance, but the heart of the matter is the way they manage risk. The distribution of returns from successful trades is generally the same for each of these traders, as shown in the figure opposite.

Most trades deliver average returns of around 10%. The analysis is correct, but the trade does not perform well. A reasonable number of trades return between 20% and 30%. The bonus returns come from just one or two exceptional trades where everything comes together. The trade analysis is correct, price leverage helps increase profits, and the exit timing is excellent.

Trading performance

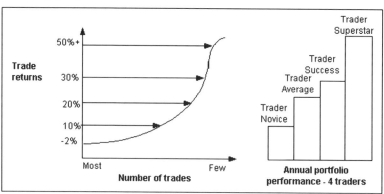

We cannot identify these exceptional trades in advance. When they happen, we need to recognize them quickly. Then we use one of several money management strategies to boost the trade performance and its contribution to our annual trading results. Trader Novice does not understand these skills, so he adds perhaps 10% to his portfolio capital during the year. Trader Superstar has a similar distribution curve to Trader Novice, but uses money management to collect a far superior return on portfolio capital. Understanding these methods is the subject of this book.

Our purpose is to explore some approaches to risk and money management that do not depend on technical and chart analysis. We assume you are already skilled at locating a trend change, recognizing an up trend, and eventually deciding when the trend changes to a downtrend. We do not cover trading techniques in detail. Instead, we explore the way money manipulation improves, or hinders, your trading performance no matter what your skill level.

We do not intend to tell you there is only one way to approach money management issues. There are many different approaches suitable for small accounts. Our objective is to show you some of the ways trading performance is boosted by better money management and by a better understanding of risk and its impact on your portfolio. Ultimately, you may choose to select just one or two, if any, of these techniques. The choice is yours and the choice is as individual as every trader.

Our focus is on the stock, or equity, market. This is the bread and butter of trading. We ignore the fancy toppings with twists and twirls available from trading options, warrants, futures, and other derivatives. These have different risk profiles and different money management strategies based on the leverage they offer. Traders interested in these particular strategies should turn to *Schwager on Futures* by Jack Schwager, or *Options as a Strategic Investment* by Lawrence McMillan, for more specialized and expert analysis.

SPREADSHEETS

The exploration of money management rests heavily on spreadsheets. In this book we keep these to a minimum and summarize results in chart displays. We use 12 Excel spreadsheet templates. They are available as the Better Trading pak from www.guppytraders.com. They are quite simple in their construction. We have not used macros or complex programming to create an eye-catching spreadsheet. We want users to modify these templates to suit their own purposes, or to use them as a base for further development. The templates are not password protected. They are locked. To unlock them, simply go to TOOLS and select PROTECTION. Then select UNPROTECT WORKSHEET.

The price charts in this book are created by MetaStock. Data comes from Just Data, KeyQuotes, and Partitech. The charts in Chapter 22, contributed by Alan Hull, are created by SuperCharts.

Our objective is to build better trades by applying leverage. The shape and content of this book has been greatly improved by the leveraged assistance provided by others. Good friends and fellow traders, Robert Deel in the United States and Sunny Low in Malaysia, contributed specialist chapters detailing the tactics used in their markets to turn analysis to success by better trade execution. Eminent technician, author, and colleague, Martin Pring, prepared the foreword. My office assistant, Leehoon Chong, ploughed through the early drafts, diligently correcting spelling and unusual grammar, and highlighting obscure passages. Ivy Batten verified mathematical accuracy. My mother Patricia proofread the final draft while noting that inserting punctuation marks in the same muddled way as letters was taking dyslexia to extremes. Without a suggestion from Dianne Maurer the title for the book might have been different. The people who read our weekly newsletter and visit www.guppytraders.com have all contributed to the production of this book. I hope it meets your expectations.

We have many newsletter subscribers, all of whom are allocated passwords with which to download the newsletter each week. To a good Chinese friend in Singapore, Nicholas Teo, I allocated a password including the combination 8884. The combination of three eights is auspicious, but the number four should be avoided. When spoken, it sounds similar to 死, the character for the Mandarin word meaning "death." Nicholas asked if the number could be changed. I explained I had deliberately included a four in the combination to remind him that every trade carries a risk of financial death.

How we manage risk determines how well we trade. Money management is the key to better trading. This book introduces you to a selection of techniques suitable for traders with small accounts. It shows you some ways to stack your trading returns so that they multiply. Please read on and prosper.

Daryl Guppy
Darwin, Northern Territory, Australia
December 2002

Part 1

Performance Profiling

ONE

BOOM OR BUST?

Rich or poor? Boom or bust? The choice is often ours, but what really makes the difference to the result? In the financial markets the difference comes from money management. This can be learned, and it uses techniques mastered with simple spreadsheets and easy rules. The objective is to take a small amount of cash and, by trading the market, consistently turn it into a larger pile. In this book our focus is on better ways to turn cash into capital through better trading.

We delude ourselves with comforting lies if we think the difference between wealth and poverty is just about being born with money. This does not explain how money is used to make money.

We all start with some cash, and we need to keep it so that it can grow. The financial markets are the most effective way of putting money to work. They are also a very effective way of losing money very quickly if you place faith in blind luck, in selected blue chip companies such as Enron or WorldCom, or in investment funds which focus on fees and commissions just for matching the performance of the market.

By selecting this book, you have shown you are ready to move beyond the commonly accepted notions that prevent ordinary people from effectively participating in the growth of capital available from the financial markets.

Money management is the secret separating average traders from successful traders, and superstar traders from successful traders. There are many different ways to use money management techniques to increase profits and returns from trading. We look at just a few and show how these are modified so that they are suitable for small traders with limited accounts. The right money management helps your trading boom. Select the wrong, and often common, approaches, and your portfolio goes bust.

Money management is not just for the funds and institutions, but it requires some modification to work for us. Our portfolios are measured in thousands of dollars, rather than millions. Our survival is important to each of us, and money management of individual trades, and of portfolios, helps us reach this goal.

We work with five traders in this book. The first is Trader Average. You probably know him, or someone like him. He has lots of fun in the market, making a few dollars in good times, and struggling in weak and nervous markets. The second is Trader Success. She trades full-time, and trading is her primary source of income. You know of these people by reputation. This is where you want to be.

The third is Trader Superstar. There are not many traders who fit this category. They represent the pinnacle of trading achievement. We know them from their books and interviews in specialist publications. We use their methods to help improve our trading success. The fourth is Trader Lucky. He is a mythical trader who buys at the very bottom and sells at the very top. He is the friend of a friend whose uncle knows the managing director. This financial media creation is an urban myth, but we can use his performance as a benchmark. Trader Novice also makes an appearance, but we do not work with her much in this book. The material we cover works best with more developed trading skills.

HOW CAN I IMPROVE MY TRADING?

This chapter is designed to answer just one question: *How can I improve my trading results most effectively?* The chart displayed in Figure 1.1 summarizes the best answer. This is the path to success for Trader Average.

Trader Average latches onto a winner 62.5% of the time. Out of 16 trades he expects to win 10. His performance is terrible when he first starts. Each of his six losing trades sacrifices 10% of his trading capital. This does not sound a lot, and many new traders lose more than this. Over 16 trades this strategy results in a 19.2% loss of trading capital. Losses are cushioned by trading successes.

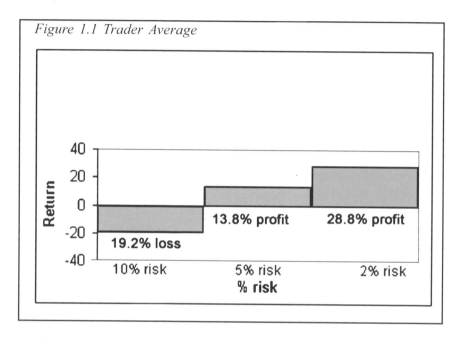

Figure 1.1 Trader Average

Apply just one money management technique and Trader Average turns the same win/loss ratio into a trading approach generating the 28.8% profit shown in the third column. He does this by reducing the loss in each losing trade to 2% of his total trading capital.

Sound too hard? Just by reducing the loss to 5% of total trading capital in each of the six losing trades, Trader Average turns a losing experience into a 13.8% profit.

This is one of the most important charts in this book. If you already completely understand and appreciate the impact of this on your trading success, then this book is not for you. If you want to find out more about how various money management strategies are used to achieve these results, then the rest of this book is written for you.

WORK SMARTER, NOT HARDER

When I first started trading I believed the best way to improve was to become more skilled. The more I could learn, the better I should perform. The result was a very large library of trading books, and a moderate increase in trading success. We all need to master the tools of technical analysis. Understanding how they work and when they are best applied is an important part of developing the skills of trading — in theory.

When it comes time to put this theory into action in the market, we discover many unexpected psychological barriers to our success. We do not have much money when we start trading, so we take a lot of time to decide on each trade. Often the first trades are easy and turn into effortless winners. This is poor preparation for the inevitable losses, because we do not know how to react. When losses do come, most times we just hold on and hope. The result is a trading portfolio littered with long-term investments in the vain hope that, given time, some of these fallen stocks may rise again.

The market provides the most expensive self-education course available. Standing knee deep in blood from losing trades, we are easily distracted by the promise of trading systems developed by other people. These approaches may work very well for others, but unless they match our growing and changing understanding of, and appetite for, risk, they work poorly for us.

Some people buy an expensive promise of trading success delivered by black box trading systems. Typically these are priced at an attractive $3,000 to $8,000. You might be told that there are only a few licensed copies left so you need to be fast. It is a sure way to a small fortune for the promoters of this software, but rarely a successful solution for the private trader.

HARD WORK

A less expensive method takes us back to the grindstone of hard work, of more study, and endless system testing and evaluation. It starts with reading about other trading approaches and testing them yourself. We do this for readers in our weekly newsletter.

At some stage we all question whether this is worthwhile. I believe the answer is "Yes," but I also recognize that this is "grunt" work. It forces us to work harder for incremental rewards, instead of working smarter for much more significant improvements in our performance. The big danger is that while we work harder, we also chew up our trading capital. By the time we know enough to succeed consistently, we may not have enough trading capital to make success possible.

Working harder also fails to acknowledge the way the burden of work increases while the return diminishes. Once I had the opportunity to climb the rigging on a tall sailing ship. The climb to the first crow's-nest at the lowest yard-arm was relatively easy. The climb to the second crow's-nest was much more difficult, even though the distance was shorter. The climb to the top of the mast was nerve-wracking and seemed almost impossible, yet it was the shortest distance of all. The same applies with developing trading skills.

Armed with just a little knowledge, Trader Novice calls the direction of a trend successfully 50% of the time. With more knowledge and skill, Trader Average finds it relatively easy to boost the success rate to 60%. This means that for every 10 trades he enters, only four are losers, or unsuccessful. Notice that we say nothing about where the four losing trades occur, nor do we say how big the profits are in the winning trades. An up-front series of four losing trades in a row is demoralizing and reduces capital significantly. A series of small winning trades does not compensate for a single large loss.

Those considering trading as a regular way to improve their income are generally working at around the 60% success rate. There are many traders in this grouping.

Getting from 60% to 70% is much more difficult. For every 10 trades, only three are failures. This success rate is sufficiently high for Trader Success to realistically consider trading as a full-time occupation. To turn this sustainable trading into a major success, we shoot for an 80% success rate to become Trader Superstar. This is like the top of the mast. Very few people make it to this level. And once they have achieved this success rate, it is very difficult to maintain. Often success comes from the mastery of just one set of market conditions. When the conditions change, the success rate declines dramatically. Most commonly this is called "confusing a bull market with brains."

There are traders who consistently achieve a success rate higher than 80%. Some of them are interviewed in Jack Schwager's *Market Wizards* books. These books are an excellent place to research trading styles and to learn about the level of successful trading enjoyed by these trading superstars. Just a few of the traders interviewed lay claim to a success rate greater than 80% — and these are market wizards. If these global masters cannot move much beyond an 80% success rate, then what are our chances?

The real answer is that our chance of dramatic improvement in skills and techniques is not great. Sure, we move from Trader Novice to Trader Average status relatively easily. Reaching the first crow's-nest, we find many others perched at the same level — around the 60% success rate. Moving to the next level is difficult. It takes a lot of time, and a lot of experience. It means honing trading skills to the extent where you understand your trading edge.

Let's say we succeed in reaching the 80% success rate. How much better is our trading going to be? The answer is "Not all that much." Figure 1.2 is based on the same set of trading results used in Figure 1.1. All losing trades lose 2% of total trading capital. The first column shows Trader Average with a 62.5% win rate. This gives a 28.8% return for the period.

The second column shows the result for Trader Success with the win rate increased to 68.75% — close to seven out of 10 trades. We retain the same winning trades as used in the first column. We change just one of the losing trades into a winner, lifting the win percentage to 68.75%. These winning trades return a profit equal to the median profit on the winning trades used in the first column. The result is a 4.8% increase in profits to 33.6% for the year. Remember, getting from average to successful — from the first crow's-nest to the second — is difficult, but not impossible. Typically it takes years of trading experience in many different market conditions.

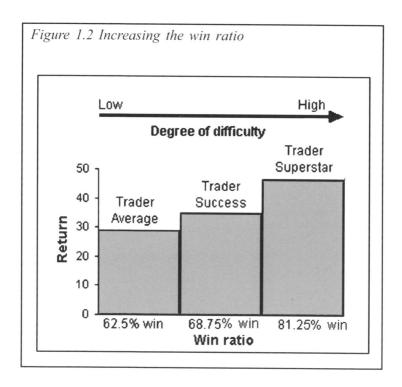

Figure 1.2 Increasing the win ratio

The final column in Figure 1.2 shows the results for Trader Superstar with a win rate of 81.25%. Again we use the same base trades, and change three of the original losers into winners and add the median profit to each. This delivers a 41.6% return for the year. It takes a long time — sometimes a professional lifetime — to get to this level. The very top of the mast sees an 8.0% improvement in performance, but it comes at great cost. This is no overnight success.

In my trading I aim for the 80% return level, but I accept that 70% is probably about as good as I am going to get. I am not Trader Superstar or a market wizard, but I lift my trading returns by working smarter. Money management is the answer.

SMARTER MANAGEMENT

There is a short-cut for improving trading results. To demonstrate how it works, we start with the base sample of trades shown in Figure 1.3. These trades were the base data for the previous charts. This Trading Performance

Summary spreadsheet is available as an Excel template as part of the Better Trading pak from www.guppytraders.com.

Figure 1.3 Trade results

The number of trades remains constant for all traders

This number of losses changes for each of the traders

Total trading capital remains constant with all traders

SUMMARY OF TRADING RESULTS	Total number of trades		Total Capital	Total profit	%%% return
	Total number of wins	16	$100,000	$28,796	28.8%
	%% wins	10			
		62.50			

STOCK CODE	COST TO BUY	$$$ PROFIT	%%%% PROFIT	WIN loss	$$$ PROFIT
SRP	$20,680	-$2,000	-9.67	loss	-$2,000
NAB	$19,933	$416	2.09	WIN	$416
SRO	$20,000	$8,000	40.00	WIN	$8,000
NABWMU	$20,100	-$2,000	-9.95	loss	-$2,000
CMLWAA	$20,000	$6,250	31.25	WIN	$6,250
TAH	$20,008	$3,977	19.88	WIN	$3,977
SME	$20,265	$3,423	16.89	WIN	$3,423
FBG	$20,284	$2,086	10.28	WIN	$2,086
TLSWDJ	$20,150	$7,000	34.74	WIN	$7,000
FBG2	$20,202	-$2,000	-9.90	loss	-$2,000
BBG	$20,081	-$2,000	-9.96	loss	-$2,000
SME2	$19,996	$644	3.22	WIN	$644
AGY	$19,996	$6,500	32.51	WIN	$6,500
NAB	$20,100	$2,500	12.44	WIN	$2,500
EGO	$20,425	-$2,000	-9.79	loss	-$2,000
ICS	$19,995	-$2,000	-10.00	loss	-$2,000

This loss figure changes to reflect the risk, 2%, 5%, or 10%

This losing trade shows a $3,977 profit when used for the Trader Success calculations.

The 16 trades are selected real trades and returns over a one-year period taken from our weekly tutorial newsletter. They are Australian stocks and warrants. We reduced the number of wins compared to the number of losses so that the results are typical of Trader Average with a 62.5% success rate. The mix of trades — ordinary stocks and warrants — and the number of trades taken, is also typical.

This benchmark of sample trades is used to show how money management affects three traders. Trader Average has a success rate of 62.5% with 10 wins out of 16 trades. Trader Success shows a 68.75% success rate. This is 11 wins out of 16 trades. Trader Superstar gets 13 of his 16 trades correct and has an 81.25% success rate. Each of these traders uses exactly the same series of trades as shown in the trading report.

This series of sample trades has six common features:

1. Total trading capital is always $100,000 to allow for a consistent risk calculation.

2. Profits for winning trades remain as shown in the base trades.

3. We do not add profits to trading capital. Profits are swept into a holding account and not used for trading.

4. We count realized gains only. These come from closed trades.

5. The risk level is always a percentage of the total trading capital. So 2% risk always equals $2,000, and 10% risk equals $10,000.

6. Losing trades always lose the full amount of risk.

Our intention is to model the impact of changes in the level of risk for each of these three traders. We show what happens when the risk level grows from 2%, or $2,000, to 5%, or $5,000, for Trader Average. This does not change the number of losing trades. It only changes the amount lost in each losing trade.

The three traders are separated by their win/loss ratio, or success rate. Trader Average has a 62.5% success rate. Trader Superstar has an 81.25% win rate. To get from Trader Average to Trader Superstar, we changed three of the losing trades for Trader Average into winning trades. We did this by calculating the median profit — $3,977 — from all the winning trades for Trader Average. We then changed three of the losing trades on the base data template into winning trades, each with a $3,977 profit.

The total number of trades remains the same for each trader, so it is easier to compare the impact of changes in risk control. The number of winning and losing trades remains the same for Trader Success. Only the level of loss, or risk, in unsuccessful trades changes. It grows from 2% to 5% and, finally, to a 10% loss.

We calculate the loss in each trade using a set percentage of total trading capital. The reasoning behind this is explained in detail in Chapter 6. For the moment, please just accept that a 2% loss of trading capital means a loss of $2,000 in these examples.

In all these trades, as in real life, the level of loss is certain. We set the figure and use it as a constant in every trade. The level of reward is never certain, and the variation in the sample profits results reflects this.

If money management is really the answer to boosting portfolio returns, then how much improvement could we expect? Let's start with Trader Average who gets it right 62.5% of the time. Often this trader risks 10% in a losing trade. Our results are based on six losing trades, each losing the maximum allowable amount. Over 16 trades, this produces a 19.2% decline in trading capital. Losses are offset by profits. This is close to the maximum amount this trader can afford to lose. If he lets risk grow out to 20%, then he loses all his trading capital based on the sample trades shown.

By simply cutting losses to 5%, this trader turns in a small profit of 13.8%, as shown in Figure 1.4. This does not sound much of a return, but when you compare it to average market performance as measured by the Australian All Ordinaries market index, it is very good. In the first years of this century, a 13.8% realized return was about as good as, or better than, the market return. Many fund managers envy this rate of return.

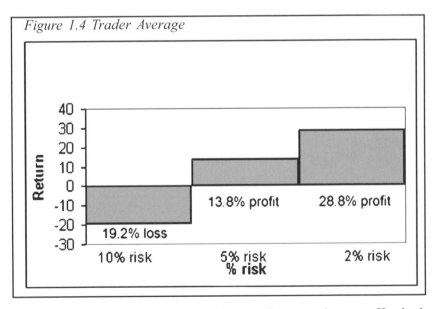

Figure 1.4 Trader Average

Cutting losses protects capital and allows profits to work more effectively.

If Trader Average aims for a maximum 2% loss rate on each of his six losing trades, then performance improves dramatically. By changing only his money management approach, using simple stop loss discipline, he boosts performance to 28.8%. These are not Trader Superstar returns, but they are achievable by average traders who get six out of 10 trades wrong.

Trader Average lifts returns to become Trader Success by applying better money management. If we combine this with an improvement in skill, then returns improve further. On the base data we change one of the Trader Average six losing trades into a winning trade showing a $3,977 profit. This brings the success rate up to 69.75%.

Even with this win rate, Trader Success cannot afford to let losses grow to 10% of total trading capital. At the end of this sample series, this blow-out in risk to 10% leaves Trader Success with trading capital reduced by 6.4%, as shown in Figure 1.5. He is going broke slowly, though probably enjoying the rush from his winners. In the long run, Trader Success destroys his trading capital, although it may take years.

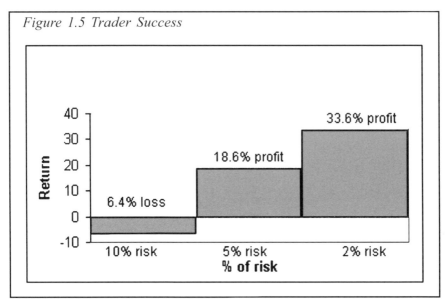

Figure 1.5 Trader Success

If Trader Success reduces losses to just 5% of capital on his five losing trades, then he turns in an 18.6% profit. Reduce losses to 2% of capital and profits grow to 33.6%. These are still not Superstar returns, but they are more than adequate to support a full-time professional trader.

These 18% and 33% returns are possible because we are not fund managers. As we explain later, we have an advantage in size and agility. We can trade stocks with increased volatility and generate these types of returns.

It is important to note that the increase in skill level from 62.5% winners to 68.75% is not sufficient to shift this trader into profit if he continues to allow losses to grow out to 10% of capital on each trade. The combination of improving trading skills and an improvement in stop loss discipline limiting each loss to 5% of trading capital is responsible for the initial move into profitable trading.

It is only Trader Superstar, with a consistent 81.25% success rate, who could allow losses to grow to 10% on losing trades and still survive. At this level, he returns 17.6%. By reducing risk to 5%, he grows profits to 32.6%.

Trader Superstar reaches this professional level because of his ability to understand and manage risk. His maximum risk on every trade is no more than 2% and is often less. Using the base trading sample, Trader Superstar collects a 41.6% return when risk is capped at 2%, as shown in Figure 1.6.

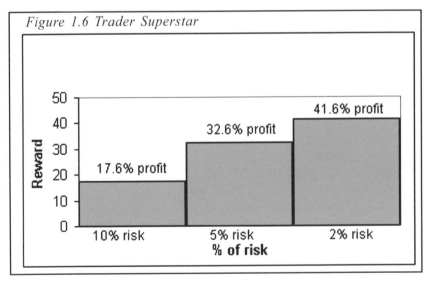

Figure 1.6 Trader Superstar

This is the essential contradiction of trading success. By the time you have enough skill to contemplate a consistent 10% loss rate, you also have enough experience and discipline to keep the losses to 2% or less.

The novice trader needs money management skills to survive, but he is the very person who is least likely to develop them. Instead, he concentrates on chart analysis and trading skills, believing they hold the secret to success. He misses the 28.8% return that launches his trading onto a sustainable path to success, because he lets losses grow to 10% in losing trades.

Trader Superstar generates returns of 41.6% when his three losses are kept to a maximum of 2% of trading capital. In reality, his potential returns are much larger. They grow because his losses are kept small in relation to his total trading capital. His trading discipline allows him to further leverage his skill and experience. By applying specialist techniques such as the Grow_Up strategy discussed in Chapter 14, he turns his winners into blockbusters.

Even with a 10% loss in losing trades, Trader Superstar returns 17.6%. This is impressive, but do you realistically think you have these skills? If you really do, then it is unlikely you are still reading this book. Reality suggests that most of us are at the Trader Average or Trader Success level, so playing with 10% losses is a path to trading failure.

We do not need to be Trader Superstar to enjoy the success generated by better money management. Money management requires knowledge and an understanding of the way losses impact on capital. Applying money management requires discipline, and this is difficult for Trader Novice and Trader Average to develop. It is part of what keeps them from becoming Trader Success. It is not a lack of charting and analysis skill; it is a lack of the discipline required to effectively implement money management strategies.

The charts in this chapter show you what is possible when money management is applied. The understanding of trading covered in my book *Share Trading*, the mastery of knowledge explored in *Chart Trading*, and the tactics included in *Market Trading Tactics* are all steps toward trading survival and success. The path to success cannot bypass these steps, but we move onto the fast track when we combine this hard work with money management. In the remainder of this book, we show how this is used to improve individual trades, to protect capital, and later to protect profits. We also show how it is used to grow portfolios in a way suitable for smaller traders.

Rich or poor? Boom or bust? The choice is yours, and it starts by understanding your trading style.

TWO
RISK WITH STYLE

Money is scattered everywhere in the market, but picking it up is not easy. Should you use a shovel, a shopping trolley, a bulldozer, or just scramble wildly with your hands? The method you choose has an important bearing on your success. The bulldozer is not much use if you do not know how to operate it. Your skill with the shopping trolley is irrelevant if the money falls through the mesh.

Your performance profile should combine style, methods, techniques, and tools in the best possible way. Too often, the combination is accidental and so too is our success, or failure. We improve our chances of success by developing a better understanding of the way money is collected from the market. We give ourselves the opportunity to make more informed choices. Stepping out and accepting responsibility for survival in the market is, initially, a bewildering experience. There is much to learn.

Before we start growing capital, we need to ensure that our performance profile is benchmarked from the same starting point. Without this agreement, confusion will follow because we talk of the same concepts but understand them in different ways.

RISK
We start with a working definition of risk and move on to examine trading and investment styles and their relationship with practical market risk.

Entire books have been written about market risk and they include some very complex definitions. When we trade the market, we can forget almost all of them. When we turn from analysis to action, the nature of risk changes. As soon as we buy stock, all the risk boils down to a single factor. If price moves against us and we start losing money, then our risk has increased. Risk, in this case, is equal to loss. It is precisely measured. In financial formula terms, risk is the product of the relationship between our entry and exit price and our trading capital.

We start defining risk by finding the exit price in a trade that is designed to tell us when we are wrong. This is called the stop loss price. The precise method you choose is not as important as making the choice. I use the count back line approach, covered in detail in my book *Share Trading*. You might apply double the average true range of recent price movements, as explained by Christopher Tate in *The Art of Trading*. Other methods use the value of an indicator, such as a moving average, or a Bollinger Band. These are personal choices and they are all designed to provide a single figure — the price at which we know our trade entry is wrong because the price has moved down instead of up as we anticipated. Once this risk level is calculated, we have a better chance of managing it.

Later we look at how some of these methods are used. At the moment, we are just interested in two market figures — the entry price and the planned stop loss exit price.

The final component of the risk calculation is capital. When Trader Average enters a trade, he thinks risk is equal to the amount of capital allocated to the trade — that capital equals position size. This is a significant distraction, because he fails to understand the relationship between each trade and portfolio performance.

HOW MUCH?
The key to risk management is how much you are prepared to lose before you admit you are wrong. This is not an arbitrary figure made up as you go along. Typically, we are prepared to lose less on a speculative trade than with a solid blue chip. We feel uncomfortable losing $1,000 with a speculative technology stock, but we are comfortable with a $10,000 loss on Wal-Mart because we believe this blue chip stock has a reliable long-term future. This

thinking suggests the acceptable size of the loss is related to the quality or volatility of the stock, rather than to the impact on our trading capital.

This is the real challenge for successful trading and investing. How can we trade volatile stocks that deliver high returns with an acceptable level of safety?

The beginning of the solution to the problem is in our understanding of what is at risk. If our total trade size, or position, is $20,000, then it is highly unlikely that the entire amount is really at risk. The only way we lose the entire $20,000 is if the stock is removed from trading by the exchange authorities. It happens, but not very often.

If prices start to fall, there is a strong chance we will get out after a $10,000 loss. It is not good trading, but the actual capital lost, or at risk, is $10,000, not $20,000. This is summarized in Figure 2.1.

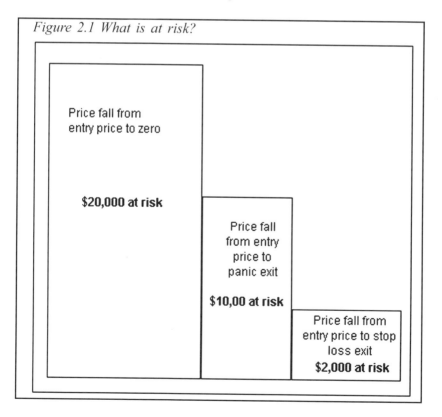

Figure 2.1 What is at risk?

Price fall from entry price to zero

$20,000 at risk

Price fall from entry price to panic exit

$10,00 at risk

Price fall from entry price to stop loss exit
$2,000 at risk

An experienced trader may exit when he loses just $2,000 from an adverse price movement. This is still quite substantial. In percentage terms, this is a 10% loss of capital involved in the trade.

If we measure the loss against the money allocated to the trade, then we exaggerate the risk. We must put this loss into the wider context of our portfolio.

THE 2% RULE

The key to this is the application of the 2% rule. This rule simply states that no single position, or trade, should put at risk more than 2% of our total trading capital. If we have $100,000, this does not mean each trade is limited to a total of $2,000. It means the actual risk of the trade — the amount we are prepared to lose before we admit we are wrong — is not larger than 2% of our total trading capital.

As we make successful trades, our portfolio capital grows, and the dollar size of 2% grows larger. As we suffer losing trades, the dollar size decreases. Every time we enter a new trade, we calculate the dollar value of 2% of our total trading capital. When we put each trade into this context, we get the result shown in Figure 2.2.

The 10% loss in the individual trade translates into a 2% loss in terms of our total trading capital or account. This result has the most significant impact on our trading. The size of the loss in the trade is not what counts. What is really important is how this individual loss relates to our total trading capital.

This understanding is fundamental to all effective risk control strategies. It allows us to capture the volatility of an individual stock while remaining within the required risk parameters of our total portfolio exposure. We trade volatility with safety. We trade high-return speculative stocks with almost as much safety as we trade blue chip stocks, when measured in terms of the impact on our portfolio value.

ENTRY AND EXIT

This takes us back to our entry and exit figures. The method we select should set the stop loss exit price to protect our trading capital. The 2% rule tells us how much this is in dollar terms.

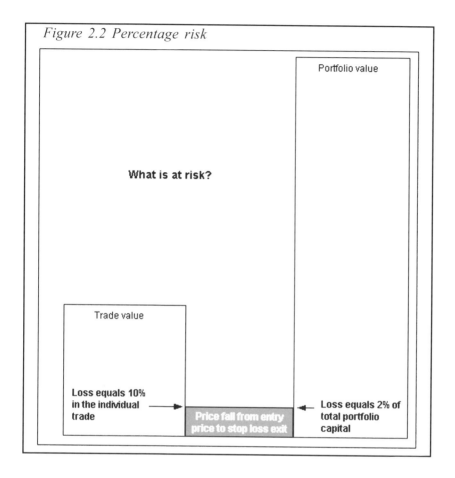

Figure 2.2 Percentage risk

For any entry and exit price combination, we decide the maximum position size we can take. The method you choose depends on the nature of the trade. These three figures — entry price, stop loss exit price, and the dollar size equal to 2% of trading capital — determine the maximum position size. We examine these calculations in more detail in Chapter 6.

RISK WITH STYLE

Does the style of trading, or investing, have a major impact on the amount of cash you make or lose? Common market myths suggest that some styles, such as long-term investing, are inherently less risky than others, such as short-term trading. This misconception breeds best when the practical nature of market risk is misrepresented.

Armed with a better understanding of how market risk is defined, we now take a clearer look at the variety of trading styles. The way you approach the market is your trading style and is imperfectly summarized when you describe yourself as a trader or investor. Trading methods, considered in the next chapter, include the combination of tools used with specific opportunities. These methods are the practical implementation of your chosen style.

Each style carries a different execution or implementation risk. With good money management, no single style is inherently more, or less, risky than another. This is counter-intuitive. Investors usually believe they have a safer approach to the market than traders. In reality, the financial risk to portfolios remains the same if good money management rules are not applied.

There is a wide range of trading styles to choose from, and few traders are adept at more than just two or three.

Does style matter? Is it sufficient just to make successful trades? Improving your style of trading is the first step in keeping your profits and protecting your capital. Style may start accidentally, but it grows into skill with consistent practice. Knowing your style means you can focus on improving your performance.

The style you adopt sets the benchmark for profiling your performance. The solution to better trading lies in selecting a single approach and applying it with subtle differences depending upon your starting point — your style.

We often talk about three trading styles — position, aggressive, and conservative — without really explaining how these are different. Other styles tend to be variations on these main methods. These styles are related to the risk taken in the market by traders, but this is not to say a conservative style carries less risk than an aggressive style. The approaches are used to determine the types of opportunities the trader finds comfortable. The risk in each trade is controlled, not by the entry point, but by the exit strategy used to limit a loss.

POSITION TRADING

Financial publications are littered with jargon. Some confusing terms for new traders are "position," "position trading," and "open positions." These are shorthand terms to describe a particular approach to trading the market.

A "position" means we own stock and have not yet sold it. As soon as we buy stock in a company — open a trade — we take a "position." In ordinary stock trading, this means we buy stock for perhaps $50 and we hope that it will go up to perhaps $75. While we own the stock, but have not yet sold it, we hold an "open position" and are, hopefully, sitting on paper profits. Traders willingly talk of open profits but are less voluble about open losses or positions that are "under water."

When the stock is sold, we "close the position" or "close the trade." The terms "position" and "trade" are used interchangeably. In futures and commodity trading, the term "position" is also related to the number of contracts being traded, but when we talk of a "position" in the stock market it usually means any stock we have bought but not yet sold.

The bad news is that the term "position" is loosely linked to the idea of position trading. Every open trade involves a "position," but "position trading" is a more precise trading technique.

Trading techniques are classified by time, as shown in Figure 2.3. Traders who aim to buy and sell within one trading session are day traders, or more correctly, intra-day traders. They intend to scalp the market using a large amount of money to generate a small percentage return each day.

This method is used by large institutional traders. For private traders, these opportunities are available in leveraged markets such as futures and options. Using just a small amount of money, these financial instruments magnify the benefit from small moves in the price of the parent stock or commodity. These traders look for a combination of leverage and momentum.

Short-term traders aim for trades lasting one to five days. They usually look for two- to three-day opportunities. These traders want to capture short, sharp price moves and rallies. They look for volume, momentum, and short-term bullish chart patterns. Their focus tends to be on low-priced stocks, as the price leverage magnifies returns. Price leverage is based on a single observation: it is easier for prices to move from $3 to $6, than it is to move from $30 to $60.

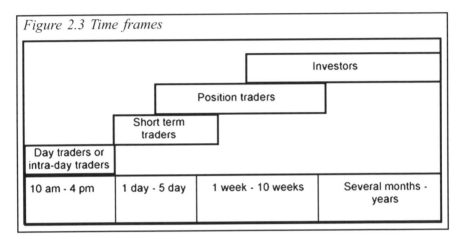

Figure 2.3 Time frames

The tools of the short-term trader focus on momentum, and include:

- bullish chart patterns;

- straight-edge trend lines;

- price and volume searches;

- volatility measures, such as those used by Robert Deel in *Trading the Plan*;

- ATR — average true range;

- Bollinger Bands;

- MACD histogram;

- stochastics;

- count back line for managing the trade, as shown in my book *Share Trading*;

- Guppy Multiple Moving Average indicator discussed in my book *Market Trading Tactics* for trend context information; and

- trading signals which use a mixture of intra-day and end-of-day data.

Position trading takes a longer perspective. The position trader is not looking for short-term returns, although he takes them if exceptional returns are offered. The chart in Figure 2.4 shows how position trading overlaps with short-term trading. The position trader is looking to join long-term trends in the market that may go on for weeks, or even months.

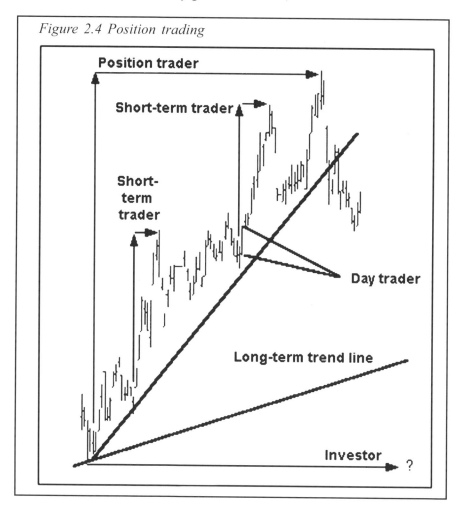

Figure 2.4 Position trading

The tools of the position trader are trend management tools, and include:

- Guppy Multiple Moving Average discussed in my book *Market Trading Tactics;*
- straight-edge trend lines;

- ADX indicators;
- Relative Strength Indicator divergences;
- price oscillators;
- count back line for managing the trade;
- point and figure charting;
- trading signals that are based on the end-of-day close data. They initiate action in the next day's market; and
- a variety of money management techniques which are discussed in the following chapters, including zero cost averaging, Grow_Up, and pyramid entry strategies.

The position trader expects to be involved in the stock for several weeks, so he is less concerned with rallies and other short-term price movements. He uses a trailing stop loss to protect open profits, but modifies these signals against other trend indicators such as the Guppy Multiple Moving Average or Bollinger Bands. Once the trend trade proves solid, he does not want to be "shaken out" of the trade by short-term fluctuations within the dominant trend. Some position traders are reluctant to accept trend change signals, so they sometimes get caught holding onto stock when the up trend switches to a downtrend.

The position trader makes better use of money management techniques, such as zero cost averaging and Grow_Up strategies, to improve the results in winning trades.

The major advantage of position trading is the way entry and exit signals are based on end-of-day data. Traders do not have to watch live screens. They may choose to use live data to improve their entry or exit decision, but this is not absolutely necessary. Very successful trades are made using the close price as the trigger signal for action in the market on the next trading day. Position trading is the most common trading approach and suits most people who still have full-time day jobs. It also suits full-time professional traders who understand that trading is about managing risk, rather than about the excitement and pressure of live screen day trading.

The investor buys a "position" for the long term. He often believes that time reduces the risk to his portfolio. When the investment performs well, he holds it for many months, or even years. This reliance on time as a means of managing risk distinguishes investing approaches from trading approaches.

AGGRESSIVE TRADING

It is a mistake to think that aggressive trading means buying depressed stocks, or stocks in a downtrend, in the hope the trend will reverse. When investors do this, it is called "bargain hunting." This strategy is often pursued with aggression and bravado. It is more properly called "fading the trend" and forms the foundation of the long-term conservative approach to the market as developed by Richard Dennis and his group of Turtle Traders. The objective of this strategy is to get into high-probability, low-risk, long-term trends. The method requires multiple entries as the trend looks as if it is changing. If the downtrend does not change, the strategy follows very precise exit rules. It requires multiple entries and rapid exits until the trend actually reverses. Then the objective is to stay with this long-term trend development.

This is a "fade the trend," or trade against the trend, approach. Other traders use it to identify downtrend reversals, or more commonly, to get out of an up trend before it changes direction.

If we call these strategies aggressive, we use financial courage and bravado as a measure of risk. This has more to do with attitude than with financial management. Putting your capital in harm's way without protection is an expression of stupidity rather than aggression.

Aggressive traders have also been described as traders who feel comfortable losing more than $40,000 of a $100,000 portfolio. This is not aggression. It is financial stupidity of the highest order, as illustrated by the results in Chapter 1 when risk was permitted to grow to 10% — not more than 40%. We mention this silly definition only because it sometimes appears as a risk control method in some trading programs.

An aggressive trading style means buying a stock in anticipation of a pattern developing, or of an indicator entry signal being generated, as shown in Figure 2.5.

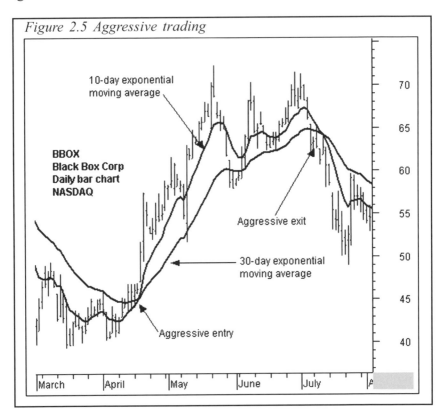

Figure 2.5 Aggressive trading

This approach is applied to both highly speculative stocks and stable blue chip stocks. The bullish flag pattern, for example, suggests a high probability of an up-move in prices. The pattern is traded in the same way no matter where it appears. If you see this pattern with Toshiba, with a speculative stock such as Simula Inc., or in a chart of a blue chip manufacturer such as Boeing, it signals the same type of opportunity.

How you trade the opportunity depends on your trading style.

Aggressive trading or investing is more closely related to the way price action develops. Price action is tracked with a price chart, or a group of indicators, or a combination of the two. The distinguishing feature of the aggressive trader is his willingness to buy the stock in anticipation of a pattern development, or an indicator confirmation.

Please do not confuse aggressive trading with foolhardy, high-risk trading that is really gambling on the market.

CONSERVATIVE INVESTING

Investors are encouraged to buy depressed stocks, or stocks in a downtrend, in the hope that the trend will reverse. This strategy relies on buying sound companies at bargain prices and forms the foundation of the work by Benjamin Graham and his most able student, Warren Buffett. The objective is to get into high-probability, low-risk, long-term up trends created when the market recognizes that the fundamental value of the company has been oversold. Some conservative investors jump the gun and buy quality stocks at bargain prices. Some call it the "pre-discovery" of value.

One unexpected problem is that a quality stock may turn into a non-performing stock of low quality — a dog. Not all analysts tell clients when this change takes place.

Traders call this method "fading the trend." The trading strategy most closely resembling this investment approach is used by the Turtle Traders, mentioned above. Here are the key differences, shown in Figure 2.6, between the trader's approach and the investor's approach to fading the trend:

- The investor holds onto the stock until it eventually starts going up.

- The trader buys the stock, and then sells it if it does not go up. He may use multiple entries and rapid exits until the downtrend actually reverses into an up trend.

If your investment approach hunts in the same area as aggressive traders, then you can improve your portfolio performance by understanding the way the trader manages risk in the same situations.

Figure 2.6 Fading the trend

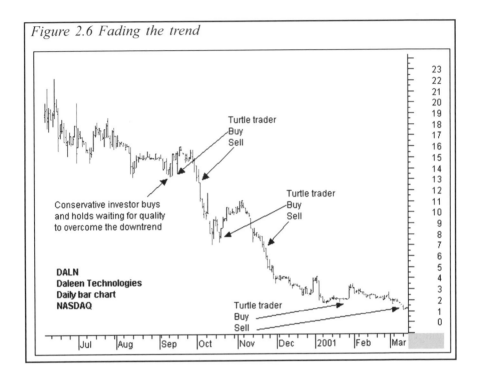

The investor uses time to manage the risk, leaving capital tied up for months in non-performing stocks. The trader uses capital to manage the risk. The size of our trading capital, account, or portfolio does not affect the way we manage the risk. Like it or not, small investors are closer to the world of trading when it comes to risk management.

The position trader buys stock today with the intention of holding it for weeks or months. This approach is more conservative than the aggressive trader and sometimes reflects a lower level of experience. The position trader waits until the pattern development is almost fully proven. The downside with this approach is that, in a fast-moving or bullish market, the position trader may end up behind the price action. He misses out on some trades because price takes off prematurely. The timing of his exact entry point varies with market conditions, but his intention remains the same. He looks for a pattern of behavior signaling a high probability of future price rises.

These traders also use indicators to assist their entry decisions. In Figure 2.7 they wait until just after the indicator confirmation on the chart of NYSE-listed Black Box Corporation.

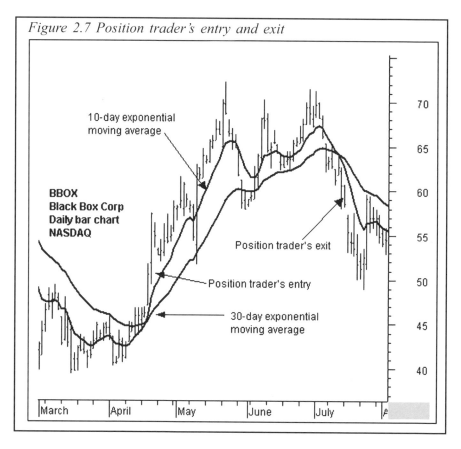

Figure 2.7 Position trader's entry and exit

Using a moving average cross-over approach, they wait until the cross-over takes place. The position trader wants evidence that his analysis is correct, but he is confident enough not to demand absolute proof.

The conservative trader demands absolute proof that his analysis is correct, and many times his trading suffers because his entry is delayed. The conservative approach has very little to do with risk control. In fact, it often increases risk because the rewards from the trade are reduced. The need to wait for absolute proof that an up trend has turned to a downtrend robs the trader of potential profits.

[31]

The conservative trader waits for confirmation that the pattern break, or the indicator signal, is correct. Using the same Black Box Corporation chart, Figure 2.8 shows the impact of this delayed entry and exit. His conservatism relates to the level of proof he requires before he takes action. Often he calls for an additional feature. He wants the price to pull back to get an entry closer to the original, and now proven, pattern.

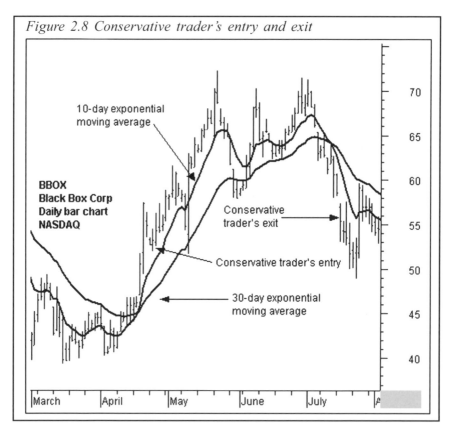

Figure 2.8 Conservative trader's entry and exit

This opportunity is sometimes available. In a weak market the breakout and retreat pattern is quite common and this provides an opportunity to get into the trade. It is not very often available in strong bullish and momentum-driven markets, so the conservative trader misses out on many opportunities.

The investor is, or should be, similar to the conservative trader. Investors are trend followers, where the objective is to find a rising stock and stay with it.

They put their capital to more effective use if they wait for confirmation that the up trend has started.

None of these strategies inherently carries more risk than the others if good money management and trading discipline is applied. Each of the approaches carries a different probability ratio of success to failure. It is easy to get a trade wrong when you fade the trend, and more difficult to make a mistake if you wait until the trend is proved. However, the risk is not in the point of entry, but in the way the trader handles a loss should his entry decision turn out to be wrong.

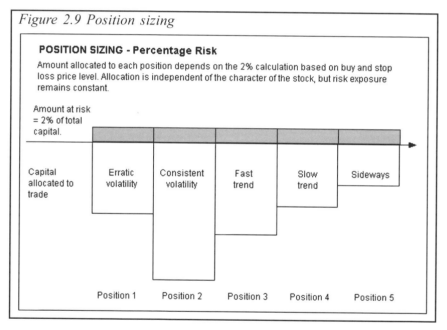

Figure 2.9 Position sizing

These distinctions — aggressive, position, and conservative trading — relate to the way traders time their entry into a stock based on their understanding of the way chart patterns or indicators are developing. Every trading opportunity provides a chance for each of these trading styles to make money. Each of these types of traders uses exactly the same type of toolkit and collection of indicators. It is the position of their entry within the time frame of trend development that helps to determine the type of trader they are. Even conservative traders become more aggressive with experience, moving to act in anticipation of indicator and chart development.

As soon as we buy stock, we open the door to risk. How we open the door — aggressively, slowly, with trepidation or bravado — does not determine the level of risk that lies beyond the door. This risk remains constant, as shown in Figure 2.9.

It is defined by the amount we are prepared to lose before we admit our entry decision was wrong.

Once we understand the nature of risk in every open trade, we can make better decisions about the most appropriate tool combination to apply in wrenching a profit from the market. These combinations are grouped into trading methods. We survey some of them in the next chapter.

THREE

MIX 'N' MATCH

Claiming you are a position trader is pointless if you still chase breakout trades using tools designed for aggressive traders with good risk control. Understanding where you are among the range of choices available in the market helps improve your trading focus. Consistency of method, style, and indicator tools with the type of trading opportunity provides a better basis for money management.

Better trading starts with establishing a personal performance profile. Know what you want, how you intend to get it, and the required combination of tools. A mismatch of trading tools and objectives destroys trading performance. A mismatch of money management solutions and performance profile destroys portfolio performance.

The previous chapter looked at trading styles. This chapter looks at some matches between trading opportunity and methods. Together these chapters are designed to encourage you to develop a clearer idea of what type of trader or investor you really are. If you reduce the inconsistency between methods, tools, and opportunity, then the money management techniques discussed in the following chapters will be applied more effectively to boost your returns.

TYPES OF OPPORTUNITIES

There are three main groups of opportunity in the market. They are:
* trend trading;
* breakout or rally trading; and
* trading based on support and resistance levels.

Each style of opportunity has its own set of rules and associated indicators. Each requires a particular personality. Some people feel very comfortable with long-term trend trades, while others fret with inaction. It is difficult to tell in advance which method will suit you best. What looks good in theory may turn out to be impractical or impossible in reality. Generally, your first reaction to the "riskiness" of the trading opportunity is a reasonable guide to how suitable it might be for you.

In this chapter we look briefly at some indicator tools and methods used to trade these three groups of opportunities. We include some chart examples of each. This is not a definitive survey. It is a starting point, or a reminder, to enable you to build a better idea of your trading profile and to match your trading methods with your trading objectives.

TREND TRADING

Trend trading is often considered the safest and easiest style of trading. It looks disarmingly simple on a chart display. An up trend is created when prices tend to move upwards in a steady fashion. On a daily chart, this move might last weeks or months. Once the trend is established, it is very easy to see and there is no doubt about the upward bias in prices.

The objective is to identify the trend once it has developed and to stay with the stock while the trend remains in place. These are usually long-term trades, and over a long period they can be very profitable.

Trend trades are designed to capture the capital appreciation that comes from a steady rise in price. Trends may be fast or slow. They also can be short-term, lasting days or weeks, or medium-term, lasting weeks or months. Long-term trends persist for months and sometimes years. A stable trend shows a steady rise with low volatility where daily price extremes remain relatively constant. When the price moves start to expand — when volatility increases — it is an early sign that the trend is becoming unstable.

Trend trades are usually defined by the way the current short-term average price is consistently greater than the long-term average price. This confirms the general direction of the price movement.

Trend trading delivers very good returns, but the weakness is the delayed entry and exit signals. The trade entry comes after the trend has started. The exit signal comes after the trend has ended, often signaled by a new sharp downtrend. The main problem with trend trading is identifying the trend in real time. In retrospect, the up trend for the Singaporean stock CEI Contract Manufacturing, shown in Figure 3.1, starts at point A, but in real time the trader does not know this.

Figure 3.1 Trend line

It is not until somewhere near point B that there is sufficient information to be confident that a trend is developing. This invariably means some profits are surrendered because the entry price, in this case around $0.15, is not the best possible. The best entry, in retrospect, was around $0.12 when the downtrend ended and the new up trend started. In this example, the time lag between the best entry and the actual entry imposes a large penalty. The delayed entry at point B is 25% higher than an entry at point A. This is counterbalanced by the prospect of a substantial return of more than 60% from a long-term trend.

In trend trading the same time lag between the best exit point and the actual exit also carries a financial penalty. Sometimes this is very costly, as prices often fall more rapidly than they rise.

Trend trading is often associated with trades or investments selected on a fundamental basis. Unfortunately, bad news travels quickly, and by the time the figures are publicly available, the price may have fallen dramatically. Charting shows the change in the trend often weeks before the relevant fundamental information is publicly available. The Enron and WorldCom charts showed clear downtrends for many months before the major fundamental problems in these companies were publicly confirmed by fundamental analysis techniques. Enron fell from $80 to less than $1 in a long, slow, steady downtrend, but it still caught fundamental analysts by surprise. They described the final collapse as "stunning in its speed and severity."

Good trend traders are usually satisfied to take a section out of the trend. This technique — "walk a mile with the crowd" — is discussed more fully in my book *Share Trading*. Those who aim to get in near the very bottom of the trend and out near the very top are usually unsuccessful.

The trend trade is controlled with technical indicators and with a stop loss strategy to set exit prices consistent with the way the trend is defined by the trader. This may be set on a straight-edge trend line as shown, or perhaps on a combination of moving averages.

Trend trading suits traders who are uncertain about their skill in picking the point of trend change from down to up. It suits those who do not want to track the market every day.

TREND TRADING TOOLS

Trend trading is at the heart of many trading techniques, so there are many indicators designed to define the trend, including:

- straight-edge trend lines;
- moving average combinations of a short-term and long-term average;
- the Guppy Multiple Moving Average indicator;
- MACD and MACD histograms;
- the ADX group of directional indicators; and
- on balance volume.

Of these, we find the straight-edge trend line, a combination of longer-term moving averages — 10 and 30-day — and the Guppy Multiple Moving Average indicator, to be generally the most useful. The other indicators are used for confirmation of the signals generated by these.

BREAKOUT TRADING

Downtrends eventually turn into up trends. Eager traders, and investors, like to buy the stock just as it finishes the downtrend and before it starts a new up trend. This is breakout trading. Every rally in a downtrend has the potential to develop into a breakout that signals the start of a new up trend. Understanding the difference between a rally and a breakout is significant, because only the breakout signals the start of a new trend. Identifying the difference in real time as price action happens is much more difficult.

A rally is a short-lived increase in price. In a downtrend, this is a desperate attempt to revive the stock and it is usually overwhelmed by selling. The rally appears when traders get fired up by a news event or rumor and push prices much higher. The downtrend rally is most often seen after a stock has fallen unexpectedly. When the NYSE-listed Greater China Fund fell from $11.40 to below $9.50, as shown in Figure 3.2, it looked like a bargain. Some traders bought at this level just because the price looked cheap compared to what it had been a few weeks before. Encouraged by this buying, a few other traders joined the party and prices moved up quickly in a short-lived rally. This delivered a 6.4% return.

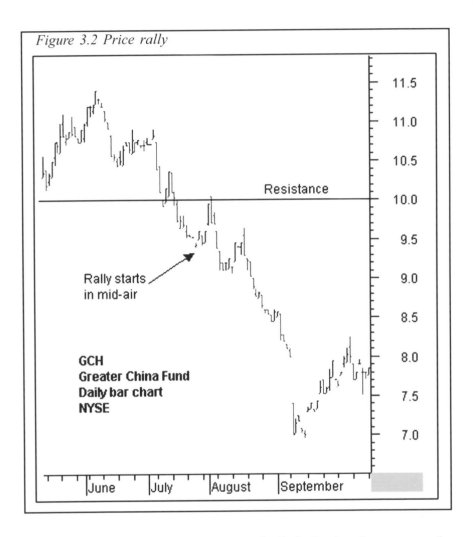

Figure 3.2 Price rally

Inexperienced traders buy the downtrend rally believing they are near the start of a new up trend. A downtrend rally has different features from a trend-break rally. Spot the difference by looking for:

- Nearby resistance levels that may act to block the price rise. These are more significant when the rally takes place in the context of a downtrend. Figure 3.2 shows this as a line at $10.00.

- Higher than average volume that drops off as price hits the resistance level.

- Rallies that start in mid-air, rather than bouncing off established support areas. The chart shows this.

- The rally that does not break above the existing downtrend as defined by a straight-edge trend line.

An indicator such as the Guppy Multiple Moving Average in Figure 3.3 shows there is a low probability of a trend change, because it is not supported by the long-term investors.

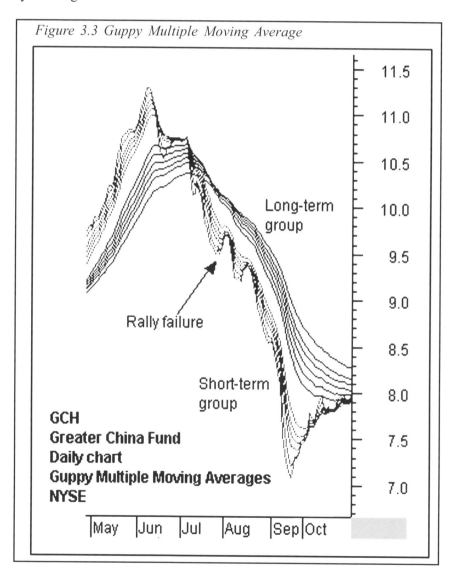

Figure 3.3 Guppy Multiple Moving Average

RALLY INDICATORS

Rally trading is part of breakout trading. The indicators are designed to define the nature of the rally. Some of these include:

- price and volume searches;
- verification with the Guppy Multiple Moving Average;
- identification of resistance levels and their strength;
- confirmation with volume behavior; and
- rally search formulas, such as those available free from www.guppytraders.com or described in *MetaStock® in a Nutshell* by Simon Sherwood.

TREND BREAKOUT RALLIES

Some rallies are immediate candidates for a downtrend reversal. They are traded in the expectation of a new up trend developing. Get this trade entry right and it delivers substantial profits.

Trend breaks are signaled by price activity moving above a straight-edge trend line. The breakout rally carries prices above the downtrend line and eventually becomes part of a new up trend. Some rallies lead straight into a new trend, but this is unusual. More often we see a test, retreat, and re-test pattern develop.

The test is when prices break above the downtrend line and move to the next resistance level. The resistance is strong enough to halt the price rise. The test of resistance is unsuccessful and this failure is shown by a price retreat toward the downtrend line. In some cases, this old downtrend line acts as a new support level. Some failures develop a standard reversal pattern, such as a double bottom shown in Figure 3.4 with Halma, listed in the United Kingdom. Others include a partial retreat of between 30% and 50% of the original price rally.

Real confirmation of the breakout rally comes with the successful re-test of the initial resistance level. Once this is achieved, there is a very high probability that a new up trend has been established.

The Guppy Multiple Moving Average is a useful indicator for assessing the probability of a rally turning into a trend break. When the rally carries the short-term group of averages above the long-term group, there is increased probability of a new trend developing.

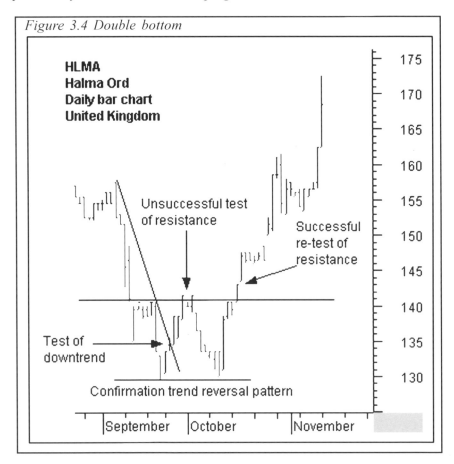

Figure 3.4 Double bottom

Traders look for these features to help identify breakout rallies:

- The rally carries prices above the downtrend line.
- Nearby resistance levels fail to completely block the initial price rise.
- Volume levels are variable. Strong initial buying is followed by a small drop in volume, increasing as prices rise again.
- The breakout rally starts from well-defined support levels.

- An indicator such as the Guppy Multiple Moving Average shows there is a high probability of a trend change.
- The rally is part of a sequence of test, retreat, and re-test.
- The retreat creates a reversal pattern, such as a double bottom.

BREAKOUT TRADING TOOLS

Breakout rallies at the end of downtrends are found with:

- price and volume searches, such as those available free from www.guppytraders.com or included in *MetaStock® in a Nutshell* by Simon Sherwood;
- confirmed breaks of the downtrend line;
- confirmed volume behavior on failure and re-test;
- rally search formulas;
- a 10-day and 30-day moving average combination to verify trend change;
- verification of a trend break using the Guppy Multiple Moving Average; and
- chart reversal patterns.

Breakout rallies are difficult to identify as they happen. They are often successfully traded after finding the initial rally and observing the failure and re-test pattern. When verified with an indicator such as the Guppy Multiple Moving Average, the trader and investor buy the stock near the start of a new up trend. This is an aggressive style of trading. Investors hunting for bargains in undervalued blue chip stocks are really applying an aggressive style of trading and should use the trader's breakout methods to improve their success rate.

Successful rally traders are not frustrated trend traders. They recognize that the trade has limited possibilities and trade it accordingly. All rally trading is short-term trading with defined price targets. The least effective way to trade rallies is to read about them in the newspaper and then try to trade them.

SUPPORT AND RESISTANCE TRADING

Up, down, or sideways? The market provides a limited range of movement but contains a multitude of opportunities. While many traders and investors focus on trends and breakouts, they ignore the ample opportunities available in stocks apparently drifting sideways.

Support and resistance concepts are among the simplest of all charting and technical indicators. They are also among the most profitable. They provide the starting point for the development of triangles and other patterns, as discussed in my book *Chart Trading*. They set accurate price targets, and are a good way of setting stop loss levels. Placing these correctly enhances trading results and trade planning.

These levels develop in response to a balance of supply and demand of stock at particular price levels. A support level is created when buyers consistently enter the market because they believe a stock is attractively priced. Markets reflect crowd behavior. Crowds tend to behave consistently, so support levels show up time and again at around the same price.

A resistance level is created by sellers. The sellers have many reasons for selling, but they often come together at a single price. As buyers bid up prices, the sellers get nervous. They worry that prices will not go higher. As soon as prices reach their target level they sell, either to lock-in a profit or because they fear the price will fall.

On a chart, these support and resistance levels appear as a series of price extremes at a single level. The more times prices move back to the support level, and then react away from it, the stronger the support level.

Support levels tend to persist over time. The support level of a few months ago is still a support level now. A support level of a year ago acts as a support level for today. Support levels are very persistent, working over many years. This allows the trader to take a single point on today's chart and verify that it has a high probability of acting as a support level. Resistance levels act in the same way, as shown in Figure 3.5.

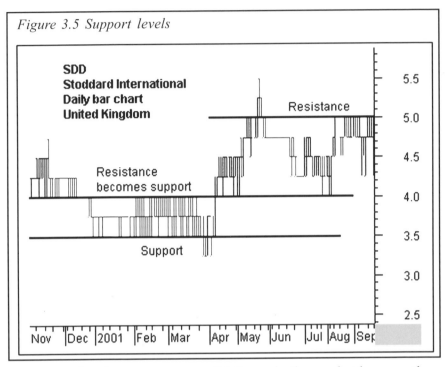

Figure 3.5 Support levels

Support and resistance are powerful forces in the market because they represent points where many stockholders make significant financial decisions about profit and loss. When judging the position of support in the current price action, we should always look at price action over 12 months or more. A weekly chart helps to confirm the placement of support levels, as does a point and figure chart.

SUPPORT AND RESISTANCE TRADING TOOLS

In placing a support or resistance level, traders note the following:

- Support or resistance lines are placed on price extremes.
- The more times the line acts as a reaction point, the stronger the support or resistance level.
- The line should capture more than 80% of the price extremes at the same level.
- Intra-day dips are not significant as long as there are just a few in comparison to the overall price activity at the support level.

- A close below support is a danger signal, particularly if a developing downtrend has dropped prices to this level.

- A single close below the support level that is part of daily volatility and not part of a developing trend warns that the support level is weakening.

- Support or resistance levels are persistent over time.

- When a stock splits and the data is adjusted for the split, the support levels on the chart remain valid.

Support and resistance form the basis of many successful trading strategies. Support helps to define safe entry points in a downtrend. Resistance helps to set profit targets in rising trends. In channel trading, where the upper and lower limits of price activity are defined by support and resistance lines, many profitable traders buy on support and sell on resistance. The Stoddard International chart in Figure 3.5 from the United Kingdom captures the initial 14% spread between support and resistance. Later this expands to 25%. Traders do not let the simplicity of the concepts blind them to the profits available from the correct application of these techniques.

A PLETHORA OF CHOICES

Where do you sit comfortably in this plethora of choices? Where we would prefer to sit and where we end up are sometimes two quite different places. This is a problem if your selected style of trading uses methods inappropriate for the type of opportunity.

A small assortment of the trader's wares has been outlined above. We select our tools from these before we proceed in the market. There are no absolute correct choices, although some choices are obviously contradictory or incompatible. If you believe you are a position trader, comfortable with trading trends, then ask yourself if you believe it is necessary to have a real-time market feed. The two are not incompatible, but they are inconsistent. The methods appropriate to one approach deliver confusing and contradictory signals when used with a different approach. You may make successful trades, but your success will not be as great as it could be. There may be advantages for you in reducing some of the time spent on trading methods that are incompatible with your style.

Some traders thrive on just a single approach, while others like to sample a variety. Traders who fail are often tempted to sample everything, creating a mix of methods, styles, and indicators in the hope that the mix will somehow magically combine and produce a consistently profitable outcome. The result is most often a continuing stain of red ink on their portfolio performance.

There is no single successful performance profile. The combination of tools, methods, and opportunities you select creates your personal performance profile. Your choice has a significant impact on the shape of your equity curve, which is the financial shape of your personal trading performance profile. Money management improves trading outcomes, but the impact is limited if your trading is a confused mixture of incompatible techniques and objectives.

FOUR
RISK IN TIME

Common thinking rarely leads to uncommon results. Nowhere is this as true as in the context of the market, and in particular in the context of money management. In this chapter we examine two related common beliefs about the way traders and investors should allocate their capital. They are the dollar cost averaging approach and the idea that *time in the market* is more important than *timing the market*.

These two related ideas rest upon the assumed inability of the private trader or investor to make good decisions. This may have been true in the past when private traders and investors were kept out of the market information loop. It is no longer the case. The private investor is potentially as well informed as her broker, because company information is now readily available to all. After the accounting disasters in the United States, all exchanges have accelerated their progress toward the objective of creating continuous disclosure rules. It is true that we will never be as close to the action as industry insiders, but for investors, this is of less importance. The intention is to capture long-term trends rather than to use traders' strategies, which rely heavily on capturing trend reversals the moment they happen.

If we assume that the private investor cannot make an informed decision, then it follows she is unlikely to catch major turning points in the market. This false assumption takes the investor to everlasting perdition. It drops her into the loser's strategy of managing risk using time in the market. This approach tells her not to worry about the collapse in DaimlerChrysler's stock price because she intends to hold the stock for the long term.

The logic of the argument suggests that the investor cannot time the market, so she should compensate by spending more time in the market. "Timing the market" means judging the end of a downtrend and the beginning of a new up trend. This is where traders like to hunt. It seems contradictory when many advisors who favor time in the market suggest buying AOL Time Warner as a long-term investment because the downtrend must soon turn into an up trend! Encouraging investors to hunt with traders is poor investment advice.

"Time in the market" means the investor buys stock in a quality company at almost any price. The intention is to hold onto it for three to five years, or even longer. Over the years the price of a quality stock is likely to increase, because over time the market generally rises. This argument appeals to lazy investors who want to make money without work. Most dangerously, it encapsulates the idea that market risk is controlled by time in the market. This is a poor strategy for a single investment. It is an unexpectedly dangerous strategy when applied to multiple investments.

Small traders and investors do not have much spare cash, but this does not stop them dreaming. Often they pick up books about Warren Buffett and think they see the path to investment riches. They forget that their small sum buys a handful of stock in the British bank, Barclays, while Buffett's strategic success depends on buying a controlling interest in a company such as Barclays. Desperately short of cash, the small investor is easy prey for such ideas.

This is the point in the investor's career where time in the market meets with dollar cost averaging. This strategy appeals to investors with limited capital. They cannot afford to buy $70,000 worth of HSBC Holdings. At best they can afford $2,000 every now and then. Dollar cost averaging encourages the investor to buy small amounts of a quality stock at regular time intervals, perhaps every three or six months. At each regular time point, they use the same amount of money. When the stock price is low, this buys a lot of stock. When the stock price is high, the same amount of cash buys less stock. These are all added to a growing portfolio, or position. This produces an average cost for the stock.

The two ideas — time in the market and dollar cost averaging — are joined by a hidden and fatally dangerous assumption. They are linked by a belief that market risk is effectively controlled by time alone. Those who believe this fallacy should talk to investors who bought into America's energy giant, Enron, or Australia's largest insurance company, HIH Insurance. No amount of time is going to recover their investment, as the companies failed rapidly. Investors who believed in the ideas of time in the market and dollar cost averaging bought more stock in these companies as their prices plummeted.

TIME COUNTS

These two ideas are major factors working against trading and investment success. Applying these ideas to market examples often produces a disappointing performance profile. The strategies are a useful starting point because they help to benchmark any improvement. If you want to drive your market performance beyond the ordinary, it is necessary to jettison common concepts designed to capture ordinary results.

To test the success of these two strategies, we use a sample period of the Australian All Ordinaries market index (see Figure 4.1). The same conclusions apply to the London FTSE, the Dow, the Hong Kong Hang Seng, or the Singapore Straits Times Index. The chart shows the performance from January 1, 1999 to June 30, 2001. This includes a strong bullish rise, a substantial market collapse, and several rally and retreat periods, as well as a period of sideways market activity. This market is traded by four volunteer investors. The first three are investors Jan, Feb, and March. They use a dollar cost averaging strategy combined with a time in the market approach. The fourth volunteer is Investor Timer. He aims to time the market to improve his investment returns.

Our objective is to assess how these four investors perform over the same period. If the time in the market and dollar cost averaging ideas are useful, then the results should be at least as good as, and preferably considerably better than, the market rise for the same period.

This is not unreasonable. After all, if risk is controlled by the passing of time, we expect no group to be seriously disadvantaged. These strategies are

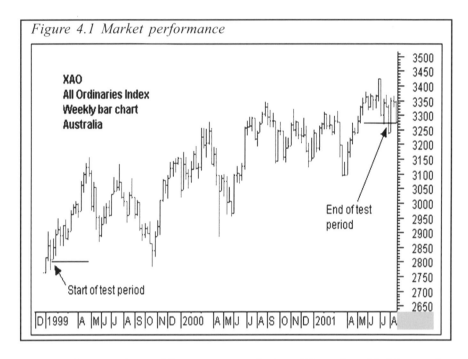

Figure 4.1 Market performance

promoted as a universal investment solution. They should ride out the impact of the market dips because they are supposed to alleviate risk. We also have the right to expect that our investments will work harder than the market — why else do we pay management fees?

We use the All Ordinaries as the base data and convert the index value into a currency reading. An index value of 3,110 is shown as $31.10. This makes it easier to compare the results of each investor. At the end of the period, we close all open investments and total the results at the July 2001 market value of $32.71.

We ask each of the first three investors to spend $10,000 on each investment every four months. This is the dollar cost averaging strategy in action. We start with Investor Jan. She buys $10,000 of the All Ordinaries at the opening value of $28.13 on January 1, 1999. Four months later, on May 1, 1999, she invests another $10,000 in the All Ordinaries at $31.01. She continues to do this every four months until her final investment in May 2001 at $32.70. We use the exact number purchased to two decimal places, so the first investment is for 355.44 shares at $28.13 for a cost of $10,000.

Investor Feb uses the same dollar cost averaging strategy, but he starts with the All Ordinaries' opening price of $28.94 on February 1, 1999. Four months later he adds a new investment costing $10,000. His purchases are offset by one month when compared to Investor Jan.

Investor March starts her investment career in March 1999, with the All Ordinaries at $28.80.

The result for each of these investors is plotted in Figure 4.2. To construct these results we take the total number of All Ordinaries stock owned by each investor and value them at the last price in July 2001 of $32.71. Each investor has exactly the same number of investments. They all spent $80,000 since January 1999.

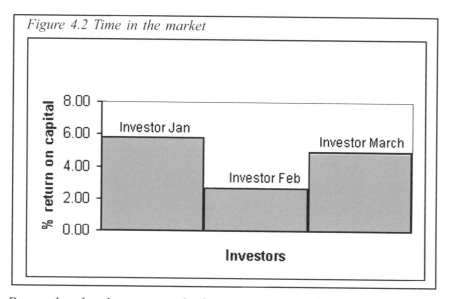

Figure 4.2 Time in the market

Remember that these are results from a generally rising market. From the January 1, 1999 low to our selected All Ordinaries exit in July 2001, the market showed a 16.28% increase. The January 1999 rise to the highest high in the period of $34.22 is a 21.65% return.

The percentage return on capital for investors Jan, Feb, and March is disappointing. Investor Jan has the best return of just 5.97%, or $4,633 in dollar terms. The worst result is for Investor Feb, with a mere 2.7% for a miserable $2,157. Investor March does a little better with an extra $3,935 in the bank for a 4.92% return. If these investors had left their money in the bank, they would have achieved comparable returns from bank interest.

These results illustrate two important points. First, the level of return from time in the market using dollar cost averaging techniques is not very good, even in a generally rising market. Imagine the results if this sample was taken from a falling market. There are better ways to manage market risk and to grow your capital. We explore them in the rest of this book.

The second feature of these results is the variability of return. The best is Investor Jan. Her 5.79% return is 114% better than Investor Feb with his 2.7% return. This very wide variation in return comes from exactly the same period of market exposure. The variation is not created by stock selection. We use the same All Ordinaries Index for all investors in this example.

It is not a result of different skill levels. In this example, all three investors buy their investments at the exact opening price for each month. We eliminate the impact of skill by selecting the same entry conditions for each investor.

Only one factor is responsible for the 114% variation in returns. It is the *timing* of the entry point for each investment. There is no escape from the inevitable conclusion: time in the market is a very poor way of investing, because the returns from such a strategy depend very significantly upon the *time* at which you choose to make your regular entries.

Buying the same dollar value of stock every three months or six months does not protect against market risk. It does not boost profits. Instead, the strategy exposes you to the vagaries of market activity without any effective risk control.

Some investors are generous with their capital. They do not like these test results, so they give the strategy another six months, or a year, or perhaps two. Perhaps then the strategies will show a better profit.

Look carefully at your portfolio. Do you keep deferring the pain inflicted by stock prices in a steady decline by refusing to sell? At some time you do have to recognize the erosion of your capital and face the fact that you might not live long enough to see a down-and-out investment actually return a profit. At the very time when you most need a return from your investments, such as during your retirement years, the neglected portfolio underperformers are unlikely to come to your rescue.

TIMING THE MARKET
We need an investment strategy to really protect us from the vagaries of market performance by managing market risk more actively. Timing the market delivers superior returns, even allowing for relatively unskilled timing decisions.

But first let us dispose of one silly myth. Timing the market does not mean buying the exact low and selling the exact high. It does not mean you are stuck in front of a computer screen all day. Commentators who suggest this sometimes have a vested interest in distorting reality. They want you to stop taking responsibility for your investment success so that they can manage your money for you for a substantial fee.

A timing the market strategy is plotted on a monthly chart using simple straight-edge trend lines, as shown in Figure 4.3. The All Ordinaries monthly chart shows three easy-to-achieve investment trades based on simple chart analysis. An entry and exit in each of the opportunities shown constitutes a timing the market approach. This is not fast trading. Entry and exit decisions are based on weekly charts.

Now meet Investor Timer, the last of our volunteer group of investors. He has seven days to make each buy or sell decision. Each trade lasts between four and 14 months. Investment monitoring is a once-a-week task. A weekly assessment of portfolio performance is not too much time to ask of any investor who is serious about improving his performance profile.

Investor Timer does not have much cash. Like the first three investors, he uses $10,000 for the first trade, but unlike his fellow investors, this is the total amount of cash he uses for the entire period. No dollar cost averaging for Investor Timer. We explain how this works as the example develops.

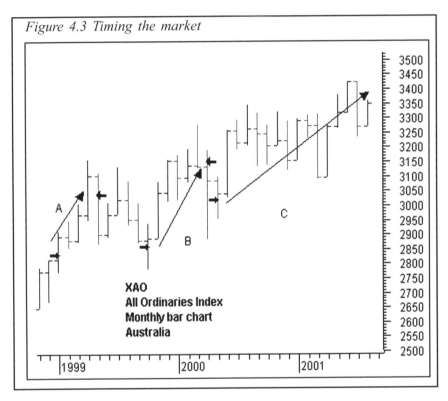

Figure 4.3 Timing the market

The first trade, or investment, starts at 2,813, or $28.13 for this exercise. It is the same starting point as we used with Investor Jan. This first trade is closed at $30.32. The timing could be a little better or a little worse. We use the opening figure for the month to keep the methods consistent with those used in the calculations for the first three investors.

In the first trade, Investor Timer spends $10,000. He collects $776.94 in profits. He also collects his original $10,000 used in this trade. He banks a total of $10,776.94.

The second trade is from $28.81 to $31.50. Again, Investor Timer spends just $10,000, but there is an important difference. Investor Timer does not need a new lump of cash worth $10,000. Instead, he re-uses the original $10,000 recovered from the first trade. This is different from the dollar cost averaging traders, who were asked to come up with an additional $10,000 for the second investment.

This second trade returns $933.34. Investor Timer banks $10,933.34.

The final trade starts at $30.85. The trade is still open at the end of the test period, so we use the last price in July of $32.71 to calculate the open profit. This delivers a $602.62 return, so Investor Timer banks $10,602.62.

The total profit from these three timing the market trades is $2,312.90. This is greater if Investor Timer re-invests his profits. We did not do this in this example because we want to keep the financial conditions of these competing strategies as equal as possible.

In dollar terms, Investor Timer's returns are slightly better than the worst-performing result from investors using the time in the market strategy — a $2,157 return. However, our focus should not be on the dollar returns, but on the percentage returns. These tell the real story of investment success.

RETURN ON CAPITAL

Why are we in the market? The novice believes it is all about making money and he counts his returns in dollar bills. The more experienced traders and investors know it is about the return on capital. The novice is blinded by large dollar figures when measuring portfolio performance. He dismisses all four strategies above because there is only a maximum $2,312.90 profit.

The experienced market players ignore the dollars and look at the percentage return on capital. They know why they are in the market and they have a more relevant question: "Which method gives a better return on capital?" A strategy with a 10% return is better than one with a 2% result. By using the first strategy, the investor turns $100,000 into $110,000 and takes a large first step in compounding capital into wealth.

Each of the time in the market investors requires a total of $80,000 to build their dollar cost averaged portfolios. Close all their open positions in July 2001 at $32.71 and the percentage return on capital varies between 2.7% and 5.79%.

Investor Timer, who is timing the market, only needs $10,000. Each time a trade is closed, he recovers the original $10,000 in capital. His $10,000 is used again and again in each of the trades. Investor Timer has a total capital commitment in this timing the market strategy of only $10,000. This puts his $2,312.90 profit into a very different perspective. This is a very effective use of Investor Timer's investment capital, with a 23.12% return. This far outstrips the returns from the time in the market, dollar cost averaging group, as shown in Figure 4.4.

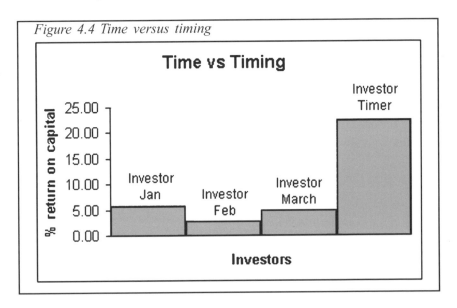

Figure 4.4 Time versus timing

The maximum market return for the same period based on an entry at $28.13 and an exit at the maximum of $34.22 is 21.65%. The time in the market strategies are well below the market return.

The timing the market strategy gives the investor a fighting chance to match — or, in this case, beat — the market performance. In later chapters we examine the issues surrounding these benchmarks and look at new money management strategies that allow even average traders to substantially outperform the market.

It does not matter how you cut the figures. We are all market timers and we all reap the rewards or the losses from our ability to time the market. There is no way to avoid this. Holding stock for a long time is not a way to manage risk.

We have been hard on these common ideas. This is no accident, because our intention is to show how better thinking about the concepts of risk and risk management leads to better trading and investment results. How you understand and apply these concepts has a dramatic impact on your portfolio performance profile.

If we cannot avoid the consequences of timing the market, then it makes sense to explore ways to time the market more effectively. Part of this solution is to apply different methods of money management so as to turn winning opportunities into outstanding opportunities.

FIVE
EQUITY CURVES

When I buy stock, it always seems to drop in price. In around 70% of trades the price recovers and the trade turns into a profit. Some trades drop immediately, and keep dropping.

Experienced traders develop a gut instinct about bad trades. They recognize losing trades early, before any charting or technical indicator signals develop. Equity curves provide Trader Average with a short-cut to gut instincts and experience by collating information for a personal trading performance profile or equity curve. The equity curve is a financial diary tracking how each trade performs day by day. When the equity curves from many trades are combined, we turn a casual observation into a powerful trading tool that provides an important way to manage risk.

The equity curve is an independent way of recognizing early trade failure. It does not rely on technical indicator values or position size and stop loss calculations.

An exceptional trade makes money from the moment you buy the stock. The price moves upward without ever looking back. The protect capital stop loss is never threatened. In just a few days the trade moves into clear profit and the trader's task switches to protecting profits. Savor these trades. They are a rare experience.

Most trades leave traders haggard for days on end. No sooner do we enter the trade than the price starts to fall. It moves perilously close to our stop loss figure. We seriously contemplate an exit just a few days after the entry. It is not a comfortable feeling, even though many of these trades recover and trend upward as we had anticipated.

Some trades drop like a stone the minute our buy order is filled. There is no doubt about our error. The price plummets below our stop loss conditions, leaving us with the agony of decision-making. We know the theory — cut the small loss quickly — but the practice is decidedly more difficult.

This repeated price behavior is not a matter of luck. It bears a direct relationship to the way we trade and make our trading decisions. It is a consistent result of our choice of trading styles, methods, and tools, and of our beliefs about the way risk is managed by time. There are many common features linking our personal trades together, including any tendency to wait too long to chase a rally, or to enter too early on a price retracement.

Rather than change our trading behavior, a useful alternative is to accept our habits and build the trading approaches around them. This is more than just matching style with method, as discussed in previous chapters. By developing a personal equity curve for our trades, we also develop a more effective stop loss strategy to confirm when we are in a winning trade and to tell us when to get out, based on our characteristic behavior.

Most times we manage a trade using stop loss techniques to protect trading capital, and later, to protect open profits. We can also manage a trade, and compare trades, using an equity curve. The curve is constructed from the closing value of each trade every day. Do not confuse this with a portfolio balance calculation. This is a total figure for all open trades every day and we use this in a different way. In Chapter 21 we show how portfolio equity curves — the combined summary of every trade — are used to improve overall trading. The equity curve is not an annual trading record of the profit or loss made on every trade.

How much money did your trade make, or lose, today? The answer is obtained by using today's closing price to calculate the value of the stock. The equity curve records the daily status of every open trade. Ten thousand shares closing at $10.00 equals $100,000. This is really good if the original trade cost $50,000. It is not so good if we started with $140,000. The final balance is the marked-to-market profit or loss for each individual trade.

EQUITY CURVE CONSTRUCTION

The equity curve could be constructed using raw dollar calculations. This makes it difficult to compare the performance of different trades and position sizes. My preference is to convert these dollar figures into a percentage, because it makes it easier to compare individual trades of different dollar values. The results are recorded daily to build a line chart showing an equity line, or curve, for every trade. Later we combine them into a personal profile using an aggregate equity curve.

Equity curves are tedious to construct because they are done by hand. Excel spreadsheet construction details are in the appendix at the end of the chapter. The Equity Curve template is available as part of the Better Trading pak from www.guppytraders.com. With only a few open positions, adding the end-of-day figures, extending the relevant formula calculation columns, and readjusting the graph does not take very long. Maintaining these spreadsheets by hand also makes it easier to adjust the calculations when new positions are added to the existing position in the same stock, or when part-profits are taken to preserve trading capital. Equity curves are a useful way of comparing trades and identifying ways to improve trading performance.

The equity curve offers two important pieces of information. The first is a graphic summary of your performance in each trade. This is not always a pretty picture and too often novice traders refuse even to take a peek.

The second important scrap of information is the average size of your loss after you buy a stock and before it goes on to make money. This draw down, or temporary loss, provides Trader Average with a statistical short-cut to experience. We often assume this temporary draw down is related to market conditions. In practice, it is more closely related to our analysis skills. Individual trade equity curves tend to show common characteristics irrespective of market conditions. They reflect our trading behavior and we use them to put a figure on gut feelings about a trade. The experienced trader draws on his experience to make this intuitive decision. The less-experienced trader draws on his performance profile as illustrated by an average equity curve.[1]

USING THE EQUITY CURVE

The equity curve in Figure 5.1 records a single trade completed by Trader Average. He has the same profile used in Chapter 1. He gets six out of 10 trades correct, but sometimes he has to wait a long time before a trade starts to make a profit.

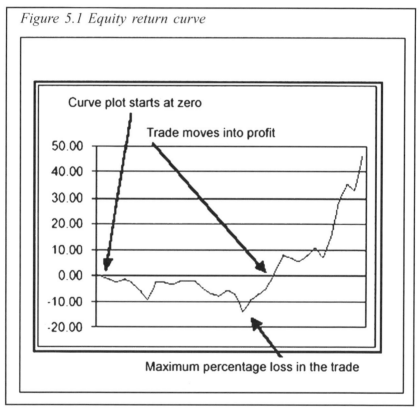

Figure 5.1 Equity return curve

The equity curve plot always starts at zero. The trade entry price is entered as the starting figure for the chart and is shown as 0%. We exclude brokerage because this factor varies from trade to trade and makes it difficult to accurately compare results across several trades.

---

1 John Sweeny, in his book *Maximum Adverse Excursion*, discusses this technique in more complex terms. We use a single aspect of this as a tool to develop performance profiling and as an independent means of recognizing early trade failure.

Each day the new closing price is used to calculate the percentage gain or loss. Ideally, the trade should start making money straight away, but the shape of the equity curve shown is closer to reality for many traders. The trade starts losing money, perhaps because Trader Average incorrectly timed the entry. Instead of selecting the low in the breakout, he selected a higher point.

The equity curve moves into negative territory and takes several weeks before moving into profit.

The shape of the curve shows that the maximum loss was 13% before this trade turned around and moved back into profit-making territory. By itself, this is just a casual, and perhaps unimportant, observation. Most traders focus on what the curve can tell them about their analysis skills.

This record of a single trade tells us a lot about our skills and our analysis techniques. The shape of this curve suggests that the trade entry was too early. If this same pattern repeats over several trades, then Trader Average needs to concentrate on timing issues. This may mean adding an additional indicator, changing the time of day when entry is made to improve the chances of getting a better entry price, or curbing the urge to chase prices rather than waiting for prices to pull back to planned buy levels.

Once this early entry characteristic is identified, the most difficult problem is to try to change our trading techniques and approaches. We use our current combination of indicators because we are comfortable with them. Even when we aim for an enticing objective, such as losing weight, it is difficult to change our behavior. The failure rate for simple dieting plans is very high. The failure rate of complex behavioral changes required for any particular type of successful trading is close to 100%.

In Chapter 1 we saw how difficult it is to grow our trading skills to Trader Superstar level. If we cannot readily change our behavior, then we need to develop solutions that allow us to use our current behavior and still improve trading results.

This individual curve is an interesting piece of a trade post-mortem. If we treat this information in isolation, we lose an important advantage. When we start trading, our performance is erratic because our skill level is low. With experience we develop a more consistent approach. Good trades start to look alike and develop similar characteristics.

Lurking in the background behind our successful trades are the losers. Any one of them can dramatically threaten our overall results. They too look alike, and by comparing equity curves, we develop a tool to distinguish between good and bad trades as they develop.

Thinking traders develop a gut feeling about their trading performance. Some shrug it off with comments such as "I always buy on the high of the day, so I expect to start with a few losing days." The experienced trader uses instincts, honed over many trades, to tell when a few losing days is OK and when it is not OK. We use the equity curve to take a short-cut to instinct.

When consistent patterns of behavior turn up on your equity curves, it provides a clear road to improvement. When we know the average shape of our personal equity curve, we have an important way to judge the early success, or likelihood of failure, in any individual trade.

HOW MANY STEPS BACK?

The classic stereotype of a drunk's progress down a footpath is described as three steps forward and two steps back. As long as this ratio is maintained, the drunk moves forward. Take four steps back and his forward progress is reversed. We have the same problem with our trading. There is a point equivalent to four steps back in every trade. Once this point is reached there is greater probability the trade will fail. The length of these steps is different for each trader and they are measured by the equity curve.

A single equity curve shows the maximum draw down in a trade and this is the second, and most significant, piece of information available from this process. A draw down is the level of loss in the trade. At the worst point in

Figure 5.1, Trader Average suffered a 13% loss. Then the trade recovered and eventually made a profit.

By itself, this information is not particularly useful. Combine this result with other equity curves for trades by Trader Average and it provides a clue to trading success. Assume the average maximum draw down on all his successful trades hovers around the 13% level. This figure provides a useful guide to setting an effective stop loss point. This is the trading performance profile for Trader Average.

The aggregate equity curve in Figure 5.2 shows the performance profile for our sample Trader Average. It is constructed from the average performance of all his successful trades. This curve tells him that when any trade takes more than a 13% loss, there is an increased probability that the trade will become a dangerous loser.

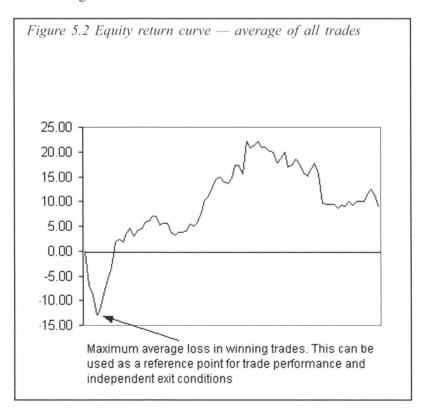

Figure 5.2 Equity return curve — average of all trades

Maximum average loss in winning trades. This can be used as a reference point for trade performance and independent exit conditions

Our objective here is not to improve our entry technique or timing. Instead, we want a better understanding of our trading behavior so that we can identify the parameters of good and bad trades. We accept that sometimes we all make poor trading decisions. The equity curve provides us with a way to quickly recognize the truly bad trade selections. The curve provides the figure we need to monitor our progress.

Two steps back is OK. Four steps back is deadly. The fourth step for Trader Average is any move beyond a 13% loss.

By examining our trading history with an equity curve, we establish when a trade is just struggling, and when it is drowning. We know what the equity curve for a good trade looks like, and we know what the curve looks like for a bad trade.

The aggregate equity curve provides a record of our repeated trading behavior. It says this trader gets in too early and, on average, he loses 13% of his trading capital before the trade turns around and starts to work in his favor. This is a consequence of early entry, but it is also a repeated consequence of about the same size for most of his trades. The really good trades only lose 6% before they start making money. The really bad trades lose 15% and just keep on going down.

The performance of every individual trade is compared with the aggregate equity curve. The curve provides an independent way to recognize and manage the risk of trade failure.

LOSING TRADE PROFILES
What does an unsuccessful trade look like? Consider the equity curve shown in Figure 5.3 of an unsuccessful trade made by Trader Average. It plots the percentage value of the trade. We use 13% as the trigger point for an exit in this example.

This trade goes straight to hell and then quickly recovers. This retreat-and-rally behavior is typical of a poorly timed entry. Perhaps Trader Average believed this was a trend breakout opportunity and used an aggressive entry in anticipation of a trend change. Instead, the market rallied before collapsing. The best return is 5%, and losses soon hit more than 20%.

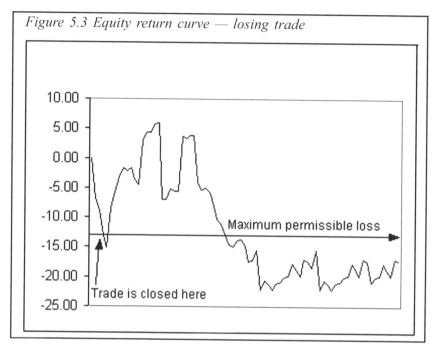

Figure 5.3 Equity return curve — losing trade

Our focus is on the percentage value of the curve, but some traders may find that a time value is also important. Perhaps trades going nowhere for more than six weeks end up as consistent losers. If this is part of your performance profile, then add this characteristic as a second cut-off point designed to lock-in winners and weed out potential losers.

Applying equity curve analysis shakes Trader Average out of this cycle of hope and disappointment. As soon as the marked-to-market loss exceeds 13%, he exits the trade. This is his personal four steps back. He uses the aggregate equity curve performance profile to calculate this figure and to make this exit decision before any charting or technically based exit is signaled.

When the equity curve for the trade passes a predetermined point, we know there is a high probability that it will remain a loser given our trading record. If we know this value in advance, we have an additional method of closing losing trades because we factor the information into our stop loss calculations.

WINNING TRADE PROFILES

What does our winning trade look like? Until we have a collection of personal winners and losers, we cannot really tell. Start by plotting an equity curve for all your past trades. Compare the curves. Look for common characteristics in the weeks after the trade entry. How much, on average, did each trade lose before starting to make money?

We delve into the records for Trader Success. He gets seven out of 10 trades correct. Many of his trades lose very little money initially and move quickly into profit. This reflects his higher level of skill and experience.

In this example we use a $500 loss as the cut-off point. Lose this amount and the aggregate performance profile for Trader Success suggests that the trade is most likely to be a loser. Sure, some trades lose more than this and bounce back. These are the lucky ones. Using luck to generate success is a good strategy in a casino. It is a losing strategy in the market.

Trader Success trades Commonwealth Bank in this example. The trade is opened at $0 on the equity curve. By day two of the trade he expects to know if he is making or losing money. Even Trader Success has an aggregate performance profile that shows he loses money before starting to make money. The equity curve for this trade, shown in Figure 5.4, reflects this characteristic behavior.

Over the next few days following the trade entry, the loss grows and creeps toward the maximum $500. Trader Success knows from experience that this is the point when a trade is most likely to go permanently and fatally bad. Trader Average does not have this experience, but by using an aggregate equity curve as a guide he takes a short-cut to experience.

Trader Success tracks the growing loss; while it is less than, or equal to, the average draw down of successful trades, he remains comfortable with the trade. In this sample trade, the loss does not exceed the loss limits and the trade quickly reverses direction and moves into profit-making territory.

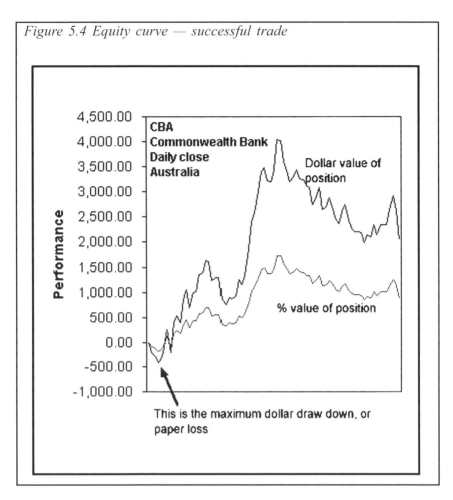

Figure 5.4 Equity curve — successful trade

Equity curves define the average draw down, as well as the maximum draw down — John Sweeney's maximum adverse excursion — for every trade. We use these draw down figures to construct and confirm our exit signals. The equity curve chart tells us when the trade is performing about the same, on average, as other successful trades. We stay with the trade with confidence.

But when the equity curve for an individual trade dips below this average — when we start to lose more than normal — we know the trade has a higher probability of disaster. This is an objective exit signal. We ignore any other signals of hope that we read into the chart, the indicators, or gather from market rumor. By constructing an aggregate equity curve over many trades, we have a tool to confirm trading success as the trade develops. Our objective is to make each trade conform to, or outperform, the best equity curve in our collection of past trades.

When we better understand the personal characteristics of our trading behavior, we develop a personal performance profile. This is the launching pad for improving our trading success. In the next three parts, we look at ways to protect capital, profits, and portfolios. These include specific techniques. How successful or appropriate they are will depend on how well you understand your performance profile.

Better money management improves results built on an inconsistent mix of tools, techniques, and methods. Inconsistency is not limited to the novice. In bullish market conditions, even Trader Success reaches for the stars from a wobbly base. Better money management dramatically improves results when applied to a consistent combination of tools, techniques, and methods.

APPENDIX: CONSTRUCTING AN EQUITY CURVE USING A SPREADSHEET

An equity curve is best constructed on a spreadsheet as soon as a trade is opened. The Excel spreadsheet template for this is available as part of the Better Trading spreadsheet pak from www.guppytraders.com. Readers may also construct this spreadsheet themselves. The layout is shown in Figure 5.5.

Column A carries the date. Column B carries the closing price. Column C is the current value of the position (position size * closing price). Column D is the return on the position at the end of the day. Formulas are inserted to produce these calculations automatically. Create an embedded chart to graph the figures in column D. This shows the dollar change in value.

Column E calculates the percentage change in value each day. The value is increased by a factor of 100 to plot it clearly on the chart display.

On day 2 of the trade, fill in the date and the closing price. Use the FILL

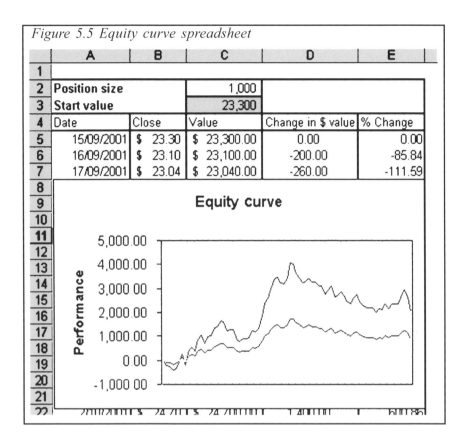

Figure 5.5 Equity curve spreadsheet

	A	B	C	D	E
1					
2	Position size		1,000		
3	Start value		23,300		
4	Date	Close	Value	Change in $ value	% Change
5	15/09/2001	$ 23.30	$ 23,300.00	0.00	0.00
6	16/09/2001	$ 23.10	$ 23,100.00	-200.00	-85.84
7	17/09/2001	$ 23.04	$ 23,040.00	-260.00	-111.59

DOWN function to duplicate the formulas in columns C and D. Ensure the chart display is updated with these changes. Continue to do this every day the trade is open.

When the trade is closed, print the equity curve and file it for comparison with other successful and unsuccessful trades.

Part 2

Protect Capital

SIX
RISK AND
UNCERTAINTY

A laddin found wealth hidden in a cave. We find it in the financial markets lurking on our computer screens. The potential wealth available turns Aladdin into a pauper. If there is a secret to gathering this wealth, it is this: do not allow yourself to be blinded by the glitter of profits slipping across your computer screen. Instead, concentrate closely on protecting your capital and profits will follow.

The novice trader ignores this advice and remains a novice or a loser. Professional traders focus on protecting capital every day against the risks that make the rewards of the markets possible. There is no reward without risk. Successful traders know the secret: the effective management of risk guarantees the reward. This is why, in the next few chapters, we start with some methods to protect capital before moving on to consider ways to protect profits.

It is our ability to identify and manage risk in the market that makes market trading so attractive. Some people believe that market traders are gamblers. It is certainly true in some cases, but gamblers do not last very long. Some people believe that market trading success is based on an ability to predict what is going to happen. This is not a long-term answer to trading success, because even the best fortune teller cannot tell when to buy a stock, or more importantly, when to sell it.

Central to the management of risk is the concept of a stop loss. Central to trading survival is the stop loss rule. Central to trading success is a correct evaluation of the risk/reward ratio. Each of these aspects of trading is considered in this chapter. Together, they provide the essential framework for trading and investment success. Trader Novice believes that success lies with proper stock selection. Trader Superstar knows that success lies with proper money management. This is the key to protecting capital, so we start with an overview of the basic calculations found in every trader's toolkit.

PROBABILITY OR PREDICTION?

When I trade the market I use chart analysis to understand crowd behavior. I also use technical analysis tools to understand price behavior. Why do you use charting and technical analysis?

Usually the answers fall into two distinct camps. One camp believes that these techniques provide a way to predict market moves and price activity. The other camp believes that the analysis establishes a probability framework. These divisions are common among professionals and amateurs. They divide traders and techniques.

When you consider applying charting and technical analysis, it is an advantage to know which camp you belong to. When reading or listening to analysts who use these techniques, it is very important to know what camp they belong to. If the analysis is based on a probability framework and you interpret it as a prediction, then you may end up with an unpleasant and costly result.

THE RISK OF PREDICTION

We all bring with us to the financial markets a different understanding of risk and a different solution to the problem of identifying and managing it. This influences the way we select and understand indicators. We talk in general terms about market risk, and this hides some important distinctions. If we believe that risk is the same as uncertainty, then the obvious antidote to risk is to reduce uncertainty. In the financial market, this typically comes in two separate packages.

The first package is neatly tied up in fundamental analysis. Fundamental ratios, analysis, and procedures provide a good starting point to focus our attention on a specific group of stocks. Many people stop there, believing they have the answer. Instead, they have just a beginning.

Fundamental analysis, in a broad sense, is useful for deciding *what* to buy. It is not very useful for deciding *when* to buy. A common solution to this problem is to buy quality stocks at bargain prices. We all like quality, and these buyers believe that the quality of the stock will overcome market retreats. They reason that good stocks always perform well, and even if they do slip a little in price, their quality means they recover quickly. These investors select quality stocks to lower risk by reducing uncertainty.

The second package contains an analysis system that generally involves some form of prediction.

The objective is the same for both the investors using fundamentals and the investors using charts and technical indicators. They aim to reduce risk by knowing as much about the future as possible, or at least by knowing more about the future than their competitors. In technical analysis, knowing the future is often associated with the use of particular indicators or indicator combinations. The objective is to identify something before it happens — every time.

An example of this type of thinking is when the Relative Strength Index indicator shows a divergence with the price chart and generates an early sell signal. Traders and investors use it as an indicator of something that will happen in the future — a prediction. Technicians spend a lot of time developing subtle mathematical manipulations which they believe help them to tell the future.

In my book *Chart Trading* I discussed the performance of these predictive techniques and I will not repeat the detail here. I agree with Larry Williams, the U.S. commodity trader who is noted for turning a $10,000 stake into $1 million in less than 12 months. He notes a survey of newsletter trading approaches in *Long Term Secrets to Short Term Trading*. He says the performance figures are very revealing: "I went back three years and found that the poorest performers in 1995, 1996, and 1997 have consistently been the Gann/Elliott/Acarne group who, as a group, have averaged a loss of close to 100% a year. This from a crowd that claims all can be known, that you really can buy bottoms and sell exact tops."

This is harsh criticism, yet some people do use these approaches very successfully. Closer inspection, though, often shows they also use good trading techniques that return good trading results under almost any system.

Personally, I believe that risk is not effectively or completely nullified by techniques designed to tell us something about the future. When I use tools designed to anticipate market action, I apply them within the context of this belief. This belief is the foundation of all the risk control strategies that follow in this book.

PROBABILITY

If risk is unable to be nullified by analysis, then where does this leave us? It doesn't mean we cannot trade the market. It means we re-focus our attention on what is easily verified and use it to construct an understanding of the balance of probability in any situation. We do not need to know the future to recognize an opportunity. Aladdin did not know he would find his cave, but he did know how to exploit the opportunity when he stumbled onto it.

This is my starting point for trading. I stand in the probability camp. I accept uncertainty, and this determines what I look for when selecting a chart and indicator combination for trading the market. I start from the proposition that I cannot predict the future, so I aim to identify the probability of one outcome in comparison to another. This is the first step in managing risk.

Probability is the ratio of favorable outcomes to the total number of possible outcomes or opportunity set. An upward-sloping trend shows a high ratio of favorable outcomes — increasing prices.

TAMING MARKET RISK

How do we turn uncertainty into opportunity? How do we turn risk into reward? Successful traders have a solution and it comes from just three numbers that accurately define and manage the risk in every trade.

It does not matter how we select a stock. The solution starts as soon as we buy, because when we turn from analysis to action, the nature of risk changes.

We introduced these concepts briefly in Chapter 1. They are the very foundation of trading success, so we consider them again in more detail before applying these calculations, in the section entitled "Setting the Stop Loss," to determine how much stock we should buy.

As soon as we buy stock, all the risk comes down to a single factor: if price moves against us and we start losing money, then our risk has increased. Risk, in this case, is equal to loss. It is precisely estimated and measured, because risk is the product of the relationship between entry, exit, and capital.

We start defining risk by noting the price we pay to buy the stock. Next we decide the exit price. This price is designed to tell us when we are wrong. Remember, we cannot predict what is going to happen, but we know when the trade is going bad — we start losing money. The aggregate equity curve from the last chapter tells us when a trade slips toward perdition.

The second important price is often called a stop loss price. The difference between our entry price and our stop loss price is the risk we take in the market. Not everybody understands this, and they often go on to lose a great deal of money. They also forget the third number in the calculation — the total amount of trading capital, or account size.

When we enter a trade, it is tempting to believe that trading capital is equal to the amount we have allocated to the trade — that capital equals position size. This is a significant distraction because it does not take into account the relationship between each trade and your portfolio performance.

If our total trade size, or position, is $20,000, then it is highly unlikely the entire amount is actually at risk. The only way to lose the entire $20,000 is if the company goes out of business. It happens, but not very often.

This is an area of confusion. Many people measure the loss in terms of the money allocated to the trade. In this example, a $2,000 loss is a 10% loss when calculated against the $20,000 used in the trade. If we measure the loss against the money allocated to the trade, we exaggerate the risk. We must put this loss into the wider context of our portfolio, as discussed in Chapter 2 and summarized in Figures 6.1 and 6.2.

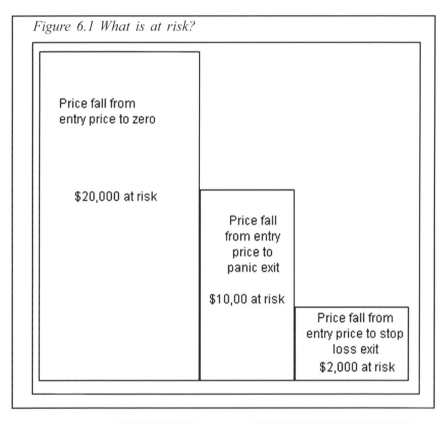

Figure 6.1 What is at risk?

Price fall from entry price to zero

$20,000 at risk

Price fall from entry price to panic exit

$10,00 at risk

Price fall from entry price to stop loss exit
$2,000 at risk

The 2% rule simply states that no single position, or trade, should put at risk more than 2% of our total trading capital. If we have $100,000, this does not mean each trade is limited to a total of $2,000. It means the actual risk of the trade — the amount we are prepared to lose before we admit we are wrong — is not larger than 2% of our total trading capital.

We use the 2% rule consistently in all our trading calculations. Chapter 1 examined the impact of changing the amount at risk in each trade. As risk grows beyond 2%, our trading has to improve dramatically just to overcome the increased level of losses in losing trades. We use 2% because testing shows that it is the optimum size for Traders Average and Success. Trader

Superstar cuts risk further, opting for 1% or less. Trader Novice treads on dangerous ground and often has no choice but to let risk grow to 5% or more.

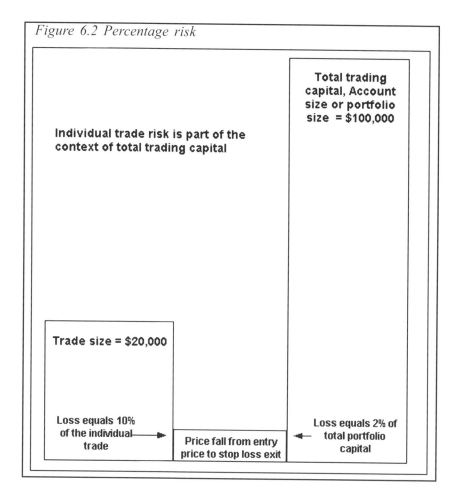

Figure 6.2 Percentage risk

Total trading capital, Account size or portfolio size = $100,000

Individual trade risk is part of the context of total trading capital

Trade size = $20,000

Loss equals 10% of the individual trade

Price fall from entry price to stop loss exit

Loss equals 2% of total portfolio capital

The stop loss spreadsheet template in the Better Trading pak provides an opportunity for readers to examine the impact of letting risk grow beyond 2%. With $100,000, Trader Average makes 194 losing trades in a row before his account is reduced to $2,000. Trader Superstar could take 390 successive losing trades. Let risk grow to 5% and Trader Novice is out of the game after 77 losing trades.

As we make successful trades, our portfolio capital grows, and the dollar size of 2% grows larger. As we take losing trades, the dollar size decreases. Every time we enter a new trade, we calculate the dollar value of 2% of our total trading capital.

This changes our understanding of risk. If risk is the amount we actually lose, then we control this using a stop loss figure. Further, if the loss is measured against our total account size, then we make sure no single trade has the power to destroy us.

We tame market risk by understanding the amount we truly put at risk in every trade. It is the amount we choose to lose. When we control this decision using a stop loss order, we tame market risk.

SETTING THE STOP LOSS

Setting a stop loss exit has two aspects. The first is the financial aspect. The second is a chart-based aspect. The objective of a good stop loss is to match the financial requirements with the chart-based requirements. When this is achieved, it makes for a safe trade because the price action trigger is related to a logical point on the chart.

We start with the financial aspect. For the purposes of this example, we join hands with Trader Success and work with a nominal $100,000 of trading capital and no brokerage fees. Trader Success always works with the 2% rule, so the most he puts at actual risk on any single trade is $2,000. This means that if the price falls after he buys the stock, he gets out if the loss reaches $2,000.

The obvious way to calculate the stop loss exit price is simply to combine our permitted loss value — $2,000 — with our proposed entry point, as shown in Figure 6.3. This provides a simple solution to the financial aspect of setting the stop loss. This is straightforward spreadsheet work.

In this example, we propose to make an entry at $5.00 and we do not want to spend more than around $20,000 on the trade. This is a reasonable trade size. This combination sets the stop loss at $4.50. If we enter at $5.00, we lose $2,000 if the price falls to $4.50. This is our exit signal.

Figure 6.3 Financial stop loss calculation

Equity name	test 1
Number of shares	4,000
Purchase price	$ 5.00
Net cost	$ 20,000.00
Av Brokerage	0.00
Full cost	$ 20,000.00
RISK PARAMETERS	
Equity risk @ 2%	2,000.00
Risk on this trade	2,000.00
Stop loss exit price based on purchase price	4.500

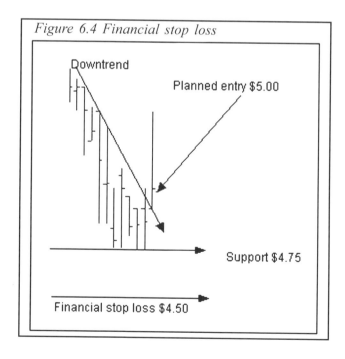

Figure 6.4 Financial stop loss

Downtrend

Planned entry $5.00

Support $4.75

Financial stop loss $4.50

This chart information provides the details required to create a chart-based stop loss condition. We plug the figures into the spreadsheet shown in Figure 6.5 and arrive at the maximum theoretical position size. The figures we need are the entry price — $5.00 — and the planned stop loss exit price — $4.75. When these are entered into the spreadsheet, we have a value for the maximum theoretical position size — in this case, $40,000.

Figure 6.5 Maximum position size: Chart stop loss

Equity name	test 2
Number of shares	8,000
Purchase price	$ 5.00
Net cost	$ 40,000.00
Av. brokerage	0.00
Full cost	$ 40,000.00
RISK PARAMETERS	
Equity risk @ 2%	2,000.00
Risk on this trade	2,000.00
Stop loss exit price based on full cost	4.750

This means that prices could fall to $4.75 and our losses will not exceed $2,000. This matches the financial risk control requirements with the logical chart-based requirements.

When we come to complete the trade, we either use this amount or make it smaller. We cannot make it larger. If we spend more than $40,000 on the trade, shown in Figure 6.6, then the exit point rises above the logical stop loss point. Look what happens when we decide to spend $100,000. The stop loss point now lifts to $4.90. Prices can only fall to this level before we incur a $2,000 loss. This stop loss is too tight. We have to get out of the trade before the chart-based logical stop loss level is hit.

Even if we decide to trade on the basis of the original financial calculations shown in Figure 6.3, we still have a significant problem. This theoretical trade is not a trade we take.

Figure 6.6 Position size too large

Equity name	test 3
Number of shares	20,000
Purchase price	$ 5.00
Net cost	$ 100,000.00
Av. brokerage	0.00
Full cost	$ 100,000.00
RISK PARAMETERS	
Equity risk @ 2%	2,000.00
Risk on this trade	2,000.00
Stop loss exit price based on purchase	4.900

We only have $20,000 available for this trade. We do not want to spend $40,000 on this trade, no matter how good it looks. In real life we might not have $40,000 available for the trade. The original financial calculations shown in the spreadsheet provide the maximum theoretical amount we can spend on the trade.

To get the best trading solution, we need to bring together the logical stop loss point — $4.75 — and the amount we are prepared to trade — $20,000 — and combine this with the amount we are prepared to lose if we are wrong — $2,000. This combination gives us the best possible outcome, shown in Figure 6.7.

Now we buy 4,000 shares at $5.00 and spend our preferred $20,000. With this combination the stop loss point is lowered to $4.50. This means that prices could drop to this level before we lose $2,000. This makes this a much safer trade, because the risk is reduced.

The chart-based stop loss level at $4.75 is still the important figure. If prices fall below this, we get out of the trade. If we exit at $4.75 the total loss in this trade is just $1,000. Instead of losing 2% of our trading capital, the conditions of this trade mean we lose just 1%.

Figure 6.7 Practical stop loss

Equity name		test 4
Maximum number of shares		4,000
Purchase price		$ 5.00
Net cost		$ 20,000.00
Av. brokerage		0.00
Full cost		$ 20,000.00
RISK PARAMETERS		
Equity risk @ 2%		2,000.00
Risk on this trade	$ 1,000.00	2,000.00
Stop loss exit price based on full cost		4.500

The results of these different approaches are shown in Figure 6.8. If we use just a financial calculation, then the stop loss level rarely coincides with a logical point on the chart. If we use just a chart-based calculation, it may require more capital than we have, or more than we are prepared to commit to the trade.

The practical trading solution brings the size of the trade — the amount spent — and the logical stop loss point together so that the actual risk is never greater than 2% of trading capital. The Excel spreadsheet template for these calculations is part of the Better Trading pak.

There are other methods for calculating the optimum stop loss size in relation to portfolio size. Our intention here is not to survey all methods, but to show how our preferred stop loss method is combined with other strategies to build effective money management solutions to boost trading returns without a significant improvement in trading skill. Readers who wish to explore other solutions will find interesting discussions in *Trade Your Way to Financial Freedom* by Van Tharp, *Trading to Win* by Ari Kiev, and *The Trading Game* by Ryan Jones.

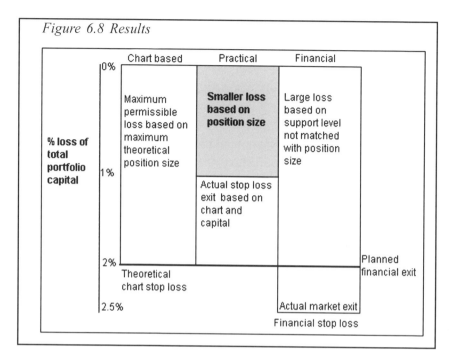

Figure 6.8 Results

CALCULATING RISK AND REWARD

Understanding risk and reward is at the very heart of trading, but few traders formally assess these relationships. One of the first steps toward market survival is to understand how risk is defined by the potential downside of any planned trade or investment. What could go up could also go down. A chart of price activity provides a logical way to calculate the potential risk and reward from each planned trade or investment.

There are a minimum of two features we need to consider:

1. Decide where the significant resistance zone or level is. This acts as a cap on the price rise and defines the likely reward. If there is no resistance, then this calculation is based on a preferred minimum return from the trade.

   This is the trade reward. It is the difference between the planned entry price and the planned profitable exit price. By itself, it means little. We need to combine it with the risk on the trade.

2. Decide where the significant support zone or level is found below the planned entry price. This acts as a safety net, and defines the

level of risk in the trade. This is usually the stop loss figure also used in the calculations discussed above.

There are several ways to set this stop loss point. My preference is to select a figure based on a logical chart point. These points include identified support levels. In some trades, it may be the value of a moving average line, the value of an average true range calculation, or the value of a count back line. The difference between the planned entry price and the planned stop loss exit price defines the risk in this trade.

The final calculation is the risk/reward ratio. This ratio is calculated by dividing the expected reward by the expected risk. The ratio tells us how much money we are risking in chasing a defined reward. We will look at three examples.

Trader Average has a portfolio littered with trades like the example in Figure 6.9. It shows a planned entry at $33 with an exit at $58. This is a reward of $25. The planned stop loss exit is at $10, giving a risk of $23.

Figure 6.9 Trader Average

Trade 1	
Planned entry price	$ 33.00
Planned profit exit	$ 58.00
Planned stop loss exit	$ 10.00
Trade reward	$ 25.00
Trade risk	$ 23.00
Trade risk/reward ratio	1.09

This is a marginal trade where Trader Average risks $23 to chase a $25 reward. The ratio is only 1:1.09. It does not matter how strong the chart pattern, how reliable the indicator, how enticing the trade, or how the company rates on the quality rankings — a trade with this risk/reward ratio is a waste of time, because the reward does not adequately compensate for the risk.

Trader Novice is attracted to trade 2, shown in Figure 6.10. The stock is not too expensive at $1.00, nor is it a speculative stock trading at $0.01. The trade has a potential return of $0.10 and a risk of $0.30. It makes absolutely no sense at all. Trader Novice risks $0.30 in pursuit of a $0.10 gain. This is a ratio of 1:0.33.

Figure 6.10 Trader Novice

Trade 2	
Planned entry price	$ 1.00
Planned profit exit	$ 1.10
Planned stop loss exit	$ 0.70
Trade reward	$ 0.10
Trade risk	$ 0.30
Trade risk/reward ratio	**0.33**

It is not just Trader Novice who makes this error. This approach is used by some black box trading systems. Unless the success rate is consistently very high, this is a losing approach. It takes three winning trades to make up the maximum loss experienced on a single losing trade. It takes four winning trades just to get ahead after a single losing trade.

Trader Success and Trader Superstar look for trades like those shown in Figure 6.11. Trade 3 shows the relationship successful traders look for. The planned entry is at $0.20, with a planned exit at $0.27. This 35% return is readily achievable in this area of the market. The risk in the trade is $0.02 because the stop loss condition is set at $0.18. This gives a risk/reward ratio of 1:3.50. Trader Success expects to get back $0.035 for every cent he risks.

Figure 6.11 Trader Success and Trader Superstar

Trade 3	
Planned entry price	$ 0.20
Planned profit exit	$ 0.27
Planned stop loss exit	$ 0.18
Trade reward	$ 0.07
Trade risk	$ 0.02
Trade risk/reward ratio	**3.50**

Good money management, tight stop loss control, and close observance of the 2% rule are all ingredients of success. Selecting trades with the best risk/reward ratio brings these ingredients together in a successful long-term survival strategy. The Risk/Reward Excel spreadsheet template in the Better Trading pak makes it easy to complete and summarize the calculations for competing trades, as shown in Figure 6.12.

Figure 6.12 Calculating the risk/reward ratio

Summary	
Trade 1	**1.09**
Trade 2	**0.33**
Trade 3	**3.50**

Setting a stop loss price is easy in theory. It is much more difficult in practice, because our emotions get in the way. None of us like losing money, so we develop a financial flinch when it comes time to act on our stop loss. The next chapter examines this flinch and suggests some strategies for beating it.

SEVEN

FLINCH POINTS

To make money, we start by saving money. To make trading profits, we start by protecting trading capital. If we avoid losing too much of our capital to inevitable trading mistakes, then we have the opportunity to make some real money.

How do you cross the road? Do you set your eyes firmly on the opposite sidewalk and boldly step out, or do you follow the road safety rules, carefully looking each way before crossing? Only a fool steps out boldly, because the trick to crossing the road and surviving is to avoid being hit by a truck. The reasons for crossing the road, good or bad, all count for nothing the moment we step onto the road surface.

As soon as we start a trade, all that counts is survival. In trading terms this means protecting our capital. If our capital is injured, or killed, we cannot make it to the other side of the trade. We do not get to enjoy profits, no matter how good our analysis and planning was. Success comes from avoiding being run over, so even the most stupid chicken makes the crossing carefully.

The reasons for each individual trade are not related to the success or failure of each trade. Even the best trades are destroyed if we fail to avoid significant capital loss. Poor traders with ill-conceived plans survive only if they can avoid being run over.

This is a disquieting conclusion. It suggests that the time spent on planning and analysis is not directly related to the success of the trade or investment.

To a significant extent, this is true. It is also true that a better understanding of the trend and its character allows you to select the better trade entry point, but this does not diminish the impact of the truck if it hits you. Noble reasons and good analysis count for little if you are squashed.

CELEBRITY CORNER

The stop loss is the celebrity of the trading world — everyone has heard of it, but few have a close relationship with it. Individually, we need to change this relationship, because a stop loss strategy is the key to long-term trading survival. This chapter explores some factors preventing us from building a closer relationship with this financial celebrity. We dealt with the mathematical calculations, the logic of chart analysis, and the arithmetic of risk in the previous chapter. Here we look at why this so often fails when we try to apply it to our own trading.

Trading survival depends on protecting your trading capital. It is protected by using a stop loss technique. The practical implementation is you place a sell order with your broker to get out of a losing trade at a small loss rather than at a large loss. Just where you place the stop loss depends on the style and method of trading you use and the way you trade, as shown by your equity curves.

Disciplined use of a stop loss order is the most important step in building trading capital. When a stock is purchased, the stop loss is designed to protect trading capital. As the trade starts to make a profit, the stop loss is used to protect profits using trailing stop loss techniques. We look at these in Part 3. In this chapter, our main focus is on using the stop loss as a means of protecting capital.

A stop loss order is implemented by using a broker who offers an automatic, electronically managed stop loss service. Or you may have to exercise your own discipline to act on the stop loss signals and contact your broker. Traders who have difficulty in picking up the telephone to act on stop losses may also find it difficult to place a stop loss order with their broker for automatic execution. Here we explore the reasons for this.

THE COWARD IN EVERY TRADER

Trading is about the management of risk. Many traders fail when it comes time to act on their risk control plans. Cowardice takes over and they back away from action. How far and how fast we retreat is tracked and calculated from our contract notes and trading records. When we make money, we plot an equity curve. When we lose money, we should plot a coward's curve because it identifies our weaknesses.

Cowardice thrives when we mismatch our intentions with our courage. It grows and dominates our trading when we place the blame on the mechanics of the trade rather than where it belongs. All stop loss strategies require discipline and a willingness to act. It is astounding just how many times we fail to act when stop losses are hit.

It is not a problem with the stop loss mechanism. Facing a loss, many traders seem to find so many convenient excuses for cowardice. Excuses range from "My stop is too close, so I had better use a more flexible approach" or "The price looks like it's getting better," to the more imaginative "The mouse stopped working" or "The telephone rang and tied up the Internet line just before the close of trading."

Try writing down your next excuse for inaction. Look at it a week or two later. Does it remind you of the dog-ate-my-homework type of excuse?

These excuses conceal the way we flinch or freeze just when action is required. The long-term prospect of financial loss is not enough to outweigh the immediate financial pain of executing a stop loss order. We back away from making the decision. The flinch factor stays our hand, and the stop loss order is never placed or acted upon.

MEASURING THE FLINCH

These flinch and freeze points are measured in the potential dollars lost; this varies from trader to trader, but the process remains consistent.[1]

---

1 An outline of this concept was published in the U.S. magazine *Active Trader* in April 2001.

By developing a better understanding of the way our fear develops and where the flinch and freeze points are located, we improve our chances of placing good intentions.

Start by identifying the size of losses in old closed trades. Go through your trading records. Organized traders look back through their collected trading plans. Make two piles of contract notes — one for winning trades and one for losing trades. Ignore the pile of winners. You probably spent enough time gloating over these when they happened.

Our interest is in the pile of losers, because they contain vital information about ourselves that we would prefer to ignore. Two important features will likely emerge:

1. We are good at selling when the loss is quite small. If the loss, for example, is $500, we sell the position easily. Stop losses at this level are easy to execute.

2. Although it does not make much immediate sense, we are also good at selling when the loss is very large. We use a figure of a $4,500 loss and above in this example.

These losses are in trades, or investments, that have gone seriously wrong. The evidence of failure is too large to be ignored and, with a shove from the tax office or our accountant, we decide to sell. The eventual sell decision is rarely related to a formal stop loss level — it was exceeded months or years ago. Once we decide to bite the bullet, we tend to dump the stock, selling at whatever price is available.

These are extremes of trading behavior. Between them we expect to see our ability to act on a stop loss signal decrease as the size of the loss increases. Small losses are easy to take. A large loss is more difficult, so we expect a curve shaped like the thin line plotted in Figure 7.1. Instead, we discover that the data plots a series of curves. Each section of the curve records our willingness to take action on our stop loss points in relation to the dollar loss incurred in the trade. The curve falls into four separate sections and their shapes are quite different. The combined curves in Figure 7.1 belong to Trader Average. We met him in previous chapters and he is just like many of us. He trades with an account of around $80,000 to $140,000.

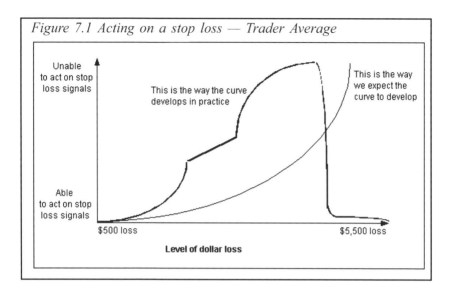

Figure 7.1 Acting on a stop loss — Trader Average

These curves match the size of his loss with his ability to act. It is a measure of the degree of courage or cowardice contained in each of his trading decisions.

Section 1 of this curve, in Figure 7.2, is the type of curve we intuitively expect to see. It shows a steady rise from our ability to act cleanly to cut a loss to the area where action becomes more difficult. As the level of loss increases in dollar terms, our ability to act on our stop loss decision decreases.

For Trader Average, a $500 loss is easy to take. Your starting figure may be different, but the shape of the curve remains the same. Trader Average has $100,000 in trading capital. By the time the loss grows to $1,500, it takes a little more thought before he clicks the mouse button to send the sell order. As the level of loss and financial pain increases, he finds his good intentions get weaker. This is a smooth process, asking for just a little more moral courage at each new and larger level of loss.

The vertical scale measures his ability to act on a stop loss signal. In the middle of this scale there is a zone of indecision. By the time the loss for Trader Average reaches $2,000 it becomes harder, but not impossible, to act on the stop loss signal. All traders know the feeling; if we give the trade just a little more time to develop, it may become profitable.

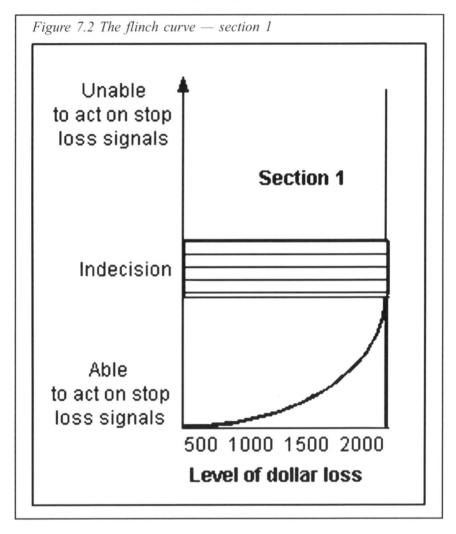

Figure 7.2 The flinch curve — section 1

You should counter this emotional response by taking another look at your aggregate equity curve and harden your resolve to cut the loser on the first stop loss signal.

Our friend, Trader Average, watches the loss grow and slowly loses the willpower to act.

PHASE TRANSITION

Physicists have long been aware of the phase transition phenomenon. Living in Northern Australia, I observe it during the Wet season when humid air turns to a curling mist running down the side of a cold bottle taken from the refrigerator. Traders feel this phase transition when a loss suddenly cracks the size barrier and paralyzes all action. By the time the size of the loss sneaks to over $2,000, Trader Average finds his ability to act is paralyzed. The shape of the plotted line, shown in Figure 7.3, changes dramatically in section 2.

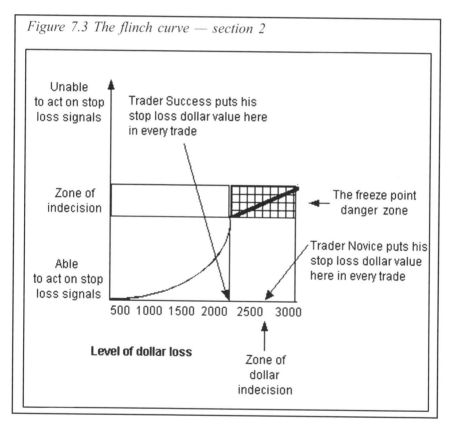

Figure 7.3 The flinch curve — section 2

We hit a "freeze" point, and this danger zone is responsible for more trading deaths than any other factor. The freeze point danger zone is at the intersection of the action indecision zone and the dollar indecision zone. It is a phase transition point where our ability to make a decision is snap-frozen.

The size and shape of this paralysis zone has a direct relationship to the size of the potential loss. For Trader Average, we show the zone of dollar indecision stretching in a $1,000 gap between a $2,000 and $3,000 trading loss. Once the loss grows to $2,000 or larger, it is very difficult to act on the stop loss signal. The larger the loss grows, the greater the probability that Trader Average will fail to act.

Your personal paralysis point may appear at a different dollar level, and stretch wider or narrower, but there is no doubt that you do have a freeze point. If you know it and understand it, you have the opportunity to avoid it. Remain unaware of it and your trading capital suffers.

The line in section 2 is shown as a straight line. It reflects the sudden phase transition that creates this freeze point. There is no gradual move from action to inaction. Our ability to act is snap-frozen. As the size of the loss grows, Trader Average moves rapidly through this zone of indecision to a stage where fatalism takes over. The exact parameters of this personal danger zone level come from your trading records.

Most traders, beginners or experienced, have a good idea of how much loss they can comfortably tolerate. Past trading contract notes put precise figures on it. These contain the trades you know you should have closed, but did not. These trades go on to become big-time losers. Pinpoint the price at the time of this indecision and calculate the loss in dollar terms. This cluster of losses defines the limits of your freeze zone.

REALITY BITES

Few people have the ability to see themselves as others see them. In many cases this is just as well, and they blithely travel through life oblivious to the distaste and disaster they trail behind them. Traders do not have this luxury when it comes to the reality of protecting trading capital. The size of the loss we think we *can* tolerate and act upon must exactly match the size of the loss that we *do* act on. This is where the flinch curve helps, because it identifies the placement of the freeze zone.

When there is a gap between where this danger zone *is* situated on the scale of dollar loss and where you *think* it is situated, then you have a problem. You may believe you can take a $2,000 loss, but your trading records will show if this is actually the case. Your flinch and freeze level may be lower than you think.

Trader Success knows the dollar value where the curve moves into section 2. At this level of capital exposure, he knows from experience that he can take a loss up to $2,000 without too much worry. As a result, his stop loss levels are at the edge of the first section of the curve and he has a high probability of acting upon them.

Trader Novice tends to consistently over-estimate his flinch and freeze level. He believes he can take a loss up to $2,500. On this sample account size, this puts the area for his stop loss decision in the middle of the danger zone on this curve. When it comes time to act, Trader Novice is frozen by indecision. Instead of looking for the best exit, he looks for reasons and excuses to stay with the trade. He looks for distractions to stop him ringing his broker or placing a sell order. The danger zone may be $1,000 wide, or as narrow as a few minutes in a fast-moving market.

The shape of the curve in section 1 gives us a solution to our inability to act on stop loss conditions. If we move the size of our dollar stop loss until it falls on the curve in section 1, then we instantly improve our chances of actually acting on the stop loss conditions. This is the way Trader Novice turns into Trader Average and then Trader Success.

The exact value used to calculate and plot the curve is an individual affair. Take the time to plot it from your trading records. Match your proven ability to act on stop loss decisions up to a particular dollar size with the planned stop loss point in your next trade. Push cowardice to one side and give courage a chance to take over when required. A glancing blow to your trading capital is not fatal.

APPROACHING THE DEEP END

Surrounded by death and destruction, the film action hero is momentarily frozen in time. Then he snaps out of it, escape plan fully formed and survival assured. The escape from our trading freeze point does not have this happy ending. Failure to act in the critical levels does not free us for instant action as the loss grows even larger. Although no longer frozen in indecision, we lack the resolution to end the pain.

The exit from the danger zone often has a well-defined trigger level and is usually plotted within just a few hundred dollars. Once the dollar loss breaks into section 3, the curve changes shape again, as shown in Figure 7.4. As the loss grows, in this case beyond $3,000, Trader Average quickly decides that it is so large he cannot afford to take it.

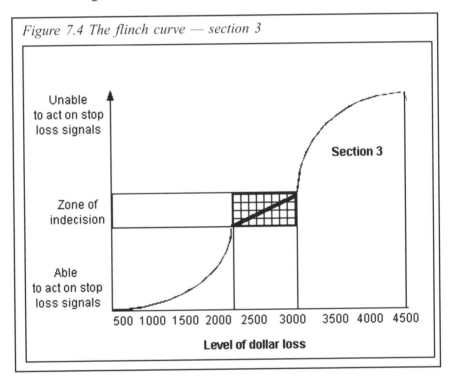

Figure 7.4 The flinch curve — section 3

Trader Average turns his back on the trade and walks away. Resolving not to take action comes with a rush of relief. The curve quickly climbs to the highest levels of inaction and stays there. The curve is concave because the closer it gets to the highest level of inaction, the more difficult it is to act. Cross the upper side of the freeze threshold and pain is avoidable. Like any shock victim, Trader Average blanks out the trauma.

Do you act like this? Of course not — or so you hope. Take a moment to flip back through the contract notes and the last portfolio statement. How much is written in red? Did you discover some old stocks purchased years ago that you had forgotten about? What about the buy contract note at the back of your record book? The company was declared bankrupt and trading halted after the 2000 tech wreck. The note represents a few thousand of your dollars that went missing in action.

How many of your current stocks are in section 3 of the curve? More importantly, how did they get there? Identify the period, defined by the dollar value of the loss, when they slipped into and then out of the freeze zone. This is the starting point for plotting your personal section 3 of the flinch curve.

Traders come up with some remarkable excuses for inaction. One of the best is, "This company has real value, but it has been unfairly lumped with all the other dot.coms." I have heard this excuse in boardrooms, not just from traders. Others claim, "This is a long-term investment" or "If I don't sell, then I really haven't made a loss." One of the least effective excuses is, "It's only speculative money, so we have to expect a major loss every now and then."

These large losses are old blood on the floor. How many of your current stocks are long-term losers? How you staunch the wounds is up to you, and some recovery strategies are considered in my book *Share Trading*. Our focus here is on how capital should be protected and what happens when it is not. If we fully understand what happens when stop loss rules are ignored, then we may be able to develop the resolution necessary to prevent it from happening again. These old, failed trades make up the third section of your personal flinch and freeze curve.

THE DEEP END

In extremes of despair, investors and traders sacrifice their trading capital. Section 4 of the curve is the last significant threshold. It is another sharp phase transition. This curve records the performance for Trader Average. The phase transition, shown in Figure 7.5, starts at a loss greater than $4,500.

In reality, the transition point is usually much greater, even for Trader Novice, often starting at around $10,000. Losses of $10,000 or more are substantial, almost catastrophic losses. They are losses too large to ignore, and it takes a lot of courage to sell.

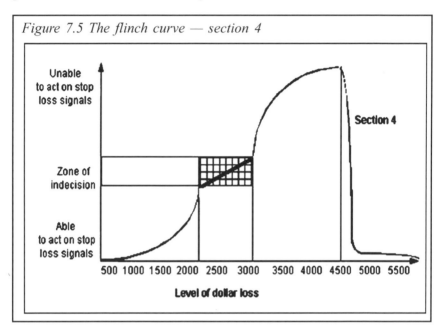

Figure 7.5 The flinch curve — section 4

The shape of this curve in section 4 is a function of time and dollars lost. It is the shape of a financial catastrophe. After a long period in a losing trade, for some perverse reason it becomes easier to sell a stock with a very large loss. Perhaps we are so long divorced from the emotion of the buying decision that our ability to act returns quickly and the large loss is locked in with grim resolution. You may have one or two of these trades in your trading records. They should date back to your days as a novice.

YOUR OWN CURVE

The shape of the flinch curve matches our ability to act on a stop loss decision with the size of the loss. Take the time to plot your own flinch curve. Adjust the figures to match your trading experience and records. As a beginner, plot the curve using figures you think are correct and then track your trading performance against the curve. Adjust the level of dollar stop loss used in your trading calculations until it sits in the first section of the curve.

Trader Average grows his skills to become Trader Success. As his trading experience grows and his trading discipline develops, the paralysis point danger zone moves to the right. Section 1 of the curve expands in dollar terms, shifting the danger zone upwards and to the right. The curve for Trader Success is shown in Figure 7.6.

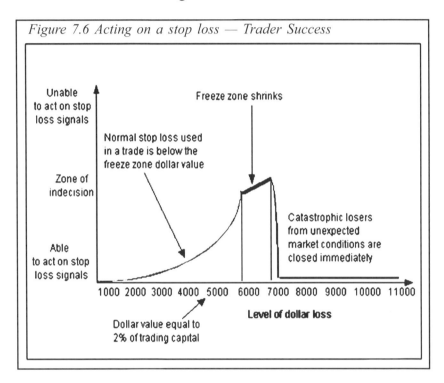

Figure 7.6 Acting on a stop loss — Trader Success

No matter how experienced or skilled we become, the shape of the first two sections in the curve remains the same. The paralysis zone never disappears, because there is always a point where losses overcome our ability to act. Successful trading is possible while we ensure that our intended stop loss remains on the curve in section 1 and that our selected dollar value is less than 2% of our total trading capital. We give ourselves a better opportunity to trade successfully, because the stop loss matches the reality of our ability to act.

Section 3 of the curve for Trader Success changes shape. Unexpected large losses sometimes happen. Traders of Hong Kong company High Fashion were caught by a three-day 38% drop in price in June 2002. When this happens, successful traders act immediately to close the trade. Section 3 of their curve moves rapidly from indecision to effective action. This behavior means there is no section 4 in their curve. They may have some major losses, but quick action prevents these losses becoming a financial catastrophe.

Good intentions are easily sabotaged by the prospect of money. We welcome the distraction from a hard stop loss decision when the possibility of abandoning a good trading plan offers potentially greater profits. Real sabotage is when our trading capital is left unprotected by the failure to execute stop loss orders. Our examination of stop loss techniques is entirely wasted if we fail to match the theoretical planning with our own capacity to buckle under the pressure of growing losses.

We all have a flinch and freeze curve. If we know where our paralysis point is, we construct more effective stop loss strategies to match good planning with real trading action to protect our trading capital.

EIGHT

SECURING
CAPITAL

The market is an experienced thief. Every trading day it steals money from investors and traders. Profits disintegrate, fear sets in, and capital losses grow. The experienced trader understands that trading is about the protection of capital at all times, not just when the trade is opened. Stop loss techniques protect capital in the first days of the trade, but what happens next?

As profits add up, it is easy to forget the capital that makes profitable trading possible. In fast-moving markets where a rally lifts price from $0.30 to $0.70, or from $24 to $38, in a single day, we are understandably distracted by profits. The question, "How do we keep maximum profits?" dominates our thinking.

Most answers concentrate on exit techniques designed to deliver an exit signal near the very top of the up-move, but our focus is on protecting capital during a successful trade. This relieves the pressure of attempting to judge the absolute high of the price move. It reduces the fear that often freezes the mouse button and the sell order at critical times. With capital no longer at risk, we are free to play with only profits. This reduces the penalty for portfolio-threatening errors.

THE ZERO COST AVERAGING STRATEGY

The zero cost averaging[1] approach uses a money management technique to recapture capital, leaving only profits at risk in the market. Unless the stock

---

1 I came across this technique in *Technical Analysis of Stocks and Commodities* magazine in 1998, in an article by T. and K. Quinn. Before applying it to my own trading, I verified it was more effective than the part-profit approach. This chapter is based on my article on zero cost averaging, also published in *Stocks and Commodities*.

is delisted or suspended, there is always a profit available from the trade.

This approach is used to build multiple trades, or positions, in a single stock. This, in turn, creates investment-style opportunities that take advantage of our skills as traders.

By quarantining and hoarding capital, we make effective multiple use of a single pile of capital without the risk of continuous capital exposure to the market.

Zero cost averaging is best applied in bullish markets where returns are at least 30%. It protects the trader against the inevitable downturn and profit collapse.

The good feeling of sitting on open profits is counterbalanced by the fear of losing them. The zero cost averaging strategy protects profits and preserves trading capital by managing trade risk. This is a particularly effective defensive strategy in a volatile market, where rallies and retreats are common. It is also a useful way to ride out substantial market falls and to still have capital when it is needed to take advantage of the new, long-term up trend.

Consider for a moment our starting point. Trader Novice is often very good at letting the losers run while cutting short profits. With more experience, Trader Average learns to cut losers early, but often he also continues to cut winners early. This method has delivered his profit stream in the past. Each trade rings up a small profit. It is difficult to shake the habit of ringing the cash register as frequently as possible.

At this point, Trader Average's trading development continues with low losses and small profits. He could grow the profits by cutting the losers early and allowing the winners to run for as long as possible. This follows the path taken by Trader Success.

THE SELL HALF STRATEGY

Trader Average often follows his broker's advice about part-profits. The broker suggests the trader sells half of the stock in a rising market — the classic sell half strategy. Readers can explore the impact of this on their own stocks using the sell half Excel template included in the Better Trading spreadsheet pak available from www.guppytraders.com.

We prefer to recover our capital, selling the exact amount of stock required to achieve this — the zero cost averaging strategy. In this chapter we compare these two approaches under similar circumstances. The base-line for comparison is the best possible outcome for a stock based on historical activity after our selected entry point.

Both the sell half and zero cost averaging strategies are defensive approaches designed to reduce risk. In terms of developing trading skills and discipline, both approaches help Trader Average scratch the itch to sell while developing the discipline to stay with a successful trade.

We know that market risk has two components. The first is the risk of losing trading capital. The second is the risk of reducing open profits. Successful trading aims first to manage capital risk, and second to capture profits. Our focus is on the way these competing money management requirements address capital risk, and then later on how they protect profits.

Experienced traders use the zero cost averaging approach to retain capital in markets where the risk of trend collapse is high or where price volatility is extreme. This frees up trading capital for use in other trades. In stocks with consistent rallies and retreats, the recovered capital is used to take advantage of "bargain" prices available when the stock price retreats or when it corrects after a speculative rally bubble. Essentially, traders grow a low-risk portfolio of quality stocks using money taken from the market. We consider the mechanics of this later in the chapter.

The sell half approach delivers profits, but it leaves trading capital at risk. It only delivers "real" profits once the stock price has gained over 100% and all trading capital has been removed from the market. The zero cost averaging approach protects trading capital, freeing it up for use in other trading or investment opportunities. It works most effectively where prices have increased by around 30% or more and is most suited to working with fast-moving momentum stocks, or stocks in strong, sustained up trends.

To compare the effectiveness of these two methods we use a single volatile stock chart — the weekly chart of the NYSE-listed Domtar Inc., which captures the strong up and down trends. Prices range from our entry point in Domtar at $10.30 to a high of $14.80 and then back to a low of $6.60. If this range from high to low sounds too great, then take another look at the charts of WorldCom, Parkway Holdings in Singapore, Cathy Pacific in Hong Kong, and others. Prices can, and do, fall much further than we expect. Many people who bought stock near the price highs are still holding them when they hit their lowest price.

Two ideal trading opportunities are shown in Figure 8.1, along with the entry and exit points for all the sample trades. Starting from trade 1, we examine how each strategy performs.

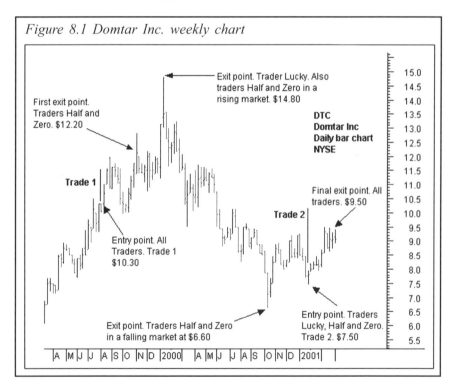

Figure 8.1 Domtar Inc. weekly chart

We introduce four new traders to show the various outcomes. Trader Lucky gets in at the very bottom of the trend and out at the absolute top of each trade. Trader ZeroCost and Trader SellHalf both jump out of the trade part-way through the first up trend in November 1999, at $12.20, but for different reasons. They leave money in the market, and we examine the impact of this in rising and falling markets.

Trader BuyAndHold rides the trend to the top at $14.80, and then all the way down to the bottom of the price collapse at $6.60, and then up again. He finally sells at $9.50 with all the other traders at the end of this sample period.

We give each of our traders $20,000 in each trade. To enable comparisons, we close all trades finally at $9.50 in January 2001. Up for grabs is a profit as low as 21.04% and as high as 70.77% from a combined two-trade strategy.

PROTECTING PROFIT

When we sell, we capture a snapshot of market action. We claw back our trading capital and snatch a profit. We hope to sell at the top of the price rise, and only later do we decide if we should celebrate or regret our decision. In this example we know that trade 1, entered at $10.30, continues to a high of $14.80. As prices reach $12.20, two of our traders — SellHalf and ZeroCost — get nervous and bail out. We need a benchmark for the effectiveness of this strategy, so we use Trader Lucky.

You remember this type of trader. Trader Lucky turned up at every backyard cookout during the late 1990s' bull market run. He told everyone within hearing range how he got into trades at the exact bottom, and out at the exact top. After the tech wreck in April 2000, Trader Lucky went to work for the promoters of a black box trading system. In this example with Domtar, he gets the best possible results from trades 1 and 2.

Each of our traders starts with $20,085 and buys 1,950 Domtar shares at $10.30. By trading from $10.30 to $14.80, Trader Lucky collects a benchmark 43.69% return, adding $8,775 profit. In total, this puts $28,860 — capital plus profit — into his bank account. A total sale of all his stocks at this level has two important outcomes:

1. It protects his trading capital. It is no longer at risk of a reversal in the trend.

2. The exit captures profits.

Trader Lucky protects both capital and profit with this exit. No alternative strategy is ever as successful as this. Every other strategy leaves some open profits, and sometimes capital, at risk. A summary of these exit strategies is shown in Figure 8.2. The bars show how much each trader recovered from the market and put in the bank.

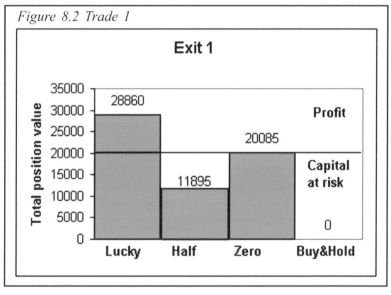

Figure 8.2 Trade 1

Trader SellHalf cannot believe his luck as prices rise. He wants to ring the cash register because he is worried about a price collapse. His broker encourages him to collect early profits, so he takes an exit at $12.20, selling 975 of his original 1,950 shares. This returns $11,895 to his trading account.

This feel-good result is an illusion. Although the strategy is often called taking part-profits, the numbers suggest otherwise.

It is true the sale generates an 18.45% profit on each of the individual shares sold, but the sale has not added any profit to the overall position. Instead, Trader SellHalf still has $8,190 at risk of market decline. He spent $20,085 to buy Domtar and retrieves only $11,895 from the part sale.

The result is substantially different from the benchmark returns achieved by Trader Lucky. This sale has not delivered any real profit, nor has it fully protected his trading capital. Although Trader SellHalf has reduced his market trading risk, he has not succeeded in protecting profits.

The second bar in Figure 8.2 shows the result. The benchmark exit by Trader Lucky at $14.80 recovers capital and profit. The exit by Trader SellHalf captures only part of his capital when assessed against his total market exposure. Until the money in the bank from his activity in these trades exceeds $20,085, he still has capital at risk.

Trader ZeroCost is just as nervous as Trader SellHalf, but he takes more effective steps to protect his trading capital. Profits help a trader grow, but protecting capital allows the trader to survive and develop his skills. Trader ZeroCost calculates how much stock he needs to sell at $12.20 to generate a $20,085 return. By selling 1,646 shares, he collects his original trading capital of $20,085. Figure 8.3 shows the spreadsheet calculations. This Excel template is included in the Better Trading pak.

Figure 8.3 Zero cost averaging calculations

STARTING TRADE

BUY VALUE		CURRENT VALUE	
DTC		DTC	
Number	1,950	1,950	Number
Buy price	$ 10.30	$ 12.20	Current price
cost	$20,085	$23,790	Current value
Trade return	**$3,705**		
%% return	**18.4**		

ZERO COST AVERAGING @ $12.20

number to sell	
to recover costs	1,646
Cash return	$20,085
Balance of	
share holdings	304
Value remaining	$3,705

Trader ZeroCost reduces the risk in the position by leaving only his profits in the trade. As we see later, no matter what happens, Trader ZeroCost cannot lose either his original trading capital or his entire profit. He captures one of the important advantages enjoyed by Trader Lucky. His trading capital is protected from any market fall.

Trader BuyAndHold is still holding on as prices reach for $12.20. He is sustained by greed and harried by fear. His performance is only judged at the end of trade 2 because he does not sell at any time during trade 1.

A summary of level and type of risk eliminated by each of these strategies is shown in Figure 8.4. We examine this summary in detail in the remainder of this chapter.

Figure 8.4 Risk for each strategy

		LUCKY	HALF<100% gain	ZERO>30% gain	BUY&HOLD
SELL DURING TREND	PROFIT	Protected	At risk	Reduced risk	At risk
	CAPITAL	Protected	Part protected	Protected	At risk
RISING MARKET	PROFIT	Protected	At risk	Reduced risk	At risk
	CAPITAL	Protected	Part protected	Protected	At risk
FALLING MARKET	PROFIT	Protected	At risk	Very reduced risk	At risk
	CAPITAL	Protected	At risk	Protected	At risk

Trader Lucky carries no risk at all at the end of trade 1 because he captures both capital and profit. Trader BuyAndHold is the exact opposite, as his open position puts at risk all his profits and all his capital. Trader SellHalf succeeds in protecting part of his trading capital, but he still has some capital at risk, along with all his profits. Trader ZeroCost carries no capital risk and has reduced risk to his profits.

Markets continue to move after we have exited the trade. What looked a good move in November looks less successful in February as prices rise to $14.80. The way each trader manages the risk to capital and profit has a significant impact on the final result.

To compare the effectiveness of these strategies we apply them to a rising market and to a falling market. In a rising market we want to maximize profits. In a falling market we want to protect profits and trading capital.

RISING MARKETS

Historical charts give us the benefit of hindsight. Regret is part of real trading life, and traders who took a November exit at $12.20 in this rising trend spent the next few months regretting their decision as Domtar prices rose to a peak of $14.80. An effective money management strategy must deliver some of these additional profits.

Our objective is to establish the effectiveness of these competing strategies. We give Trader Lucky a second life. His trade starts at $10.30 and ends at $14.80, so he takes the top benchmark score with a 43.69% return. This adds $8,775 in profits to the benchmark result. The summary of the results for all traders is shown in Figure 8.5.

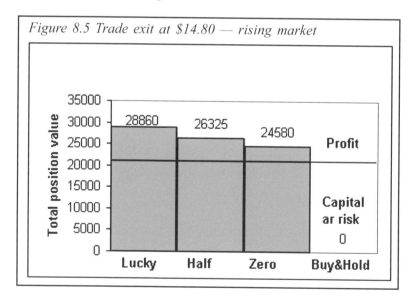

Figure 8.5 Trade exit at $14.80 — rising market

By the time prices reach the top of the rise, Trader SellHalf is still looking good. A sale of his remaining 975 shares at this level returns $14,430. We add this to the total from his first sale — $11,895 — to get a total return of

$26,325. In terms of the total capital allocated to the original position, this is a 31.07% return and puts $6,240 profit into the bank account. The total bank balance is $26,325. This is not a bad outcome for what is essentially a series of trading exits driven by habit and fear.

Compare this with the result for Trader ZeroCost. He retains 304 shares and, when sold at $14.80, they return $4,495. Add this to the $20,085 recovered in the first part of this trade and this puts a round total of $24,580 in the bank. On the original position, this is a 22.38% return. The dollar difference between Trader ZeroCost and Trader SellHalf is $1,745.

This difference is the cost of insuring or hedging risk in a rising market. For $1,745, Trader ZeroCost purchases total trading capital protection and significant profit protection. This is a very effective way to control market trading risk. By selling an appropriate quantity of stock, Trader ZeroCost recovers his trading capital and is truly in a position to let his profits run.

In a rising market it is easy to forget the risk of loss. We look for strategies to maximize profits and ignore the need to protect trading capital. On this basis the zero cost averaging strategy looks less successful. The cost of insurance seems too large.

Insurance premiums always seem too large until the house is flooded or burned down. Then the focus shifts abruptly to the problem of loss and under-insurance. Past quibbles about the cost of premiums seem unjustified. A falling market has the same impact on our trading success.

In a continually rising market, the gap between the outcomes for Trader SellHalf and Trader ZeroCost continues to widen. As expected, the gap between these two results and Trader Lucky remains a gulf in a rising market, as traders who catch the very bottom and the very top always provide the benchmark for the best possible trade. Again, we ignore Trader BuyAndHold, because he is still sitting on his stock.

FALLING MARKETS

In a rising market everybody is happy, but what happens when prices fall? Paper profits burn quickly in the market, as the 2000 tech wreck illustrated. Trader Lucky, who took an exit in a rising Domtar trend at $14.80, watches with undisguised satisfaction when prices quickly turn and retreat.

Here we consider the impact of a theoretical fall from the exit point at $10.30 on the chart in trade 1. This allows us to compare the effectiveness of the competing strategies. The lowest point on the chart highlights the impact of a falling market.

As prices fall from $14.80 to $6.60, Traders SellHalf, ZeroCost, and BuyAndHold are frozen with fear. They did not sell the balance of their stock at the peak price of $14.80. They fail to sell on the way down, but Traders SellHalf and ZeroCost both muster the courage to sell the very low at $6.60. Stop loss applications are important, but in truth, many traders still find themselves holding losing stocks. If a particular money management technique helps reduce the pain of stop loss inaction, then it is worth investigating.

Trader Lucky is true to his name. He got out at $14.80. This benchmark 43.69% return adds $8,775 to his bank account. He protects both capital and profit.

Trader SellHalf quickly finds himself in serious trouble. With half of his original position remaining, his 975 shares are sold at $6.60 for $6,435. He collected $11,895 from the first sale and $6,435 from the second. His total recovery is $18,330. He loses 8.745%, or $1,755, of his original trading capital.

In a falling market the sell half strategy exposes the trader to the risk of capital loss and the complete destruction of profit. Trader SellHalf is poorly protected in a falling market. His profits on the total position start to disappear quickly, as shown in Figure 8.6.

Trader ZeroCost is a much more effective risk manager. He still holds 304 shares. Selling these at $6.60 adds $2,004 to his trading account. All of the stock sold in this second parcel, or lot, count toward profit. The sale of the first and second batches puts a round total of $22,089 in his bank account. The overall return on the total trade is reduced to 9.98%, but this is much better than the return for Trader SellHalf in the same situation.

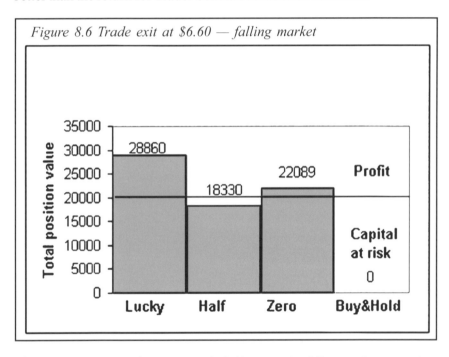

Figure 8.6 Trade exit at $6.60 — falling market

The zero cost averaging approach delivers a significant advantage in a falling market. It delivers total protection of trading capital and absolute profit protection, although not profit preservation. Unless the stock stops trading, Trader ZeroCost always shows a profit on the overall position. His trading capital was retrieved when he sold at $12.20. No matter how low prices fall, Trader ZeroCost always shows a profit, as plotted in Figure 8.7.

This is the most significant feature of the zero cost averaging strategy. By protecting trading capital, it helps the trader to effectively manage and protect open profits. As part of a defensive strategy used at the top of bull markets, or in trading significant volatility, zero cost averaging is an effective way to capture profits in the face of adversity.

When trading an uncomplicated rising trend, the zero cost averaging technique protects trading capital and allows profits to run. This technique removes the stress associated with a single exit required to protect both trading capital and profits. At some stage in our development as traders, we all have the experience of letting a good profit slide into a dreadful loss. The end of a strong up trend is often treated with initial disbelief, partly because we have made so much in paper profits. It hurts when these are chewed up by falling prices.

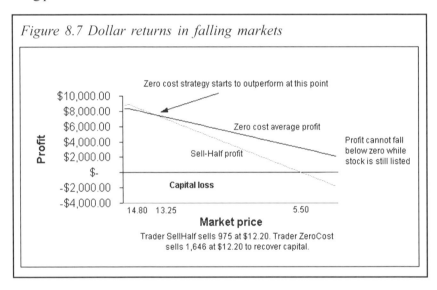

Figure 8.7 Dollar returns in falling markets

Zero cost averaging limits the damage caused by our indecision, no matter what its reasons. Because our trading capital has been stripped from the trade, we have the freedom to play with just the profit component of the trade. It provides the opportunity to fine-tune exit decisions without risk to our original capital.

The template taken from the Better Trading spreadsheet pak and shown in Figure 8.8 allows traders to calculate the impact of the zero cost averaging strategy in rising and falling markets.

Figure 8.8 Zero cost averaging calculations

STARTING TRADE				
BUY VALUE			**CURRENT VALUE**	
DTC			DTC	
Number		1,950	1,950	Number
Buy price	$	10.30	$ 12.20	Current price
cost		$20,085	$23,790	Current value
Trade return		**$3,705**		
%% return		**18.4**		

ZERO COST AVERAGING @ $12.20	
number to sell	
to recover costs	1,646
Cash return	$20,085
Balance of	
share holdings	**304**
Value remaining	**$3,705**

COMPARISION OF OUTCOMES - Rising market		
ORIGINAL TRADE	**ZERO COST TRADE**	
new price	$14.80	$14.80
New value	$28,860	$24,580 Total ZC return
return if sold	**$8,775**	**$4,495**
%% return	**43.7**	**22.4**

COMPARISION OF OUTCOMES - Falling market		
ORIGINAL TRADE	**ZERO COST TRADE**	
new price	$6.60	$6.60
New value	$12,870	
return if sold	**-$7,215**	**$2,004**
%% return	**-35.9**	**10.0**

For some traders this advantage is enough. For others this approach provides a way to turn trading skill into longer-term investments that continue to make money. This happens in the short term with stocks such as Domtar, which show consistent up trends and downtrends lasting several months at a time. It is also applicable in the long term where up trends and downtrends may last many months or years.

We summarize these additional strategies by using another sample trade based on the developing opportunity in 2000 when the Domtar downtrend reverses and trends upwards. This is trade 2, shown in Figure 8.9. Our traders enter at $7.50. We close it at $9.50 on the right-hand side of the chart.

Figure 8.9 Trade 2

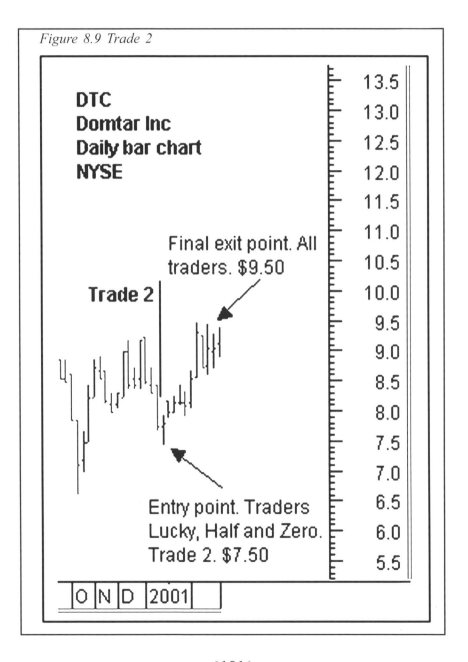

But what of Trader BuyAndHold? As prices fell to $6.60 in late 2000, he turned the computer off and stopped looking at the screen. We force him back to reality in the final part of trade 2.

MULTIPLE TRADES TRIGGER INVESTMENTS

Good traders capture rallies, retire during price retreats, and then enter again on new trend reversals. Successful implementation depends on having trading capital available to take advantage of the opportunities. In this example we see a new trading opportunity in Figure 8.9 as Domtar prices rise from the low of $6.60 to $9.50. Ideally, we want to be buyers and take advantage of the new up trend. Our trading rules prevent our four traders using trading profits to trade this opportunity, so they must reach into their trading capital, or what remains of it, to take advantage of this new up trend.

In this trading comparison we assume Trader Lucky entered trade 1 at 10.30 and got out at $14.80. This is the money he has available to trade the opportunity in trade 2. Trader SellHalf sold half his position at $12.20 and Trader ZeroCost sold part of his position at the same price. Neither sold at $14.80.

Trader Lucky has his original $20,085 available — excluding trading profits — to buy 2,680 shares at $7.50 as the new up trend starts. Lucky trader that he is, he sells at the top of the new trend in trade 2 at $9.50. This returns a 26.67%, or $5,360, profit. Total return is $25,460 added to his bank account. For comparison, we use the same exit price for all our traders.

Trader Lucky used just the one amount of trading capital — $20,100 — for the second trade, and slightly less for the first trade. It is useful to compare the total outcome. This is a total profit of $14,135 — $8,775 from trade 1 and $5,360 from trade 2 — from total trading capital of $20,100. This is shown in Figure 8.10.

Trader Lucky has a return on capital of 70.32% for the two trades. This is an impressive benchmark. Our other traders cannot beat this, so we should aim for the best possible real-world results.

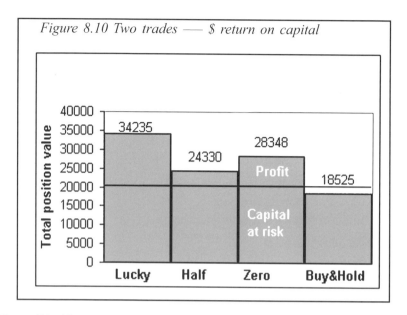

Figure 8.10 Two trades — $ return on capital

The sell half strategy advocated by some brokers now reveals further practical weaknesses. Trader SellHalf has a problem. He wants to take advantage of the new trading opportunity in Domtar C, but in total he only has $11,895 available from the sale of half his stock at $12.20 in trade 1. Remember, although this strategy is often called taking part-profits, in fact it does not return a profit until the price rise exceeds 100%. He buys 1,586 shares. We compare the total outcomes of these combined trades.

This time he sells his entire position at $9.50, including the remainder of stock still held from trade 1. This is a total of 2,562 shares — 975 remaining from trade 1 and 1,586 from trade 2. This adds $24,330 to his trading account, but only part of this is real profit.

Just how much did Trader SellHalf make from this series of trades? He starts with $20,100. His first sale of half his stock does not make a profit and returns only part of his trading capital. By selling 2,562 shares at $9.50 in trade 2, he picks up a total of $24,330. At the end of this series, Trader SellHalf has a total return on capital of 20.9% and adds $4,230 to his account. This result is significantly worse than the benchmark result posted by Trader Lucky.

Trader ZeroCost is in a much more comfortable position. At the end of trade 1, he recovered all of his trading capital — $20,085. He has the same buying power as Trader Lucky when the trade 2 opportunity develops. In this recovering market, Trader ZeroCost is fully cashed-up and ready to take full advantage of new trading opportunities. Both Trader Lucky and Trader ZeroCost had the luxury of full capital protection as the market collapsed. Trader SellHalf and Trader BuyAndHold have always faced the threat of capital reduction in a falling market.

In this recovery trade, Trader ZeroCost is in an even more powerful position because he still holds 304 shares from the first trade. They are pure profit. The sale of these returns $2,888. The sale of the second parcel purchased at $7.50 in trade 2 delivers $5,360 profit. This is the same return as Trader Lucky achieved for the second trade. In total, this adds $8,248 in profits to Trader ZeroCost's bank account. This is $4,018 better than Trader SellHalf. More importantly, this better return is obtained with less risk.

Trader SellHalf, who makes exactly the same entry and exit decisions in trade 2, carries a much greater capital risk because a portion of his original capital has been fully exposed to the falling market since his first entry in trade 1. Additionally, he has a reduced ability to take full advantage of the new opportunity in trade 2. Even at best, his profit potential is less than that of Trader Lucky and Trader ZeroCost. The overall returns on capital in percentage terms are shown in Figure 8.11.

The return for Trader ZeroCost is good, but, even better, it is achieved at minimum risk to his trading capital. Trader Lucky was, well, lucky. If you believe you can pick the absolute top of each move, then Trader Lucky's strategy gives better results than zero cost averaging.

Trader BuyAndHold has fared terribly in the face of these events. He lost 7.77%, or $1,560, by selling at $9.50 in what was trade 2 for the other traders. His trade took over a year to complete and exposed him to extended time risk. It carried him to the heights of delight and the depths of despair. We assume he enjoyed the ride, because so many novice traders seem to duplicate it. For the duration of the entire trade, both his capital and his profits were at full risk. The buy and hold strategy is the least reliable trading approach.

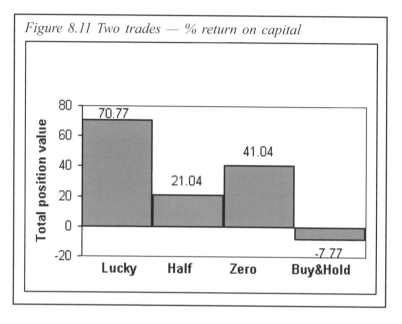

Figure 8.11 Two trades — % return on capital

WHAT ABOUT INVESTMENTS?

In these examples, all trades were completely closed at the top of the second up trend in trade 2. Trader ZeroCost sold all his stock, recovering both the capital and profit components. A better application of this technique is when this trader again applies the zero cost averaging approach by selling only 2,116 shares to recover his capital.

In the long term, this builds an ongoing trade in a single stock made up entirely of profits. They are profits generated by just a single amount of capital, applied and reapplied consistently to a single stock.

By leaving profits in the trade, we lose the opportunity to turn those profits into trading capital and to use them elsewhere. This is not a problem if we aim to build a substantially risk-free, long-term investment that consistently remains in profit.

The sample series of four zero cost averaging trades shown in Figure 8.12 details how the strategy is applied in the long term to the Malaysian utility company, YTL. Each trade uses around $20,000. The initial $20,000 capital is recovered after each trade and applied to the next trade in the series.

Figure 8.12 YTL monthly chart

The first zero cost averaging trade is entered in 1997 at $2.60. The zero cost strategy is applied to the exit in early 1998 at $5.50. This leaves 4,060 YTL shares in an open position. The second trade starts at $2.00 and ends at $7.00. It leaves 7,143 shares in the open position. Trade 3 starts at $5.00, closes at $7.50, and adds another 3,333 shares. Trade 4 starts at $3.40, and adds 1,888 shares with the exit at $5.00. The final trade is taken in mid-2001 at $11.70 and closes a few months later at $5.20. There are 1,880 shares left over from this transaction.

After five trades for a total capital commitment of $20,000, this trader now has 18,304 shares in YTL. They are pure profit. Even on the most recent prices shown on the chart, this represents a profit of $75,180 at $5.20. This is a 376% return on capital. If prices drop dramatically, perhaps to $2.00, the total trade is still in profit with an 83% return.

If prices fall to $2.00, then Trader ZeroCost has $20,000 — his original capital — available to buy into any new recovery up trend.

ZERO COST GROWTH

The zero cost averaging approach has three main advantages:

1. Trading capital is fully protected.
2. If prices continue to rise, profits grow.
3. If prices fall, profits are protected against total loss.

The impact on capital and profits for each strategy is summarized again in Figure 8.13.

Figure 8.13 Risk for each strategy

		LUCKY	HALF<100% gain	ZERO>30% gain	BUY&HOLD
SELL DURING TREND	PROFIT	Protected	At risk	Reduced risk	At risk
	CAPITAL	Protected	Part protected	Protected	At risk
RISING MARKET	PROFIT	Protected	At risk	Reduced risk	At risk
	CAPITAL	Protected	Part protected	Protected	At risk
FALLING MARKET	PROFIT	Protected	At risk	Very reduced risk	At risk
	CAPITAL	Protected	At risk	Protected	At risk

If you have difficulty in picking anywhere near the top price in fast-moving stocks, then the zero cost averaging approach gives a more effective outcome in a volatile market. If Trader SellHalf delays selling until prices have risen by more than 100%, then in effect he is following a similar strategy to zero cost averaging and results improve accordingly.

In the real world of the market, the zero cost averaging approach is an effective way to preserve trading capital and protect profits. In rising markets, the strategy reduces the full profit potential. However, it is a useful way for traders who have a habit of selling too soon to effectively lock-in profits and participate in the remainder of the trend.

In volatile markets, or markets where traders worry that the trend is nearing exhaustion, the zero cost averaging strategy protects profits from total destruction. It also completely protects the trader's capital, giving many more options for effective trading in new opportunities.

By removing the original trading capital, the trader has the ability to enter into new trades while waiting for a general market recovery. Later, he has the capital on hand to participate in any new rally, perhaps building multiple positions in a single stock, which turns his trading skills into an investment strategy.

The zero cost averaging strategy is useful for investors who want to build essentially cost-free multiple positions in a single stock. Because these positions consist only of trading profits, the investor collects a continuous low-risk dividend from the market at any time while preserving capital. When combined with strategies for matching money management with trade risk, the results are particularly encouraging.

The zero cost averaging strategy is a very useful strategy for teaching traders to break the habit of selling early. It is a much more effective solution than the sell half approach.

TAX CONSEQUENCES

All money management strategies have taxation consequences. We have not considered these impacts because the individual taxation circumstances vary among readers and often depend on the quality of taxation advice. Understand which money management strategy is most likely to deliver the results you want for your trading, and then ask your accountant to develop appropriate tax strategies to assist you in achieving your goals.

The zero cost averaging strategy leverages our trading skill into better returns by using money management. Some traders believe they achieve the same result by trading with a margin loan. We consider this dangerous detour in the next chapter.

NINE

DANGER ON THE DETOUR

Just how good is your trading performance? Can you afford to take 8% to 12% out of every winning trade and give it away to somebody else? Can you afford to find 8% to 12% extra cash for every losing trade and hand it over to your broker? For most traders the honest answer is "No." For Trader Average, this is just another version of financial suicide, yet the appeal of a margin loan still beckons. Margin trading has benefits because it allows traders to use the value of a stock as collateral for borrowing money to buy more stock.

MARGIN TRADING

Margin trading[1] means borrowing funds to trade, or invest, in the market. Traditionally, this has been a loan facility offered by brokers. Now it is also available from banks and leads to the turn-the-upstairs-bedroom-into-a-stock-portfolio advertising line. Collateral for the margin loan can now come from property, which puts your house at risk from the vagaries of the financial markets.

This is one facet of the danger in this detour. Traders take out a margin loan facility in an attempt to lift profits. At the same time, they put their trading capital at increased risk. This impact on capital makes it appropriate to consider margin trading in the "Protect Capital" part of this book.

---

1   The terms "margin lending," "margin trading," and "trading on the margin" are used interchangeably in this chapter, as they are in the financial market. They all mean trading with borrowed money. Futures traders are always involved in margin trading, as each contract is controlled by a small margin — the market price of the contract. Futures markets use the term in a different way to equity or stock markets. This chapter deals only with the stock market.

The second facet of danger is the unintended reduction of trading profits. Margin lending provides a link between this part of the book, which deals with protecting capital, and the next, which deals with protecting profits.

Raise a margin loan from a bank or a broker and the mechanics are much the same. The value of the shares in a company, the value of your portfolio, or the value of your house is used as security against a loan.

We start with a simple example of the broad process. Trader Average wants to buy another $10,000 worth of stock in the Hong Kong developer, Cheung Kong Infrastructure, but she currently does not have the cash available. Margin lending is usually limited to a group of secure blue chips, although in a bull market, margin loans are made available for many companies outside the blue chip grouping.

The ratio of lending to the capital value of the asset — in this case, Cheung Kong Infrastructure — is always less than 100%. For some blue chips, the lender only counts them as 70% of the current market value. So, for a $10,000 trading loan, our friendly bank advances Trader Average only an additional $7,000. If the investment has a market value of $10,000, the maximum she can borrow under this margin example is $7,000. This is the first part of the risk with margin trading.

The bank, or the broker, reserves the right to change this lending ratio — the margin — at any time during the course of the loan. Changes in rates may also be mandated by the Federal Reserve or central bank. This change may reflect a change in the lender's or central banking system's assessment of risk in the market and may have nothing to do with actual changes in the stock price. This is an unusual event, but in very volatile or prolonged bearish markets it cannot be ruled out.

Again, to simplify, once Trader Average has borrowed funds, she is required to maintain the agreed ratio between the market value of the stock and the money she borrowed. This is a loan-to-valuation ratio or a debt-to-value ratio. It remains constant and leads to an obligation to repay part of the loan if the value of the stock investment falls. There is a buffer zone included to allow market value to move down to a minimum level before a top up margin call is made. Commonly it is 10%, although it varies between stocks and is based on the lender's assessment of volatility. In this example, if the value of the stock Trader Average purchased with her cash and borrowed funds falls below $9,000, then she is required to restore the original lending ratio.

Once the value of her collateral — her Cheung Kong Infrastructure stock — falls 10% or more below her original purchase level, she no longer has the required ratio between what she owns and what she borrowed. Her original portfolio value falls to $7,000. Seventy per cent of this new market value for the stock is $5,600. This is now the new maximum amount the margin lender will lend against this stock. Trader Average has an obligation to reduce her loan to $5,600. She is required to top-up the value of what she owns to maintain the agreed lending ratio. She does this with an immediate payment of $1,400.

This is a margin call. It is rare to hear it in a bull market, but it is the call of the sharks in a bear market. The call also excites receivers, liquidators, and bankruptcy managers.

LEVERAGE

Margin means leverage. Your small current collection of cash is combined with the broker's, or bank's, larger cash reserves. This larger pile of money is used to buy a lot of stock in the company you are certain has hitched a ride with rising prices. Margin lending gives you the ability to buy more stock than you could by using just your own cash. Instead of $10,000 profit you could have $20,000 profit from exactly the same trade. These are glittering numbers and the glare often conceals the piper standing on the sidelines. The piper works for the lender. When it comes time to play a tune, it is the lender's choice, not ours.

Margin trading is an activity I have always avoided, although, like many others, I have been tempted by offers. I do not use margin lending because it alters the risk profile in every trade. I cannot make effective trading decisions while looking over my shoulder to see what the tax man is thinking, nor do I want to look over my other shoulder to see what my margin lender is thinking. Small losses are an inevitable part of trading. Margin lending inflates the impact of these losses.

Some traders use margin lending facilities successfully, so readers are entitled to wonder why I class them as a dangerous detour. This is a personal view rather than a guide to the services available. The objective in this chapter is to increase your understanding of the risk involved in trading on the margin so that you can make a better decision when these facilities are offered to you.

TYPES OF LEVERAGE

The appeal of margin trading is the leverage. Just a small amount of cash, or an asset such as the new bedroom extension, could be turned into a large amount of profit in the market. But leverage is a mixed curse in equity markets. The curse comes in three forms.

The first is price leverage, where a low-priced stock moves quickly to a much higher price. It is easier to lift a stock trading at $3 to $6 than it is to lift a $30 stock to $60. The percentage gain is the same, but the amount of work required is quite different. Price leverage makes low-priced stocks appealing.

The second form of leverage comes with trading instruments purchased on the lay-by system. A high-priced stock such as U.S. aerospace and defense contractor, Northrop Grumman can be purchased using a low-priced option, a single stock future, or a warrant. A substantial commodity contract is available on the futures market for a fraction of its cash value. For just a few cents in the dollar, the trader has the opportunity to participate in magnified losses or profits. If you do not have a million dollars, then the leverage available in these derivative markets allows you to trade as if you did.

Derivative markets call for specialized risk control and money management techniques. They are drawn from the lessons learned in equity markets, but they include additional refinements and some quite new structures. Jack Schwager in *Schwager on Futures* covers this area with authority. Larry McMillan provides more detail in *Options as a Strategic Investment*, as does George Fontanills in *The Options Course*.

The third type of leverage is promoted by the money lenders, including banks and brokerages. This is margin lending and it is based on using the value of the stock purchased as collateral for the loan. It is the equivalent of a home loan for stocks, although with several significant differences:

- *Home or apartment loan.* A home loan allows you to use the equity in your house as security for the loan.

  Margin loan. A margin loan uses stocks or other assets as security. This can include your home.

- *Home or apartment loan.* A lender typically gives you 20 or 25 years to pay off a home loan with regular payments based on interest rate movements.

  Margin loan. A margin loan has a lump-sum repayment facility triggered by changes in portfolio value driven by fast-moving financial markets. Repayment or top-up demands always seem to come at the most inconvenient time — when the market is declining. Repayment demands are due within a few days and are in addition to any regular interest payments.

- *Home or apartment loan.* The home loan repayment schedule is not related to the market value of the house. In a falling real estate market, the level of repayment does not increase. The repayment schedule is based on the amount borrowed.

  Margin loan. The margin loan is directly related to the market value of the stock or portfolio. The repayment schedule is linked to the state of the market. In a falling market you are asked to make new and increased payments to maintain the balance between your borrowings and the market value of your equity. This is the margin call. It has sounded the death knell for many traders, because once interest is added to the repayments, the loss in the trade sometimes grows to more than 100%.

TRADING DETOURS

Good traders are terrified by losses because they destroy trading capital. Good traders protect trading capital by retaining the freedom to make buy and sell decisions based on their analysis of market conditions. They set stop loss conditions based on a range of market-related factors, as discussed in Chapter 6. They feel uncomfortable surrendering this independent decision-making to fund managers, money managers, and others who claim, for a commission, to make their money grow. Traders accept the responsibility for the growth or failure of their capital but, in return, demand the freedom to make these decisions.

Operating with borrowed money reduces this freedom because there is always a need to pay the piper — the lender — before we pay ourselves. The shadow of the lender's hand alters our ability to make a decision even in a rising market.

All successful traders use their analysis of individual stocks to make an exact decision when to buy, and later, when to sell. They believe in the accuracy of the trading approach they have selected. They are confident that it works. In a winning trade these traders wait for the exit signal to develop. At times it takes exceptional patience. It always requires discipline to capture profits. When the sell signal comes, they sell without a quibble or a second thought.

The reward for this skill, discipline, and hard-earned experience is a profit of 10%, 20%, 50%, or more. It is deposited directly into their bank account. Some of this profit is ambushed by the tax man, and a small amount is nibbled away by brokerage fees.

But what happens when the trade is based on borrowed money? Borrowed cash comes at a cost. The loan is serviced from the profits. Suddenly, all you make is not your own. The 20% profit is less satisfying after the lender is paid. The 10% profit won from difficult trading may deflate to a 3% contribution to your bank balance.

The sell decision is now complicated by the need to pay the piper. The trader must shoot for higher returns from every trade with borrowed money to offset the interest fees. He may stay in a trade beyond his exit signals in an attempt to collect just a little extra to pay the piper. Inevitably, his successful trading approach is under pressure and attacked by demands that have nothing to do with his ability to trade.

The moment we start trading with borrowed money, we start trading for somebody else and must take into account their demands. I value the independence trading brings, so I avoid this detour.

In a bull market, many traders believe they can live with the demands of borrowed money, but all traders experience losing periods. Sometimes it is just an extended run of losses consistent with the overall behavior of their trading approach. Trader Average in Chapter 1 had a 60% success rate, but this does not stop him experiencing eight losing trades in a row. Eight losers out of 20 trades is still a 60% success rate. At other times, the trader simply loses touch with the market. Trading with our own capital means we work through the losing streak, or stand aside from the market, until we are comfortable with trading again.

These are important decisions. They are made more difficult when a money lender constrains our action, or demands repayment at inconvenient times. It shifts trading on our own account to trading for somebody else, and the result is sometimes devastating. For those who believe that lifestyle is one of the prime benefits of trading, the intrusion of these demands is unsettling.

FALLING AND LOSING CONTROL

The most important problem with margin trading is the collateral damage created in a falling market. This is an additional risk created by a disinterested third party. In a falling market we carefully manage the market risk, the analysis risk in each trade, and the execution risk where our sell order may be filled at much lower prices than we planned. These three risks are unavoidable and we plan each trade to take these into account.

When borrowed money is involved, a new layer of risk is added which, while associated with the market, is not directly related to the market. It becomes a multiple-car pile-up. You may succeed in avoiding serious damage when you hit the car in front, but the truck traveling behind wipes you out.

Traders who used margin trading facilities to buy more tech and dot.com stock in the last weeks of March 2000 found that their ability to react in the best way possible to the April tech wreck was limited because of the need to raise additional cash. As prices fell, they were hit with demands from their margin lenders for additional cash to maintain the margin between the value of the stock and the amount they had borrowed. A few met these calls with cash. Most met the calls by selling stock into a falling market. Instead of getting the best price, they were forced to take the worst price. And with others reacting the same way, the selling pressure rapidly gathered momentum as the disaster accelerated.

This destructive cycle occurs, in part, because margin lenders are not traders. They are not interested in the market other than as a measure of collateral for loans. When prices fall, this simply means your broker, or lender, rings you and demands that you deposit enough additional cash to maintain the ratio. Sometimes this must be transferred by the end of the next day, particularly in fast-moving volatile markets.

There are two ways to meet these demands. The first is simply to transfer cash to the broker's loan facility account so that the value of your stocks and your cash is sufficient to maintain the required ratio between your borrowed funds and the asset — the stocks. In a falling market, people are reluctant to add more money, and in some cases, they do not have spare cash to meet this margin call. Figure 9.1 shows how funds are distributed.

The second way to raise funds to meet the call is to sell some of your existing stock. This is where the margin lending document you signed gets dragged out again. The margin lender does not entirely trust you, so the contract gives him the right to sell the stock without your direct permission. He sells enough stock to retain the margin on the loan. He acts to protect the broker's, or the bank's, position. He is their representative acting in their interests. Your interests come a distant second.

When the value of the collateral falls, they want money quickly to protect their loan asset. In a falling market, they dump stock just to raise the funds. Dumping means selling "at market," rather than trying to get the best possible price. Forced margin selling often means stocks are sold at the worst possible price.

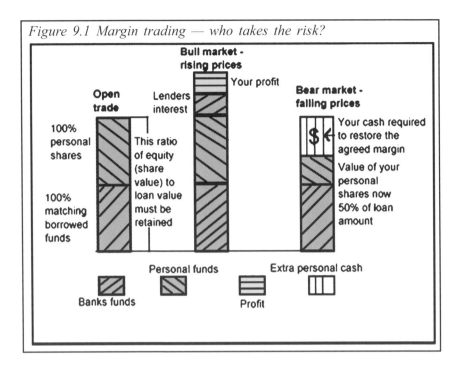

Figure 9.1 Margin trading — who takes the risk?

Very quickly this becomes a nightmare scenario out of a B-grade loan shark thriller. If the market continues to fall the next day, the trader may get a second margin call. Few people are prepared to put up additional cash in this situation, so more stocks are dumped by brokers to satisfy margin calls. This forced selling feeds the bear and quickly traps the market in a downward spiral where margin call is made on top of margin call.

The precise mechanics of margin lending and margin calls vary from broker to broker and bank to bank. The general mechanics remain the same. The winners are the brokers and bankers, because they get to sell your stocks and keep the money. The lucky traders put only their stock portfolio at risk. The unlucky ones have pledged their stock portfolio, their house, their second mortgage, and other assets.

Margin lending introduces a risk over and above that created by the market you are trading.

MARGINAL RISK

Hamlet is advised by his father, Polonius, "Neither a borrower, nor a lender be." Excellent advice had Hamlet been about to venture into the financial markets. In previous chapters we suggested that the ability to identify and manage risk lies at the very heart of successful trading and investment. In a rapidly falling market, traders who fully own their stocks are able to consider all the alternatives because there is no pressure to come up with extra cash. These alternatives include refusing to sell into market panic and waiting for the inevitable rally to sell at higher prices. Strategies include riding the stock all the way down, and then using price leverage to take new trades and make up the loss from the first trade.

These strategies, and others, are not available to those who borrow money to trade and who face margin calls they cannot easily meet. The margin loan limits the range of options, strategies, and tactics available to the trader.

Traders who do not borrow funds have a wide choice of options and strategies when markets fall dramatically. They survive because they do not have the additional risk imposed by borrowed money. They have the freedom to take appropriate action to protect their trading capital and profits. Some of the methods used to protect profits are considered in the next part of the book.

Part 3

Protect Profits

TEN

EXIT GREED

Protecting profits has an intimate relationship with greed. We all lust after the best possible returns and, unless we are careful, this clouds our trading judgment. We forget that the primary trading objective is to capture as much of the trend as possible — not all of it. Collecting the very bottom and the very top of a trend or a rally is an almost impossible task, but this does not stop us from attempting the feat, and regretting when we fail.

It is easy to look at the behavior of others in the market and identify just where greed sets in for them. It is much more difficult to observe this behavior in ourselves, even though, ultimately, it is more important. We need to understand this behavior so that we can recognize it. Then there is a chance that we may do something about it.

Before we examine specific strategies to protect profits, it is appropriate to consider a detailed post-mortem of the way a trade is destroyed by greed. Having defined the problem, we can then adapt or adopt one of the solutions in the following chapters best suited to tackling our particular variation on greed. Understanding failure gives us the opportunity to plan for success.

It is difficult to transfer a paper plan to trading reality when the market beckons with the potential of higher prices. Perhaps we aim for an exit at $36.00. Prices reach this level, and then trade higher at $36.30. This single upward blip on a price chart has the power to destroy our willpower and our good intentions. Should we stay with the trade and aim for higher prices? Should we just take the money and run?

The right answer adds to profits. The wrong answer destroys profits, sometimes slowly and sometimes very rapidly. If we cannot make the exit decision at the time it needs to be made, then perhaps we could lessen the destructive impact of this delayed exit decision by taking defensive action earlier in the trade. We consider some solutions in the following chapters. We make a start by examining the problem we wish to solve. Come with me and greet greed in a real trade.

GREED AND THE EXIT

Find any trade and greed is sure to be close by. We start with a trade that delivers a clear exit signal. Trader Success shows how the trade is most effectively managed. Then we give the same trade to Trader Average. He shows how greed delays the exit as he hopes for higher prices, and then as he prays for higher prices when the trend collapses and takes his position with it.

There is no better way to explore these issues than by using a real trade rather than a theoretical example. I am most active in the Australian market, so these notes come from a trade followed in real time in our weekly Internet newsletter, *Tutorials in Applied Technical Analysis*. The principles apply to every trade in any market, because greed is the trader's constant enemy.

Sirocco Resources is a small Australian mining company, shown in Figure 10.1. Trader Success likes the volatility, the leverage available from low prices, and the potential for substantial changes in price. The entry point is at $0.16. His trading plan rides the parabolic trend. The exit target is based on past price action. Several months earlier, Sirocco Resources developed a downward price gap on the chart. This sets the new sell target zone between $0.29 and $0.32 based on the bottom and the top of the price gap.

Some trades hit the sell target and then go much higher. If this happens regularly, traders are inclined to let greed take over, delaying the exit until prices move above the original target prices. The Sirocco Resources trade is not like this. Instead, prices hit the lower band of the target area, and then collapse. Greed encourages traders to hang on and hope that prices will reach the upper target levels.

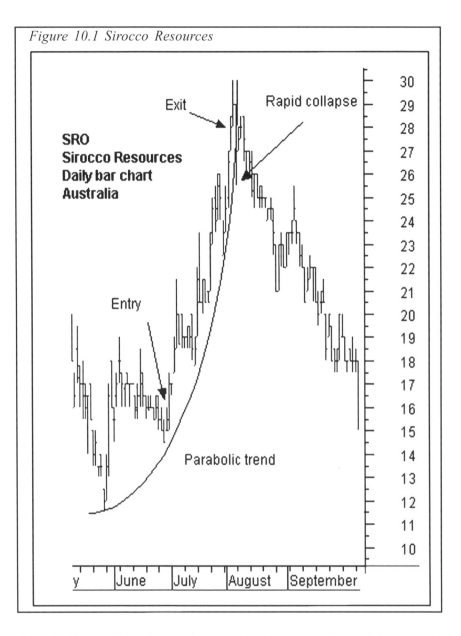

Figure 10.1 Sirocco Resources

A parabolic trend develops in fast-moving price rallies. It provides a way of managing momentum-driven trades. The trend is best described on a chart by using an arc or parabolic curve. The curve starts off slowly, then accelerates very rapidly until the activity on the price chart is almost vertical. Parabolic trends end very rapidly, often with substantial price pullbacks gapping well below the previous close.

While parabolic trends are most frequently seen in fast-moving stocks, they are also present in fast-moving indices or markets, such as the NASDAQ in early 2000. A parabolic trend is not adequately described by a single straight-edge trend line. The trend line is constructed from myriad short-term straight-edge trend lines, as shown in Figure 10.2. The curved trend line has the same impact as a more conventional straight-edge trend line. The price action uses a parabolic curve as a support level.

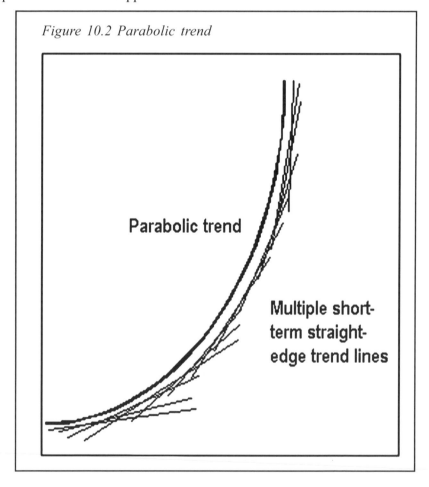

Figure 10.2 Parabolic trend

Parabolic trend

Multiple short-term straight-edge trend lines

OPTIMUM AND ACTUAL EXITS

Sirocco Resources is not an unusual stock. It offers four exit opportunities. They are:

1. The best theoretical exit — the absolute high of the trend move.

2. The planned exit price — established when we entered the trade.

3. The optimum exit — the best price available after the planned exit price is hit.

4. The actual exit — what we get when the trade is closed.

Greed has a wide playground. The optimum exit is rarely the same as the best theoretical exit or the planned exit. The Sirocco Resources chart shows that the planned exit at $0.29, based on the price projection, was achievable. Greed is thrown into sharp relief with historical charts. The best possible theoretical exit is at $0.30 on the absolute high. Trader Success aims for the optimum exit at $0.28. This is the optimum exit given market conditions and price behavior. It is easy to see in retrospect but much more difficult to achieve in real time.

The optimum exit at $0.28 provides a 75% return. The important point is not the size of the return. Focus on this and greed creeps in undetected. The important point is the way this exit at $0.28 is consistent with the original trading plan established when the trade was first entered.

A parabolic trend is made up of a series of increasingly shorter straight-edge trend lines. The Sirocco Resources trade exit is also defined by the last of the short straight-edge trend lines, as shown in Figure 10.3.

The first close below this short straight-edge trend line is an exit signal. It comes after two other indications suggesting that Trader Success needs to be ready for action:

- the increasingly vertical slope of the parabolic trend; and

- the way prices have entered the target sell zone.

A close below this most recent trend line is acted upon because Trader Success is primed to act on any additional signal that increases the probability of a trend break.

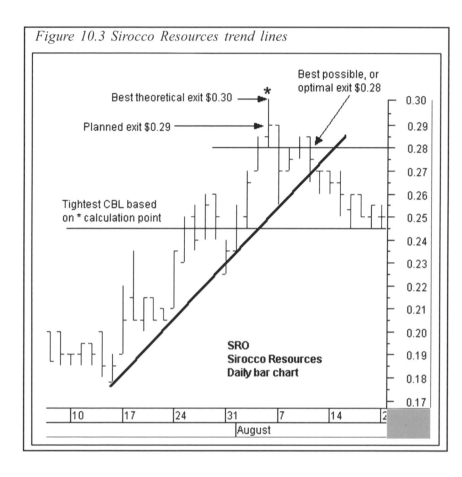

Figure 10.3 Sirocco Resources trend lines

This is a frightened-rabbit approach. It protects rabbits from predators, and nervous traders from large profit surrenders. Trader Success wants to exit at $0.28, but market action prevents this. The best price he gets is an actual exit at $0.265 as prices close below the trend line. This is a 65% return.

This exit is not as good as the optimum exit at $0.28, but it is the best exit available given the way price behaved once it moved below the straight-edge trend line.

Greed starts with the feeling that we should have achieved an exit at $0.29 or higher. Regret follows as we lament missed profits because our actual exit was lower than the historical high.

Speculation about exit conditions yields many possibilities. The spreadsheet extract in Figure 10.4 maps some outcomes based on the high of $0.30, the exit at $0.265, and the stop loss at $0.245. It assumes that 125,000 shares were purchased at $0.16 for an initial cost of $20,000. Change any one of these figures and profit grows or shrinks. The Exit_Greed spreadsheet includes calculations for the part-profits strategies discussed in Chapter 8. This spreadsheet puts definite figures on alternative exit strategies. Use these calculations with caution. They have the potential to inflame emotions.

Figure 10.4 Comparison of outcomes

			Return	Profit on sale	%% return
Sell all at estimated best price	125,000 $	0.300 $	37,500 $	17,500	87.50%
Sell all at current price	125,000 $	0.265 $	33,125 $	13,125	65.63%
Sell all at estimated worst price	125,000 $	0.245 $	30,625 $	10,625	53.13%
Summary strategy A - sell 50,000 and market rises			35,750 $	15,750	78.75%
Summary strategy B - sell 50,000 and market falls			31,625 $	11,625	58.13%

HOPING FOR NEW HIGHS

Unless there are convincing chart- and price-based reasons for amending the plan as the exit point arrives, traders are better off staying with the plan. As soon as we second-guess the exit plan, we start to reduce profits significantly. Greed more frequently takes us to loss than to additional profits. This effect is leveraged into greater profit reductions when we deal with overpriced stocks in momentum-driven trades where price leverage is high.

Hoping for new highs uses seductive reasoning. We could assemble many reasons to explain why Sirocco Resources was bullish, ranging from general market conditions to moving averages. A more bullish trader looks for prices to move toward the upper levels of the target zone at $0.32.

When we start to speculate and calculate how much higher the price could go once initial targets are reached, we open the door to emotional trading based on hope. With Sirocco Resources, an exit at the upper target of $0.32 rather than $0.29 yields an extra 19% in potential profit. This must be balanced against the downside risk.

Traders make the most effective exit decisions when they are not exposed to the heat of the moment. When we enter the trade we have a clearer idea of the objectives of the trade and the exit conditions. If we try to make the exit action closer to the exit point, or if we try to second-guess an established trading plan, in most cases we get it wrong. Too many of these exit modifications are based on hope rather than sound chart and price signals. Unless traders are very disciplined, it is easy to turn managing a profit into managing a loss.

ONCE WERE PROFITS

Turning a profit into a loss is a strategy based on greed. Trader Novice is the most likely victim of this strategy, but Trader Average falls for it as well. When Trader Average trades Sirocco Resources as the action develops in Figure 10.5, it may work like this.

The price dips below the straight-edge trend line. Rather than accept this sell signal, Trader Average looks for another sell signal at a lower price. This defers any action, and with luck this gives time for prices to rally back to the old highs. He selects a count back line calculation. The stop loss value is $0.245. A close below this line is the new exit signal, and it comes with a close at $0.24.

Trader Average is disappointed and decides to get out the next day. As prices open lower at $0.23, he decides to wait for the usual daytime recovery. Instead of placing a sell order, he decides to micro-manage the trade from a live screen. Prices creep up to $0.235, but he is not quick enough to grab this trade. Prices move down quickly from what was the high of the day and close at $0.225.

Trader Average is not trading well. His decision not to place a sell order is based on hope and greed. He hopes that prices will lift back to the level where he first decided to sell — the close at $0.24. In his heart, he lusts after an exit around $0.265. Greed encourages him to "get even" with the market for taking away previous profits.

When trends collapse in these types of stocks, the price moves are often substantial. Sirocco Resources opens the following day at $0.23 and falls steadily and quickly to $0.21. Get out here and the profit is 31%. This is very small when compared to the 81% available from the original planned exit at the target price of $0.29.

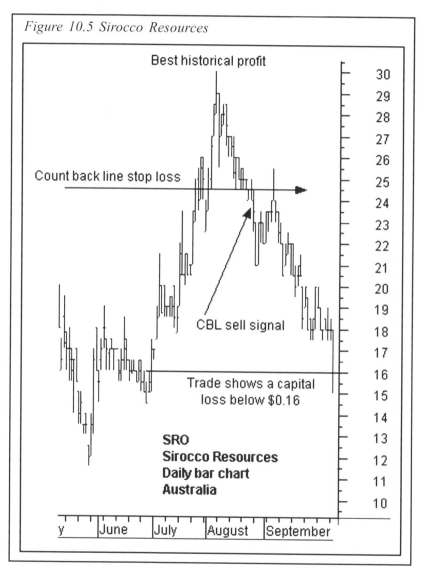

Figure 10.5 Sirocco Resources

Best historical profit

Count back line stop loss

CBL sell signal

Trade shows a capital
loss below $0.16

SRO
Sirocco Resources
Daily bar chart
Australia

y   June   July   August   September

When profits more than halve, Trader Average starts thinking about not selling. Greed whispers seductively. Instead, he decides to wait until prices move back up to $0.24. Reluctantly he decides to ride the trade until it recovers. In just a few days he shifts from managing a profit to managing a recovery, or even a loss.

When prices lift to $0.24, Trader Average finds another excuse not to sell. Often he wants revenge for lost profits. If Sirocco Resources' price recovers to $0.24, then it could also climb back to $0.29 — and this time, he lies to himself, he will sell. Instead, the price collapses, falling to $0.15. What was once a profit is now a loss of trading capital.

Playing with greed is a dangerous activity, as summarized in Figure 10.6. If we change the rules to protect profits, we have a much better chance of success.

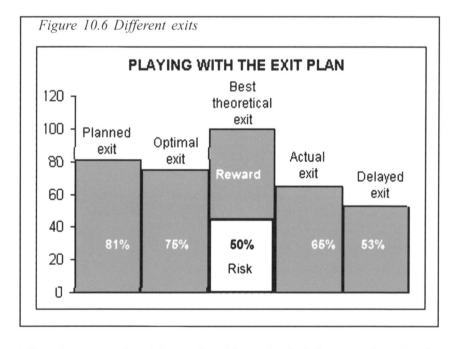

Figure 10.6 Different exits

All traders struggle with greed and it marks their journey from Trader Novice to Trader Success. Success depends on understanding how greed destroys our exit strategy. Our analysis of the trade is often correct. The failure comes from the way greed encourages us to second-guess our planned exit, suggesting we could capture profits from the highest high.

The first planned exit decision made when the trade is entered is most often the best. Good traders develop the discipline to act on the signals when they arrive. They do not use the signal as an opportunity to second-guess their original decision.

Protecting profits is not only a matter of judging the best exit point. Many traders believe this and concentrate on fine-tuning indicators to shift the exit signal as close as possible to the ultimate high in any trend. The risk of failure is always high, and is compounded when greed encourages us to stay with the trade to recover lost profits.

Protecting profits requires more than mechanical skill and chart-based exit points. Our profits grow as our skill in using these techniques improves. Profits grow as our trading discipline improves. Profits take off when we put greed to one side and apply a range of money management techniques to our trading.

In the following chapters, we consider techniques to prevent profit erosion and methods to help the trade grow with the developing up trend. These involve a combination of chart-based and financial calculations.

ELEVEN
PROFIT AT RISK

It hurts when profits slip through our fingers. The difference between Trader Success and Trader Average, who is on the brink of success, is the way they capture profits. The erosion of profits in good trades undermines long-term trading success. Our objective is to improve the way we take profits by combining financial money management calculations with chart and price action.

Perfect profits glitter at the end of every up trend. They are the profits available from an exit based on the absolute high. Some traders pursue perfect profits out of greed. We use perfect profits to provide a benchmark for our trading performance. The high price of the trend or rally makes it easier to compare what could have been with the actual result from the trade.

I have yet to discover a method to consistently identify the top of a trend or rally. By combining luck with judgment, I sometimes exit a trade near the top of the trend. More frequently I am either a little too early or a little too late. I close the trade and the price keeps moving upward, or I exit the trade after prices fall from their peak. I always surrender some of the potential profit available from each trade.

Profit erosion is a problem for every trader and we have a choice in how we deal with it. Some traders keep fine-tuning their exit conditions in an attempt to consistently exit near the top of a move. This is time consuming and, ultimately, not consistently successful. Stocks behave in too many different ways, so it is difficult to fine-tune a single solution to fit all.

Other traders explore ways to protect profits to the best extent possible given the individual circumstances of each trade. They accept that they cannot collect 100% of the profits available, so they are interested in techniques that help them collect at least 80% of the available profits. In some trades, the chart-based stop loss and protect-profits methods are satisfactory. In many trades these are also balanced against financial objectives to determine the level of profit at risk in each trade.

We tend to pursue profit as if it were separate from other aspects of our trading — somehow not related to capital or risk. After all, it is the reward side of the equation. It comes with trading success, so the risk seems to be in the past. There are advantages in treating reward as another aspect of risk because, in preserving profits, we have to determine how much profit we are prepared to give up before we decide it is time to get out.

When we start a trade, we know how much capital we are prepared to risk in dollar terms. This risk is also transferred to the reward side of the equation. It makes no sense to risk losing more in open profits than we are prepared to risk in capital with a failed trade.

THE CONCEPT

The problem we want to solve is how to protect our open profits and take an exit as close to the top of the up trend as possible. The relationship between the 2% rule, the stop loss condition on entering the trade, and trading capital sets the position size and provides the starting point for a solution. When planning to enter a trade, we adjust the position size, as discussed in Chapter 6, so that when prices fall to the stop loss level we put at risk no more than 2% of our trading capital. This approach uses a logical stop loss based on chart activity, such as a support level or count back line calculation.

The significant feature of this risk control method is the way we define in advance how much we are prepared to risk on the trade — no more than 2% of our total trading capital. In some trades, we may decide to risk less, perhaps 1%. The risk is related to our total trading capital, not the individual trade.

The strategy at the heart of this chapter takes the initial method of risk control used at the start of the trade and applies it to the end of the trade. If 2% of trading capital is the maximum amount of loss we are prepared to tolerate when we buy the stock, then the same dollar amount is also used to define the maximum amount of loss of profit we are prepared to suffer. If a $2,000 loss was acceptable on entering the trade, then only a $2,000 loss of open profits is acceptable on closing the trade. This is a Profit Dollars at Risk strategy.

Voluntarily surrendering part of our trading reward does not sit comfortably with all traders. Our reaction is colored by the difference between the loss of committed money — money used to buy the stock — and the attack on our "reward" — the full potential profit. For the moment, we put these considerations to one side.

The Profit Dollars at Risk strategy is an effective additional tool for protecting profit, particularly in fast-moving rallies and momentum-based trades. It is less effective in slower moving established trends where traditional protect-profit chart-based methods work well. In these trades, the Profit Dollars at Risk strategy is applied as a back up. We compare examples from both market situations.

FAST MOVERS

Fast-moving stocks whip away profits in a flash. In fast-moving stocks it is difficult to capture the top of the move. These are speculative bubbles and short-lived rallies. We need a more effective exit method than those based on luck, courage, and guesswork. Our concern with these trades is to lock-in the maximum profit without being taken out of the trend too quickly. Traditional exit conditions often leave the stop loss too far away from the current high in fast rally and momentum trades.

The Profit Dollars at Risk strategy starts with the dollar amount of risk calculated on the trade entry. This figure is used to cap foregone potential profits as the trade develops. This has the advantage of tying the stop loss dollar figure to a rational calculation so that it leaves less room for fear and greed to edge into the exit decision.

For comparison purposes we use a single trade in Hong Kong-listed Wah Tak Fung and show how three traders apply three different exit methods. We assume the same entry point, position cost, and position risk for all of the trades. We look at three possibilities for each trading example:

1. The first is using the same dollar risk on the exit as with the trade entry — $2,000 in these examples. When $2,000 of potential profit from the most recent high is lost, then Trader Success leaves the trade.

2. The second compares this exit using a 2xAverage True Range protect-profit exit point calculated from the same recent high as discussed by Christopher Tate in *The Art of Trading*. These rising stop loss values are shown as dots on the chart display. Trader Average uses this strategy.

3. The third places half as many dollars at risk on the profit exit — in this case, $1,000. Trader Novice applies this approach.

We show the calculations for each example, both on a spreadsheet and a chart. The Dollars at Risk spreadsheet Excel template is included in the Better Trading spreadsheet pak from www.guppytraders.com.

We start this comparison with momentum and rally trades. Wah Tak Fung highlights the problem with this type of opportunity. The impact of the exit decision is exaggerated in this penny dreadful stock, where price leverage builds rewards quickly but demolishes profit just as rapidly. The full trade opportunity is shown in Figure 11.1. It includes the exit points for all three options.

Why do we apparently waste time at this end of the market? At best this trade from $0.30 to $0.80 returns 166% in 20 days. We like a good profit as much as the next trader, and with the risk management solution discussed in Chapter 6 we trade this volatility with low risk.

For this example, all traders take an entry into Wah Tak Fung at $0.30. Each buys 67,000 shares for a total cost of $20,100. We start with Trader Success who applies the first risk management option using the same dollar risk on the exit as with the trade entry. When $2,000 of potential profit from the most recent high is lost, she leaves the trade.

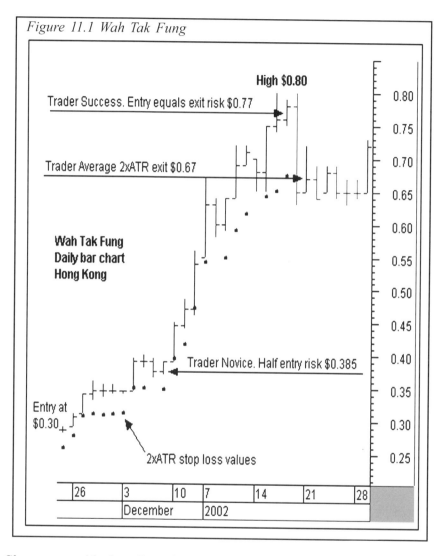

Figure 11.1 Wah Tak Fung

High $0.80

Trader Success. Entry equals exit risk $0.77

Trader Average 2xATR exit $0.67

Wah Tak Fung
Daily bar chart
Hong Kong

Trader Novice. Half entry risk $0.385

Entry at
$0.30

2xATR stop loss values

| 26 | 3 | 10 | 7 | 14 | 21 | 28 |
| | December | | 2002 | | | |

She wants to ride the rally and momentum action on this small speculative stock. Every time a new high is made, she turns to the spreadsheet to adjust the calculations. Wah Tak Fung hit a high of $0.80 and the calculations are shown in Figure 11.2.

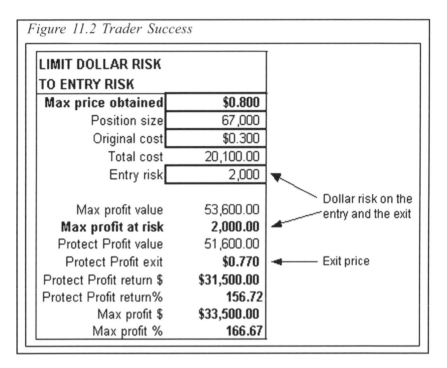

Figure 11.2 Trader Success

LIMIT DOLLAR RISK TO ENTRY RISK		
Max price obtained	$0.800	
Position size	67,000	
Original cost	$0.300	
Total cost	20,100.00	
Entry risk	2,000	Dollar risk on the entry and the exit
Max profit value	53,600.00	
Max profit at risk	2,000.00	
Protect Profit value	51,600.00	
Protect Profit exit	$0.770	Exit price
Protect Profit return $	$31,500.00	
Protect Profit return%	156.72	
Max profit $	$33,500.00	
Max profit %	166.67	

If prices close below $0.77, then Trader Success takes an exit because the loss is greater than $2,000. Prices close below this level, so Trader Success exits the next day at $0.77, taking a loss as planned of $2,000. This trade returns 156.7%.

The second protect-profit stop loss option uses twice the value of the average true range indicator to plot the stop loss. Only the highest value is used. Lower values are ignored and are not shown on the chart. Trader Average uses this approach and it is not an ideal solution to these fast-moving trades. As shown in Figure 11.1, the stop loss lags a long way below the highest high. The 2xATR stop loss is based on the ranging activity of price, but there is no exit signal until price closes below $0.67.

Waiting for this signal puts a lot of profit at risk. Acting on this exit signal, Trader Average surrenders $8,710 of profits. This hurts. His return on the trade is reduced to 123%. The results are shown in Figure 11.3. In fast momentum and rally trades, the Profit Dollars at Risk strategy appears more successful.

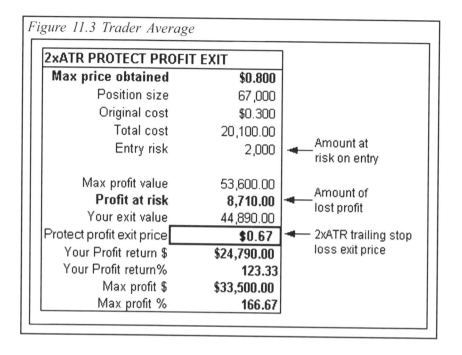

Figure 11.3 Trader Average

2xATR PROTECT PROFIT EXIT		
Max price obtained	$0.800	
Position size	67,000	
Original cost	$0.300	
Total cost	20,100.00	
Entry risk	2,000	◄— Amount at risk on entry
Max profit value	53,600.00	◄— Amount of lost profit
Profit at risk	**8,710.00**	
Your exit value	44,890.00	
Protect profit exit price	**$0.67**	◄— 2xATR trailing stop loss exit price
Your Profit return $	**$24,790.00**	
Your Profit return%	123.33	
Max profit $	**$33,500.00**	
Max profit %	166.67	

WORKING THE PROFIT SQUEEZE

Traders always try to squeeze the maximum out of every trade. Getting out of Wah Tak Fung at $0.77 still hurts because the absolute high was $0.80. Some traders believe it makes sense to limit the profit loss to less than the risk on the entry. This is the third possible approach and is used by Trader Novice. Instead of using the full amount of risk, he puts half as many dollars at risk on the profit exit.

This often moves the exit price very close to the current price. Many trades are closed too early. This is a false exit. The Wah Tak Fung example shows the impact of reducing the Profit Dollars at Risk amount. Trader Novice chooses to use half the entry risk, so he gets out when the trade loses $1,000 of open profits. Based on the high of $0.80, this locks in a 161.67% return. This is 4.95% better than Trader Success, whose exit was based on a $2,000 profit reduction.

This result is deceptive, though, because it ignores an earlier exit signal. Seven days after the entry, price topped out at $0.40. On this day, the Profit

Dollars at Risk calculation for Trader Novice sets the exit trigger at $0.385, as shown in Figure 11.4.

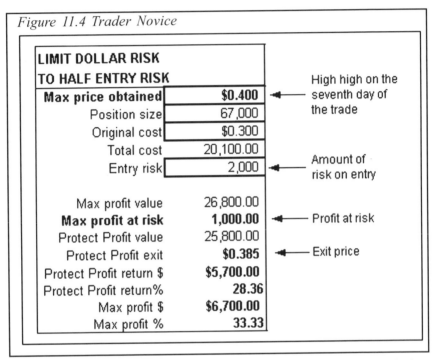

Figure 11.4 Trader Novice

LIMIT DOLLAR RISK			
TO HALF ENTRY RISK			High high on the
Max price obtained	$0.400	◄—	seventh day of
Position size	67,000		the trade
Original cost	$0.300		
Total cost	20,100.00		
Entry risk	2,000	◄—	Amount of risk on entry
Max profit value	26,800.00		
Max profit at risk	**1,000.00**	◄—	Profit at risk
Protect Profit value	25,800.00		
Protect Profit exit	$0.385	◄—	Exit price
Protect Profit return $	$5,700.00		
Protect Profit return%	28.36		
Max profit $	$6,700.00		
Max profit %	33.33		

Shortly after Wah Tak Fung opened the next day, the price fell well below these exit conditions. In this particular example, this exit technique is best based on the end-of-day closes, so Trader Novice has to ignore this intra-day low. Traders watching real-time trading screens need strong discipline in this situation. The temptation is to act on the intra-day signal rather than wait for end-of-day confirmation. The eventual close at $0.37 takes Trader Novice out of Wah Tak Fung before the trend has a chance to reach the final high of $0.80.

The Profit Dollars at Risk approach is much more successful than volatility- and range-based exit conditions in fast-moving trades. In this example, the trader surrenders 9.95% of the potential profit, compared with 43% surrender for the 2xATR approach, as shown in Figure 11.5. Using the half entry risk approach is theoretically attractive, but this result ignores the early exit triggered at $0.37.

Figure 11.5 Relative performance

ENTRY RISK EQUALS EXIT RISK	Profit surrender	$2,000.00
	% surrender	9.95
2xATR EXIT	Profit surrender	$8,710.00
	% surrender	43.33
EXIT RISK HALF ENTRY RISK	Profit surrender	$1,000.00
	% surrender	4.98

Using the Profit Dollars at Risk approach gives the trader an effective way to control profit erosion in momentum trades. It also provides a good way to protect open profits in long trend trades, particularly when used in conjunction with other standard trend trading tools and signals. While traders might choose to ignore the Dollars at Risk signal, they have a back-up in a trend trade provided by moving average exit signals.

Good trading suggests we act on the first signal to limit our loss, but practice suggests that we are more likely to use this as a preliminary alert.

SLOW MOVERS

Slow and steady trends carry less risk of sudden trend collapse. Trend identification tools include the Guppy Multiple Moving Average, trailing protect-profit stop loss calculations, moving average crossovers, and other standard indicators such as divergence signals in the Relative Strength Index. All have the potential for improvement when applied alongside a Profit Dollars at Risk calculation.

We use the strong up trend in Malaysian-listed AmCorp in Figure 11.6 as an example to illustrate the impact of these techniques. Trader Success applies the Profit Dollars at Risk strategy, and Trader Average uses the crossover of a 10- and 30-day exponential moving average to signal entry and exit conditions. Both traders start with an entry at $3.55.

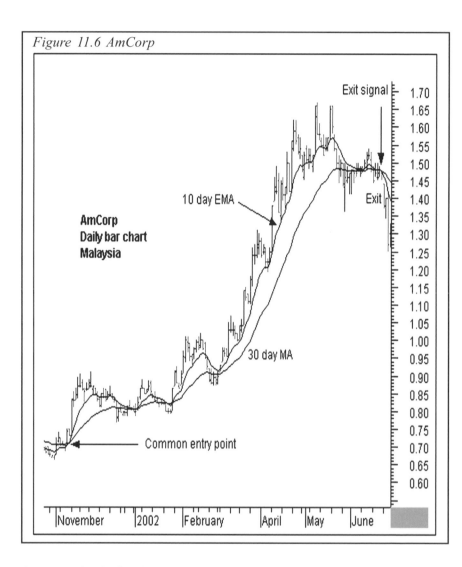

Figure 11.6 AmCorp

Our attention is fixed on the end of the trade. The best exit method should deliver the maximum potential profit. An exit at the absolute high of $1.67 puts $27,168 profit into our account. The moving average crossover trigger price is at $1.47, but Trader Average cannot act on this signal until the next day. This delivers an exit at $1.43 for a profit on the trade of $20,376, as shown in the spreadsheet extract in Figure 11.7.

The difference between the maximum profit obtainable and the actual exit based on the moving average crossover exit signal reduces the potential profit by $6,792. This is more than three times the amount Trader Average was prepared to risk when the trade opened.

Figure 11.7 Exit at $1.43

MA Exit	1.43	
Position sale	40,469	
Profit	20,376	
Maximum sale	47,261	Based on exit at $1.67
Maximum profit	27,168	
Surrendered profit	6,792	

Trader Success uses the Profit Dollars at Risk strategy. It offers the potential for a more effective exit that captures more profit. When the maximum potential profit is reduced by $2,000, the trade is closed. The chart in Figure 11.8, however, shows a significant problem with the Profit Dollars at Risk strategy in slow-moving trends. When prices peak at $0.92 a few weeks after the trade entry, the trailing stop loss exit point calculated with this method is at $0.85. Should prices fall to this level, then open profits are diminished by $2,000. A few days later, Trader Success exits at $0.85 to protect his open profits, as shown.

The result is shown in the spreadsheet extract in Figure 11.9. The strategy is successful in achieving the protect-profit objectives, but it bears no relationship to the developing trend. In a slow trend, where price volatility is lower, we effectively limit profit erosion to preferred levels. However, this strategy does not help Trader Success to stay with growing trend strength. Relying only on financial considerations for the exit signal is not satisfactory.

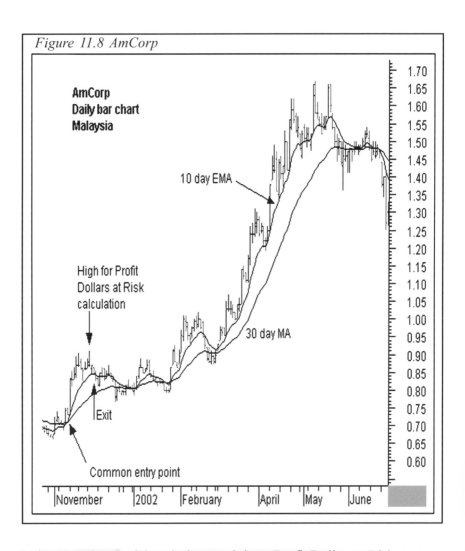

Figure 11.8 AmCorp

AmCorp
Daily bar chart
Malaysia

10 day EMA

High for Profit
Dollars at Risk
calculation

30 day MA

Exit

Common entry point

November   2002   February   April   May   June

In slow-trend trades it is pointless applying a Profit Dollars at Risk strategy based on an exit signal using half the initial entry risk. This strategy, used by Trader Novice in the Wah Tak Fung example, is a complete failure with AmCorp. Trades based on this method are closed just a few days after the very beginning of the trend development. The exit signal is just too close to the current highs.

SELECTING THE BEST EXIT
It is useful to compare the results of the Profit Dollars at Risk strategy with

your usual protect-profit strategy as a trade moves toward the end of the trend. This is most easily completed on a comparative spreadsheet, as shown in Figure 11.10.

Figure 11.9 Exit at $0.85

Dollars at risk exit	0.85	
Position sale	24,055	
Profit	3,962	
Maximum sale	47,261	Based on exit at $1.67
Maximum profit	27,168	
Surrendered profit	23,206	

The trade in this example was entered at $19.50. We purchased 1,050 shares for a total cost of $20,475. The entry risk was $2,000. The current high price is $27.20 and we are nervous about the stability of the trend. These figures are entered into the upper section of the spreadsheet in section A.

This exit requires close management to prevent the rapid destruction of profits. These starting figures provide a trading solution for the Profit Dollars at Risk strategy. Sell at the current high and the maximum profit is $8,085. This is a 34.49% return.

If we allow profits to fall by $2,000, the exit trigger price is $25.30. The spreadsheet calculates this price automatically. We show this as $25.295. We need this price detail when comparing exit strategies in low-priced stocks. This reduces the profit in the trade to 29.72%. Compared to the maximum profit available from the trade, this strategy surrenders 9.77%.

The results in section A of the spreadsheet provide a comparison point for alternative strategies. The base figures — entry, current high, risk on trade entry — are automatically transferred to section B. Only the lower section of the spreadsheet changes value. The changes are triggered by a single variable — the exit price determined by an alternative exit strategy.

Figure 11.10 Comparative spreadsheet

	Section A		Section B	
LIMIT DOLLAR RISK TO ENTRY RISK		**YOUR PREFERRED METHOD OF TRAILING PROFIT STOP**		
Max price obtained	$27.200	Max price obtained	$27.200
Position size	1,050	Position size	1,050
Original cost	$19.500	Original cost	$19.500
Total cost	20,475.00	Total cost	20,475.00
Entry risk	2,000	Entry risk	2,000
Max profit value	28,560.00	Max profit value	28,560.00
Max profit at risk	**2,000.00**	**Profit at risk**	**3,885.00**
Protect Profit value	26,560.00	Your exit value	24,675.00
Protect Profit exit	$25.295	Protect profit exit price	$23.50
Protect Profit return $	$6,085.00	Your Profit return $	$4,200.00
Protect Profit return%	29.72	Your Profit return%	20.51
Max profit $	$8,085.00	Max profit $	$8,085.00
Max profit %	39.49	Max profit %	39.49
RELATIVE PERFORMANCE			
Profit surrender	$2,000.00	Profit surrender	$3,885.00
% surrender	9.77	% surrender	18.97

The strategy with the lowest profit surender is the most effective

You might base the stop loss on a count back line calculation, a 2xATR stop loss technique or on the current value of a long-term moving average. The stop loss price you select determines the efficiency of your exit strategy. Compare your results with the best possible exit based on the current high and the Profit Dollars at Risk strategy.

In this example, we select an alternative exit price of $23.50. We do not intend to act until there is a close below this level. Under the conditions displayed on the spreadsheet, this reduces the profit in the trade to 20.51%. This is 9.21% lower than the alternative strategy. It is 18.97% worse than the best possible exit.

The bottom line of the spreadsheet compares the exit efficiency of the selected strategies. In this example, the Profit Dollars at Risk strategy is more effective. Equipped with this information the trader who is already worried about the stability of the trend may decide to act on an exit signal generated by the Profit Dollars at Risk solution.

The Profit Dollars at Risk strategy is a money management approach that imposes a financial calculation on the exit conditions of a trade. It is designed to stop the erosion of profits. When financial calculations are applied to a trade entry, we have a well-defined mechanism to match financial and chart-based calculations to determine the optimum position size for each trade. This is an effective way to manage risk, because we control both the entry price and the quantity of stock purchased. This is a precise relationship where many variables are brought into agreement.

It is more difficult to match financial calculations with real trade conditions when it comes time to exit the trade. The position size — the quantity of stock held — has already been determined. The variables have been reduced, so the solution is not always as relevant or the fit as elegant. However, in fast-moving, momentum-driven trades, the Profit Dollars at Risk strategy provides a very effective way to manage the exit. It is a useful tool to add to the standard protect-profit toolkit in these situations.

In trend trades, the strategy is best applied when other indicators also suggest that the end of the trend is developing. In this situation, the strategy is applied as a back-up rather than as an initiating condition for the exit.

Effective trading requires more than just the mechanics of chart analysis. Applying financial and money management considerations helps prevent the erosion of hard-earned profits. Profits still slip through our fingers, but the loss is much smaller.

TWELVE
WINNING
ADDITIONS

When a trade takes off, we boost performance by adding more capital. Cutting losers and riding winners is a survival strategy. To really get ahead, we need a method to leverage returns from winning trades. Winners should add even larger amounts to our total portfolio capital. Getting the most out of winning trades is the subject of the next two chapters.

Increasing the number of successful trades is a hard path to trading success. If we increase the level of return in every successful trade, we have a better method of gathering more profits. It is not enough just to have a profitable trade. We want to turn it into a *very* profitable trade. In the previous chapter, we considered how protect-profit methods assist in achieving this objective. A better solution uses money management techniques to grow profits more effectively. This leverages profits, giving them a lift by using the acceleration effect of trending behavior.

The commonly accepted solutions are built around pyramiding trades. These solutions are remarkably unsuccessful at boosting returns on capital. However, these ideas are so entrenched that it is necessary to take some time to examine them in greater detail. These strategies ask the trader to add new positions as the trade starts to make a profit.

This increases the profit, but it has an unexpected level of risk that may significantly reduce profits, and, at times, eat into trading capital. The outcome is not what we expect. The reason for this is found in the nature of all trends. In the next chapter we examine a better solution, which matches money management techniques with trend behavior.

The pyramids of Egypt have stood for thousands of years and the classic pyramid trading approach suggests the same stability. In this chapter, we show how risk changes even with exactly comparable positions and stop loss exits. A significant level of risk is directly related to the money management technique selected.

Fund managers and institutional traders have a selection of well-defined money management formulas. Ralph Vince in *Portfolio Management Formulas*, Fred Ghem in *Quantitative Trading and Money Management*, and Ryan Jones in *The Trading Game* provide a good coverage of this area. Their solutions are designed for traders with large amounts of capital, and for fund managers whose portfolio calculations start with millions of dollars. Trader Average and even Trader Success would like to have a million dollars, but until they do, they need to use different methods to manage risk.

We start with three classic strategies for loading up winners. We join hands again with our three traders. The strategies are:

1. Pyramiding with constant position size. This is used by Trader Success.

2. Pyramiding with constant dollar size. Trader Average applies this strategy.

3. A benchmark return based on a buy and hold strategy. This is an opportunity for Trader Lucky to show why he is unwelcome at parties.

Our objective is to increase the total position size as the trade continues to move in our favor. The ultimate outcome is to have most of our trading capital tied up in money-making trades, rather than having capital trapped in trading opportunities which are doubtful or losing money.

Most traders reach for one of two common strategies. The first strategy, used by Trader Success in this example, calls for traders to add new positions to a winning trade. These are the same lot or parcel size as the initial position. The second strategy encourages traders to add new positions keeping the same dollar size. Trader Average takes this approach. Both these strategies appear successful while the trend continues, but they expose the traders to significant risk when the trend reverses.

For comparison purposes, we use a single stream of data and a common series of entry points for each additional position. Just like real-world trading, we assume the traders have slow reflexes when it comes to the exit. The exit signal comes today, but they do not get to act on it until the next day. We use Spotless Holdings as an example, but the relationships are more important than the security selected. Our sample traders each have $300,000 available for trading, and this figure becomes more significant as we consider effective risk control measures. The traders put at risk no more than 2% of this figure on any individual trade. With total account size at $300,000, this translates into a maximum loss of $6,000 in any single trade.

A SUCCESSFUL TREND TRADE

All strategies start with an initial entry at $5.00. All strategies end with an exit at $7.30, where all open trades are closed. Trader Lucky gets the benchmark result.

The Spotless chart in Figure 12.1 shows the benchmark progress of this successful trade based on a buy and hold strategy. Trader Lucky enters at $5.00, just after the 10- and 30-day moving average crossover signal. His exit at $7.30 is also triggered by the crossover of the 10- and 30-day exponential moving average. This is a simple and successful trade. For the first trade in all strategies, we buy a parcel of 6,000 shares for a total cost of $30,000.

We use the terms "lot" and "parcel" to define the first trade, or position, taken with Spotless. Later we add multiple entries in the same trade, so it is clearer to call them lot 1, lot 2, and so on.

The buy and hold benchmark strategy results in the sale of this lot of 6,000 shares at $7.30. Trader Lucky collects $13,800 profit for a 46% return on capital employed in the trade.

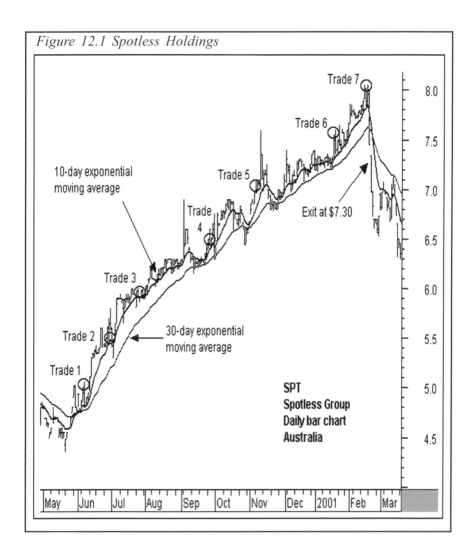

Figure 12.1 Spotless Holdings

The equity curves, expressed in both dollar and percentage terms, for this buy and hold strategy are shown in Figure 12.2. The equity curve, or line, traces the growth of our position size — capital and paper profits — as the trade develops.

Can we improve on this 46% return using pyramiding strategies? The answer depends on how we add to the initial position — trade 1 — taken at $5.00.

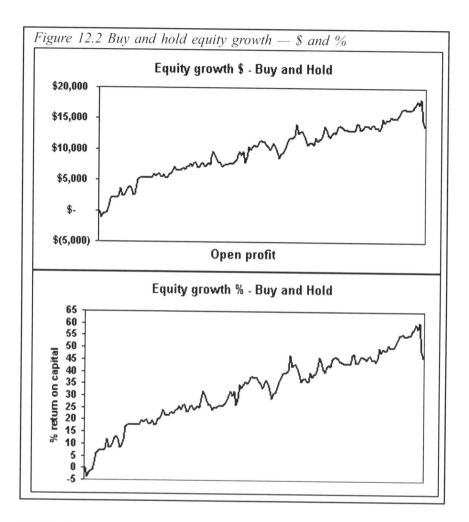

Figure 12.2 Buy and hold equity growth — $ and %

PYRAMID BUILDING BLOCKS

We selected Spotless because the chart shows a clear rising trend. In this benchmark chart example, we have the advantage of hindsight. In real time, it is difficult to decide when to add to winning trades. We did consider some options in Chapter 8 and we consider some other strategies in the next chapter. In this example, we want to keep the new entry decision as simple as possible so that we can focus on the comparative outcomes.

The steps on this pyramid entry are set at intervals of $0.50. Trader Average and Trader Success add a new trade, or position, at every

$0.50 interval. This gives six additional entry points after the first trade at $5.00. New trades are added at:

1. $5.50
2. $6.00
3. $6.50
4. $7.00
5. $7.50
6. $8.00

This gives a total of seven trades, or lots. Adding new trades is a clear strategy in retrospect, but much more difficult in real life. This variation between theory and reality adds a risk we need to manage in an effective way. These seven entry points are the base conditions for comparing the two money management strategies below.

This add to winning positions strategy comes with two choices:

1. *Constant position size.* Trader Success keeps the amount of stock in each parcel the same as in the first parcel. This makes seven parcels, each of 6,000 shares in this example. The cost of each parcel is different, depending on the current price.

2. *Constant dollar size or dollar cost averaging.* At each entry point, Trader Average spends the same amount of money. The first parcel cost $30,000. When she adds the next parcel using this strategy, it costs around $30,000. The number of shares in each new parcel changes, depending on the current price.

New trades are added at regular price intervals. We use $0.50 as the trigger price. The true dollar cost averaging strategy adds new positions at regular time intervals, such as once a month.

CONSTANT POSITION SIZE

When a stock starts rising in price, many brokers encourage traders to buy more. This is a money management strategy, as well as a trading or investment tactic. Some traders keep the number of shares purchased in each new lot the same size as the original parcel — 6,000 shares in this example. They believe this is an effective approach to build profits and lower risk, mainly because the price is rising. Each time the Spotless price moves up $0.50, Trader Success buys more stock.

When Spotless goes to $5.50, he adds another 6,000 shares, spending an additional $33,000. He collects another parcel of 6,000 at $6.00. This costs $36,000. This strategy calls for deep pockets. By the time seven positions are opened, Trader Success needs $273,000. This is often beyond the reach of small traders.

Our sample traders each have $300,000 available to meet the demands for additional capital to load up on the winning trade. Unfortunately, by maintaining the same lot size, this strategy distorts the risk profile in the trade by reducing the reward. When it comes time to exit the trade at $7.30, all open positions are closed.

The exit signal comes from the moving average crossover. The exit is lower than the entry price in the final trade at $8.00. This is a theoretical example, but we do not want to step too far away from reality. Often we add to winning positions just before the trend begins to reverse. Additionally, our reaction to the exit signal is often delayed. To ignore this reality means that money management strategies that work on the pages of books do not work when transferred to our trading records.

Many traders intuitively believe this is a winning strategy. They are wrong. The return on capital in this strategy is dismal. Keeping a constant position size with new trades costs Trader Success real money even though he bought into a rising trend.

The results are assembled in Figure 12.3. Trader Success has an impressive $33,600 in profits. However, total return on capital committed to the trades is just 12.31%. This is well below the 46% benchmark return from the buy and hold strategy pursued by Trader Lucky.

Figure 12.3 Return on capital — constant position size

Total trade capital	$ 273,000.00
Current value	$ 306,600.00
Total open profits	$33,600.00
%% Return	12.31

This strategy works if the trader gets out of the trend before it collapses. This is easy on historical charts, but much more difficult in reality. Many traders have trouble with the exit. Even if they act with discipline on exit signals, the signal often comes too late.

Readers who want to run the mathematics can use the Pyramid Growth spreadsheet templates included in the Better Trading pak available from www.guppytraders.com. The performance of this pyramid strategy is destroyed by the poor exit at $7.30. We improve the result by taking an exit above $8.00. Readers who manipulate the spreadsheet results in this way need to ask an important real-time trading question: How do you know at the time that an exit above $8.00 is appropriate and that the trend is not going to carry prices to $9.00 or higher?

An honest answer has a big impact on the final result of this strategy.

At the exit point on the chart, the equity curve for the trade collapses dramatically by any criteria. It does not support the commonly accepted idea that adding to winning positions in a rising trend is an effective way to build trading profits.

Successful trading depends on discipline, and this comes from trade planning. Every trade plan contains a consistent set of conditions specifying the exit. The plan our sample traders use is a crossover of the 10- and 30-day moving average. It captures the bulk of the Spotless trend. It is convenient to look at the Spotless chart and point to where the best exit should have been, but the reality of this trading plan called for an exit when a different set of conditions was met. If we take an exit without adhering to the original plan, we are in danger of relying on emotional guesswork to deliver consistent profits.

This constant position size pyramid strategy fails because it skews risk toward the wrong end of the trade. As the trend develops, the dollar value of each position increases. As the trend weakens, this strategy calls on Trader Success to add even more cash. The 6,000 shares purchased in the final parcel at $8.00 cost $48,000, or $18,000 more than the original parcel. This adverse risk is even more pronounced if our actual exit is poorly timed, as in this example.

DOLLAR COST AVERAGING

By accident, by design, or by necessity, many traders add new positions to winning trades by using the same dollar size for each.

We use Trader Average to demonstrate this approach. The initial position in this example cost Trader Average $30,000. The dollar cost averaging strategy calls for her to spend just $30,000 on each new parcel of stock.

The total position costs less to build. Intuitively, she believes the risk is also contained more effectively. For this example, she uses the nearest round number of shares at each entry price to keep the position size as close to $30,000 as possible — the original cost of entry.

Trading results are shown in Figure 12.4. They are more encouraging than the first approach, but still not as successful as the buy and hold benchmark provided by Trader Lucky. Trader Average needs a total of $210,090 to implement this dollar cost averaging strategy.

Figure 12.4 Return on capital — dollar cost averaging

Total trade capital	$ 210,090.00
Current value	$ 241,776.00
Total open profits	$31,686.00
%% Return	15.08

This is still a poor strategy. Total profits returned are just $31,686, or a 15.08% return on the total trading capital committed. This is less than the 46% available with the buy and hold approach used by Trader Lucky who, as expected, is exceptionally lucky in this trade.

If we measure the return in dollar terms it looks better. She gets $17,886 more than Trader Lucky, but it takes significantly more capital. This approach controls risk slightly more effectively than the constant position size model used by Trader Success, but the return on capital is still marginal. Most traders look for better results from a trade costing $210,090.

The pyramid built with dollar cost averaging is better than the one built with a constant position size. Not only is the return on capital 2.76% better, but it is achieved with a smaller amount of cash. For many small traders, it is impossible to build either of these pyramids because they do not have $200,000 or $300,000 available to allocate to a single stock.

They favor the buy and hold strategy which calls for just $30,000 and delivers an effective 46% return on capital, as shown in Figure 12.5. This is good trading, but the buy and hold strategy does not help to boost returns when trades are successful. The buy and hold model does not give Trader Lucky the opportunity to exploit winning trades.

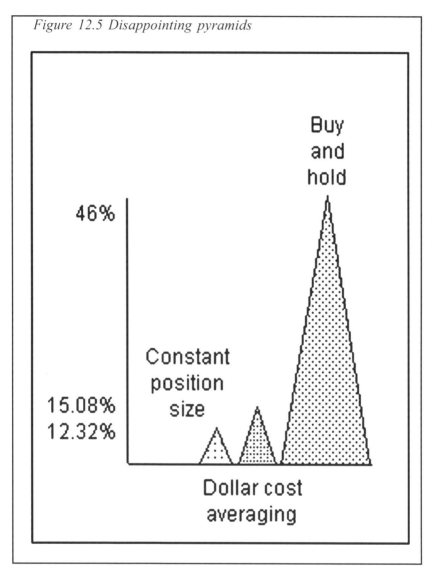

Figure 12.5 Disappointing pyramids

The results obtained from the Spotless example are not definitive. Choose another stock, change the entry or exit conditions, or modify the combination of position size and entry points and the outcomes change. Use the Pyramid Growth spreadsheet templates to explore these options. A common feature soon emerges. These popular pyramiding strategies do not substantially increase return on capital when we find ourselves on board a winning trend trade.

PYRAMIDING RISK

As traders, we look for a better risk and reward equation than 12% or 15% return from a successful analysis of the trend. The trades should add substantially to profit growth.

The exit at $7.30 from Spotless should conclude a nicely profitable trade. Instead, the choice of an ineffective pyramiding money management strategy destroys the opportunity.

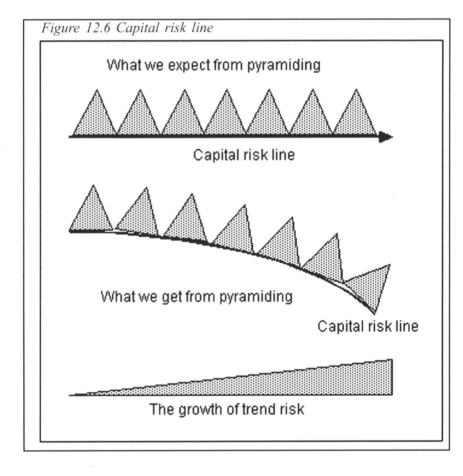

Figure 12.6 Capital risk line

What we expect from pyramiding

Capital risk line

What we get from pyramiding

Capital risk line

The growth of trend risk

The poor performance of these pyramiding methods rests on a poor understanding of trend risk. Just at the point where the risk of trend failure is greatest, these strategies ask the trader to add a new parcel of stock based on the same assumptions of risk behavior as when the trend was young and strong. When the trend fails, we have an increased sum of capital at risk and our potential losses are large. We expect the capital risk line shown in Figure 12.6 to hold steady and strong. Instead, the capital risk line bends down as the risk of trend failure increases. We push this to snapping point when we add new positions pyramided at the same size. When the capital risk line breaks, it takes a large amount of capital in the fall.

We need a method of adding new positions, or pyramiding, to match the risk of new positions with the risk of the trend failure. Just because we get the direction of the trend right, it does not mean the trend is invincible, nor that it will continue for a sustained period.

Both the constant position size and dollar cost averaging approaches to profit growth assume trend continuity. While there is no trend reversal, these add-on approaches are quite successful. These strategies collapse when the trend reverses. Just when we need the protection of a good money management strategy, these strategies desert us.

We match risk and position size more effectively by separating our ability to get the trade right from our understanding of the trend. Pyramid strategies work when we match the changing nature of risk with our financial reaction. The Grow_Up strategy is a better way to exploit winners.

THIRTEEN
TRENDING
TOWARD RISK

Trends vex traders at the beginning and the end. In the middle, it is true that the trend is your friend. At the start and end, the trend is an unreliable friend. Trends have two points of high risk where failure is a real possibility. The first is as the downtrend turns into an up trend. The second is as the up trend turns into a downtrend. The section in the middle provides low-risk trading opportunities because the trend is well-established and sound.

Every now and then it is good to return to the basics and remind ourselves of what we are doing. As traders, our objective is to buy low and sell higher. The most effective way to do this is to trade an up trend in prices. From this basic observation comes a range of trading tools, indicators, and strategies, all designed to identify the beginning and end of a trend. These do not interest us at the moment, and they are covered in detail in my books *Market Trading Tactics* and *Chart Trading*.

We are interested in the common features of trends. All trends go through four phases, as shown in Figure 13.1. Immediately after the breakout from a downtrend, the young up trend is strong and vigorous. This is often the period with the greatest increase in value over time. Here we see rallies and explosive up-moves, followed by consolidation periods and momentum patterns. Measured by angle, the trend line may move between 45 degrees and 60 degrees. These are steep slopes.

Later the trend is robust. This is a well-established, respectable, and consistent stage 2 trend. The slope of the trend line becomes shallower, and the rate of change decreases. Typically, the trend moves between 30 degrees and 45 degrees.

In the third stage the trend matures. The rate of trend growth slows. Traders see consolidation patterns develop. Rounding tops and head and shoulder patterns are found during this stage. Some trends break out of this maturity with a new lease of life. Most nibble away at our trading profits before collapsing. There is little growth in returns, and the stock does not appear on any market scan designed to select trending stocks.

Trend failure in stage 4 sometimes comes quickly, with a sudden collapse and no recovery. In other circumstances, prices simply stumble steadily day after day. This graceful curve signals the slow destruction of trading capital. Like daylight fading from noon through dusk, to black night, it is difficult to pick the exact point of change. Quite suddenly it appears that our trading profits, and sometimes our trading capital, have disappeared into a black hole.

The observation about growth, robustness, and maturity in trends is not new. Victor Sperandeo uses a similar concept to measure the probability of a trend reversal in *Trader Vic.* He uses a statistical measure. The growth and collapse of the typical trend has a rigid inevitability even though it is within an indefinite time frame.

These general observations define the behavior of most trends, but they do not determine the time frame, or length, of each stage. Robust behavior may last for weeks, or months. As in all trading, it is easier to see these trend stages in retrospect than in real time. Our objective is to use our understanding of the life story of a trend to develop more effective money management approaches to grow our trading profits.

When these observations are directly coupled with a better understanding of the risk of trend success or failure, we have a method of matching our trading exposure with the changing risk. The diagram at the bottom of Figure 13.1 shows how risk changes during each stage of trend growth.

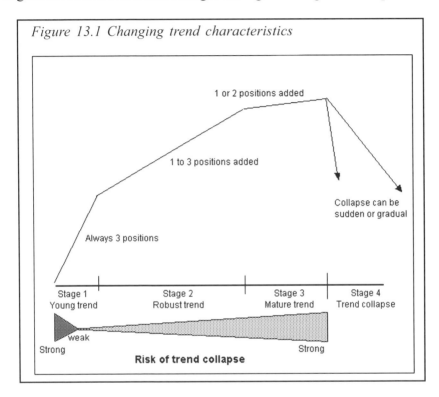

Figure 13.1 Changing trend characteristics

By combining our knowledge of capital- and profit-protection methods with our understanding of trend growth and changing risk, we better match our trading activity with developing price action. We develop a logical approach to trigger the decision to add more of the stock to our portfolio. Get this right and we take full advantage of the growth of the trend. Get it wrong and the results are still better than the pyramid approaches in the previous chapter.

In this chapter, we examine a Grow_Up money management strategy to match capital risk with trend risk. The key to success is to keep the purchase of each new position or parcel consistent with our preferred rules for protecting capital and profits.

TRADING WITH HOPE

Our objective is to combine four factors to develop a comprehensive Grow_Up money management strategy to magnify the return from winning trades. The four factors are:

- our knowledge of the typical character of trend growth and decline;
- our understanding of the way the nature of risk changes in each stage of trend growth;
- our emotional shift from hope to confidence to certainty; and
- a mechanical entry and stop loss approach based on ranging activity in the developing trend.

The Grow_Up strategy is designed to match our position size with our level of confidence in the growth of the trend or with our fear that the trend may be ending. In this chapter, we consider the way the young trend is traded with multiple positions to build and form the base for trading growth.

There are many mechanical methods of determining trend entry. We use the count back line technique in this example. The method you select should identify three critical stages in the young trend. These are:

1. *The period of hope.* This is where you have completed your analysis, and you hope it is correct. This is where you first buy stock.

2. *The period of confidence.* This is when the trade starts to move in your direction. It starts to make a small profit, and your stop loss exit conditions, if triggered, actually lock-in a profit.

3. *The period of certainty.* We all know when a trade becomes a sure thing. There is no doubt about success. This is when our attention really shifts from protecting capital to protecting open profits. It is a great feeling, and we give it expression by adding a new trading position.

Hope, confidence, and certainty match the decline of trend risk, as shown in Figure 13.2. When the trade is first entered, there is often a high risk of trend failure.

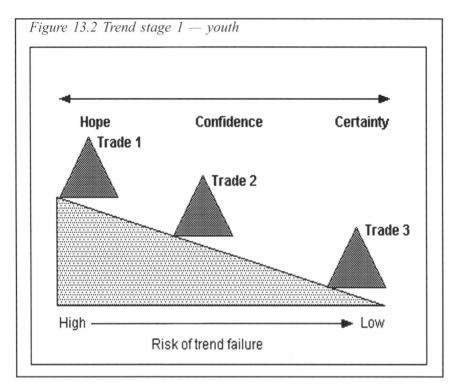

Figure 13.2 Trend stage 1 — youth

We use the mining company Sons of Gwalia as an example of how the Grow_Up strategy is applied. Total trading capital is $100,000 and maximum risk on each trade is $2,000, or 2%. The compressed daily line chart in Figure 13.3 shows the price action traded in this example. The young trend starts in April 2000 and ends in June. There are quite specific conditions for defining this part of the trend, as shown by the single vertical lines. They provide a framework for action and are the subject of this chapter.

The change in the trend from robust to mature is a more difficult period to pinpoint. This is a judgment call more easily made retrospectively than in real time. The changeover is most often a zone, or area, rather than a particular set of conditions. This zone is shown as a vertical box in Figure 13.3. A mature trend may show unexpected signs of life, and the April 2001 rally is like installing a pacemaker. This new burst of life carries Sons of Gwalia to new highs but with increasing risk of trend failure. We consider appropriate trading strategies for these later stages of the trend in the next chapter.

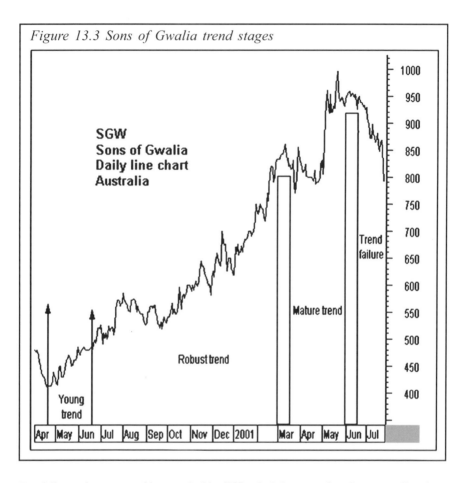

Figure 13.3 Sons of Gwalia trend stages

Deciding when a trend has ended is difficult. Many traders have a collection of horror stories about their inability to act when the trend ends. Some stocks, such as Hong Kong company High Fashion, drop off the precipice, falling 38% in just a few days. Most times the trend slowly rolls over, as shown with Sons of Gwalia.

TRADING THE YOUNG TREND

We start with the methods required for trading the young trend. When does the downtrend prior to April 2000 turn into a new up trend? We use the count back line calculation, shown in Figure 13.4, to set the value of this change.

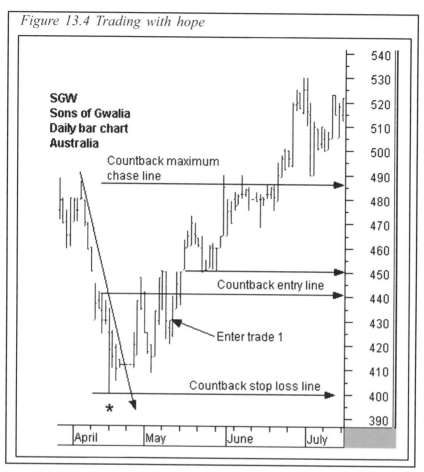

Figure 13.4 Trading with hope

The count back line has two separate roles to play. It is mainly used as a trading entry tool, and this is discussed fully in my book *Share Trading*. The count back line is designed to follow the existing short-term trend and to confirm when the trend changes. We apply it to trends lasting days or weeks. The count back line works by using the ranging activity of price to establish a hurdle which must be overcome before we believe the current up-tick is really a trend break, rather than just a normal up and down within the existing trend. Prices move up and down all the time, and not every up-tick, nor every low, is important. Our task is to identify those that are.

The standard entry condition on a breakout trade is established when the closing price is above the count back line. This value is calculated by selecting the most recent low in the current downtrend. Move to the top of this bar, then travel to the left until you intercept the next bar. Move up this bar to the top, then travel to the left until you intercept the next bar. Travel to the top of this bar. The value at the top of this bar gives the count back line value. We show this by projecting a line to the right across the chart. Prices must close above this count back line before we assume the trend has changed.

In calculating the placement of the line, we ignore any price gaps in the current trend. Instead, we move to the next highest bar in the current trend. Readers interested in the full construction rules will find them in *Share Trading*. Traders using the Guppy Traders Essentials toolkit have access to an automatic count back line breakout tool.

We start the count back line process with the Sons of Gwalia chart by taking the bar with the lowest low in the existing downtrend. This bar, marked with "*", is the starting point and becomes the pivot point low. We move to the top of this lowest bar in the downtrend, and then across to the left until we hit the next highest price bar. Again we move to the top of this bar, and across to the left until we intersect the next highest bar. Price bars of equal height are ignored, as are intervening days with lower highs. Price gaps are ignored by moving up to the next bar in the current trend. When the third-highest price bar is located, we move to the top of this bar and project a line to the right. A close above this level confirms the trend break.

The entry trigger snaps with a close above the count back line at $4.41.

This is an end-of-day entry signal, so we act on this the next day. We enter on the close, adding the first trade at $4.30 and spending $9,004.20 to get 2,094 shares. The calculations shown in Figure 13.5 are taken from the Grow_Up spreadsheet template. This is available as part of the Better Trading pak on www.guppytraders.com. We could have done better than this by delaying our entry, as prices fell to $4.20 over the next few days. We do not have the luxury of hindsight when acting on entry signals, so our trade suffers a small loss for the first few days.

Figure 13.5 Trade 1 — based on hope

Stock	SGW	
current price	$	4.30
Trade 1		
price	$	4.30
number		2,094
Cost	$	9,004.20
Current value	$	9,004.20
Open profit		**$0.00**

We enter a trade with hope, not certainty. We hope our analysis is correct, but we protect ourselves with a stop loss condition. Again, we use the count back line calculation and the position size risk calculations discussed in Chapter 6. The initial stop loss level is set at $4.00. With this combination of entry price and stop loss, we could afford to spend $28,666 and still remain within the limits of the 2% rule. Our entry cost of $9,004 keeps the risk low on this trade entry. We stand to lose $628 if we are wrong.

TRADING WITH CONFIDENCE

Traders move from hope to confidence, but when do we know the shift has taken place? Do we rely on gut feelings, on instinct, or sheer guesswork? There is a time and price that identifies this shift. It is usually best seen retrospectively on the chart. The count back line technique provides a mechanical way to establish this shift.

The count back line calculation provides the second trigger to confirm the up trend and it is contained in the way the stop loss line moves upward as the trend rises. When the stop loss value moves above the initial entry point for the trade, we normally just breathe a sigh of relief. Under these conditions, if we had to act on the stop loss signal, the trade, at worst, is break-even. Our stop loss exit is equal to, or slightly better than, our original entry price.

This sigh of relief overpowers a significant message. When the stop loss value rises above the initial entry point, it represents a significant shift in the balance of probability. The nature of the risk of trend failure changes. This is a key trigger point where we match our confidence in the trend with added positions. This is the start of the Grow_Up money management strategy designed to match the risk of additional positions in a developing trend with the growth stages of the trend.

The second entry point is triggered when the count back line trailing stop loss value closes above the original count back line level. This develops quickly with Sons of Gwalia. The count back line breakout level is $4.41. When Sons of Gwalia prices hit $4.73, as shown by the "*" in Figure 13.6, the new count back line trailing stop loss value moves above the old count back line break-out value. The new count back line stop loss value is at $4.50. This is a mechanical signal based on the ranging activity of price and it confirms our confidence in the strength of the growing trend. This young trend stands upright and takes its first steps.

Once this signal is delivered, we add a new position to the trade. We buy the next day at $4.65. How much should we spend?

The question has a logical answer. We were prepared to spend around $9,000 based on the *hope* that our analysis was correct. Now that we are *confident* our analysis is correct, we add another trade at the same value. This position size, or cost, reflects our confidence. We are not worried about the imminent danger of a trend collapse. We recognize this is still a young trend, and we want to invest in its future. This is not the time to quibble, so we add 1,936 shares for a total cost of $9,002. At this stage, we keep each new position around the same dollar size.

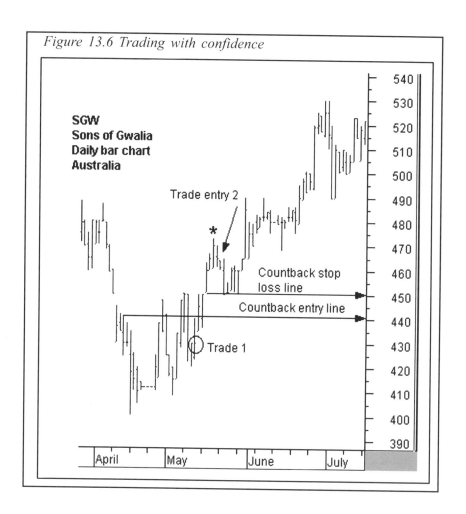

Figure 13.6 Trading with confidence

The spreadsheet extract in Figure 13.7 shows the developing outcome for what is now two open positions in Sons of Gwalia. The first trade shows a $732.90 profit with the Sons of Gwalia price at $4.65. As the young trend continues to develop, the second trade will also add to profits. At this stage in the development of this strategy, the trader is exposed to the same level of risk in all open positions.

If an exit signal is delivered by a close below the count back line stop loss at $4.50, we take home around $128 in profit. A trend collapse puts two equal amounts of capital at risk, as each trade costs around $9,000.

However, our growing confidence suggests this is unlikely to happen.

Figure 13.7 Trade 2 — added with confidence

Stock	SGW		
current price	$ 4.65		

Trade 1		Trade 2	
price	$ 4.30	price	$ 4.65
number	2,094	number	1,936
Cost	$ 9,004.20	Cost	$ 9,002.40
Current value	$ 9,737.10	Current value	$ 9,002.40
Open profit	$732.90	Open profit	$0.00

Theoretically, our cumulative risk is 4% of total trading capital, but in practice the risk is less than 1%. Consider the calculations. Assume we take an exit based on the stop loss level calculated when the second parcel was purchased. This is set at $4.50 and is above our initial entry price used to buy the first parcel. The loss in the second trade is $290, compared with a maximum permissible loss of $2,000 based on the $100,000 of total trading capital.

The portfolio risk of the second position is always 2%, because it is not added until the stop loss level has risen above the entry level for the first trade.

TRADING WITH CERTAINTY

After a few weeks, or sometimes months, in a successful trend trade we develop a feeling of certainty about the trade. We are on a good thing and we know it. This feeling signals the end of the young stage of the trend. It is still a safe entry point into trend development, as the probability of trend collapse is very small. The reduction of risk is shown at the bottom of Figure 13.1. Just as we matched our confidence with a new trading position, we also match our sense of certainty with a new position.

The count back line calculations made when the trade was first entered provided us with a logical, rather than emotional, method to make this decision. Every count back break-out line calculation includes a maximum chase line. This is initially used to set the level that tells us we missed the early stages of the trend. When prices move above this level, it helps to confirm our confidence in the trend. We shift to certainty when the count back line stop loss calculation also moves above the count back line maximum chase line. This creates a level of certainty, because any stop loss exit signal still captures most of the new, young trend.

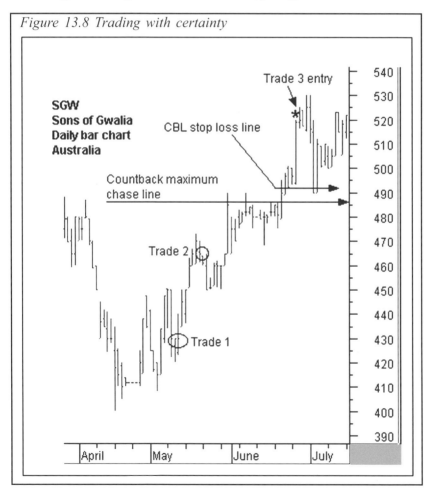

Figure 13.8 Trading with certainty

The maximum chase line is set at $4.81, shown in Figure 13.8. The trailing stop loss calculation starts at $5.20 on the bar marked with "*" and sets the trailing stop loss at $4.93. This is a signal for the third and final entry into the young trend. With Sons of Gwalia, this is made on the next day at $5.19. We add 1,735 Sons of Gwalia shares for a total cost of $9,004, as shown in Figure 13.9.

Figure 13.9 Trade 3 — completed with certainty

Stock	SGW						
current price	$	5.19					
Trade 1			**Trade 2**			**Trade 3**	
price	$	4.30	price	$	4.65	price	$	5.19
number		2,094	number		1,936	number		1,735
Cost	$	9,004.20	Cost	$	9,002.40	Cost	$	9,004.65
Current value	$	10,867.86	Current value	$	10,047.84	Current value	$	9,004.65
Open profit		**$1,863.66**	**Open profit**		**$1,045.44**	**Open profit**		**$0.00**

At the end of the young trend, our three positions have a total of $3,543 in open profit based on the high of $5.30, summarized in Figure 13.10. The first position from trade 1 contributes most to this profit result. As a group of three trades taken early in what turns out to be a long-term trend, these contribute most to the final result when the trend comes to an end. By purchasing three positions of the same size to match our shift from hope to confidence, and then to certainty, we set up the conditions where they can have the maximum impact on the final results. The size of these early positions leverages the final result. Ideally, we could use $27,011 to buy Sons of Gwalia at the first entry price of $4.30, but we lack the confidence to do this at the time because we are not certain the young trend is sustainable.

In every trade, we shift from hope to certainty. If we have a method of identifying these emotional changes in real time, then we leverage this analysis in the early stages of the trade.

Figure 13.10 Return on capital

Total trade capital	$ 27,011.25
Current value	$ 30,554.50
Total open profits	$3,543.25
%% Return	13.12

RISK CAPTURES REWARD

With three open trades, the portfolio risk is not 6%, but 2%. Our stop loss conditions allow trade 3 to lose 2%. It also triggers the close of all open positions, and this serves to limit risk. An exit at this level locks in profits from trades 1 and 2.

Step through the calculations. Assume a stop loss exit signal is generated at $4.91 just a few days after we buy the third parcel at $5.19. Parcel 1 is closed. Originally purchased at $4.30, it shows a $1,277 profit. Parcel 2 is closed. Purchased at $4.65, it now shows a $503 profit. Parcel 3 shows a loss of $485. This is well inside the 2% of trading capital limits. This small loss is easily compensated for by the locked-in profits. The full outcome for each trade is shown in Figure 13.11.

Figure 13.11 Stop loss exit based on trade 3

Stock	**SGW**					
current price	$ 4.91					
Trade 1		**Trade 2**		**Trade 3**		
price	$ 4.30	price	$ 4.65	price	$	5.19
number	2,094	number	1,936	number		1,735
Cost	$ 9,004.20	Cost	$ 9,002.40	Cost	$	9,004.65
Current value	$ 10,281.54	Current value	$ 9,505.76	Current value	$	8,518.85
Open profit	**$1,277.34**	**Open profit**	**$503.36**	**Open profit**		-$485.80

Cumulative risk is at its worst when spread over three trades in different stocks. If we have three equal size positions in three separate stocks, each showing the potential to break into a new up trend, then the cumulative trade risk is 6%. The practical risk is even higher despite the apparent diversity of this portfolio structure. The nature of the risk is much the same in each trade and is complicated by the skill factor.

Trader Average gets six out of 10 trades correct. What if these three trades were all taken from the losing end of his skill range? There is a higher probability that all three trades could be stopped out, and thus he would lose 6% of total trading capital.

This is different from the three parcels we accumulate with Sons of Gwalia. Each trade captures a different stage of trend risk as we move toward certainty in our analysis. If an exit trigger comes, it crystallizes the risk in the most recent position and captures the profits in the previous two. Risk is kept at 2% of total trading capital.

There are usually three opportunities to add to positions in a young trend. Once the third position is added, we shift our focus to trading the robust trend. This trend is unlikely to deliver the same rate of return, as the acceleration of prices slows. The potential rewards start to slow and this is a signal to reduce our risk. The common pyramiding approaches ignore this signal, which is why they perform so poorly. The Grow_Up strategy recognizes the way reward starts to diminish as risk grows again. There is a growing risk of a trend slowdown and eventual collapse. We recognize this developing risk by changing the size of the new positions we take in stages 2 and 3 of trend development.

By combining appropriate money management with our existing level of analysis skill, we create an effective path to greater success. The previous chapter showed that simply adding new positions to a developing trend is not a particularly effective strategy. The next chapter shows how the analysis in this chapter is combined with money management to deliver increased returns.

FOURTEEN
EXPLOITING
TRENDS

A robust trend is an apparent haven. The high-risk period of a young trend is behind the trader. Now he concentrates on pyramiding into the robust trend. This is the point where the pyramiding strategies discussed in Chapter 12 unintentionally start to increase the overall risk. To safely trade these developing trends, we look for an inverse relationship with the risk taken in each new position and the slowly growing risk of a trend collapse.

At the beginning of the trade the risk of trend failure is high. We manage this using the count back line calculation. As the young trend develops robust features, the risk of trend failure is low. We match this certainty with new trading positions. As soon as the trend starts to move into a mature period, the risk of trend failure starts to grow again, although usually more slowly. This relationship is shown in Figure 14.1.

As the risk of trend failure grows, we reduce our trading size. This is the key principle in this approach to the management of risk.

In this chapter we continue the Sons of Gwalia example. We add new trading positions in the robust and mature states of the trend. Finally, we look at the impact of an exit from the sample trade as the trend fails. We exit at $9.00 based on a count back line signal. A summary of these new trades is contained in Figure 14.2.

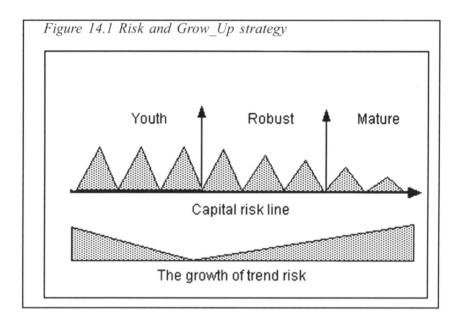

Figure 14.1 Risk and Grow_Up strategy

ROBUST TRADING

In a young trend we have a precise method of identifying each entry point. This is not so easy in a robust trend. The combination of indicators we select is based on experience, skill, and judgment. Our interest is the impact of money management on risk and reward. The method we choose to identify when it is time to add new positions is only a means to this end.

In trading robust trends, our preference is to apply the Guppy Multiple Moving Average. This helps establish the strength and characteristics of the trend. When prices dip back toward the long-term group of averages, we see an opportunity to buy more stock at lower prices.

In this example we use a 10- and 30-week moving average to provide entry signals. They provide a clear short-cut and the buy areas broadly match those generated with the Guppy Multiple Moving Average on the daily chart. Applying these two moving averages in real time by themselves does not provide full analysis of the trend. It does not help the trader identify the balance of probability and provide the confidence necessary to add to existing open positions. The chart in Figure 14.2 shows three new entry points in this robust trend. They are at $5.28, $5.92, and $6.27. Each is an example of price weakness in the trend. Each is more clearly identified and assessed with a Guppy Multiple Moving Average.

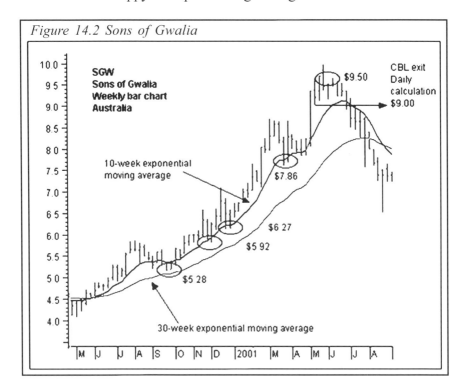

Figure 14.2 Sons of Gwalia

We have the opportunity to add more stock at good prices. How much stock do we buy? Our objective in adding a new trade is to select a position size consistent with the growing risk of trend failure. Although we feel increasingly confident at this stage of trend development, we need to recognize that the risk of trend failure is slowly growing. Any new trades should reflect this feeling. The Grow_Up strategy reduces the size of each new position in the robust trend to half that of the original trades, as shown in Figure 14.3. This is very different from the pyramid strategies considered in Chapter 12, where position size bears little relationship with the changing nature of trend risk.

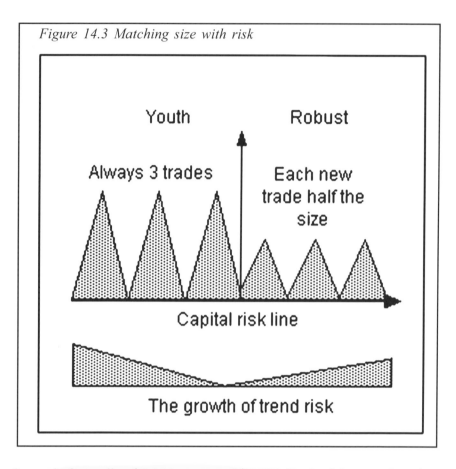

Figure 14.3 Matching size with risk

Instead of spending $9,000, we spend $4,500. Each of these trades takes $4,500 of new capital. We add three new trades in this section of the trend. There is no set number. In long trends like those shown by US-listed Supervalu Inc. or Singapore's HTL Holdings, the trader might add four or five new trades. In short-lived robust trends found in stocks such as Marathon Oil on the NYSE or Naluri in Malaysia, there may only be time to add one or two new positions. The robust nature of this trend phase is defined by its character and not by time. Many robust trends last many months, but some prevail for just a few.

This reduced dollar size has an important impact on the risk of each new position. In this sample trade, the value of the moving average is the exit trigger. The financial stop loss point based on the 2% rule is well below the current value of the long-term moving average. The practical impact is, if we exit when prices fall below the long-term moving average value, then the actual loss is often much less than 2% of trading capital. This is a characteristic of a robust trend. Price activity tends to cluster around or above the short-term moving average line.

Any exit signal is also a signal to close every other open position in the stock. This captures profits and limits losses. Figure 14.3 summarizes the way our capital exposure decreases as the risk of trend failure increases.

The spreadsheet summary in Figure 14.4 shows how each of these three robust trades affects the portfolio, based on a closing price of $7.00. The initial three positions — trades 1, 2, and 3 — contribute most to overall portfolio performance. The more recent half-size positions — trades 4, 5, and 6 — show substantial profit growth, obtained with a reduced level of risk.

Some traders further reduce risk by scaling down each new position in the robust trend. If we apply this approach to this sample trade, we might reduce trade 4 to $7,560. This is around 16% smaller than the original trade size used in trades 1, 2, and 3. Applying the same reduction factor, trade 5 costs $6,120 and is 32% smaller than the first positions. The final trade meets the overall target of 50% reduction in position size, costing around $4,500.

Figure 14.4 Robust trend — three trades at half size

Stock	SGW							
current price	$	7.00						

Trade 1			Trade 2			Trade 3		
price	$	4.30	price	$	4.65	price	$	5.19
number		2,094	number		1,936	number		1,735
Cost	$	9,004.20	Cost	$	9,002.40	Cost	$	9,004.65
Current value	$	14,658.00	Current value	$	13,552.00	Current value	$	12,145.00
Open profit		**$5,653.80**	**Open profit**		**$4,549.60**	**Open profit**		**$3,140.35**

Trade 4			Trade 5			Trade 6		
price	$	5.28	price	$	5.92	price	$	6.27
number		853	number		760	number		718
Cost	$	4,503.84	Cost	$	4,499.20	Cost	$	4,501.86
Current value	$	5,971.00	Current value	$	5,320.00	Current value	$	5,026.00
Open profit		**$1,467.16**	**Open profit**		**$820.80**	**Open profit**		**$524.14**

This is excellent in theory and it works well on historical charts. The only catch is, when the first trade in the robust trend is opened, we do not know how long the trend will last, nor do we know the number of trades we will eventually take. Do we reduce each new trade by 16% on the assumption of three new trades? Or do we reduce each new trade by 12.5%, assuming we will add four new trades during the robust trend stage? Truth is, we do not know in advance how many new trades will be added. It is more practical to immediately reduce position size by 50%. If it turns out that only two trades are made, we still get the full benefits of the Grow_Up strategy.

Readers can play with these figures and combinations using the Grow_Up spreadsheet template in the Better Trading pak.

TRADING WITH MATURITY

As the trend matures, the nature of our market risk changes. Now we are really concerned the trend might end. Our attention shifts to indicators used to signal that the trend is slowing, or turning. As the risk of trend failure grows, we again apply the count back line to the daily chart. We use it as a trailing stop loss condition.

We know two important things about the nature of the trend in this mature stage. First, the trend will end. Second, a close below the trailing stop loss usually provides early warning of a change in trend direction, and, potentially, the end of the trend. By combining this knowledge with appropriate money management, we control the risk in the developing trade by reducing position size with each new entry.

Our position size bears a direct relationship with the changing nature of trend risk.

How much should we reduce these final trades? We have many choices, all leading to the same destination. The smallest position size worth trading is around $2,000. Trade smaller than this and brokerage and slippage chew away at any profits. Trades very rapidly turn marginal. You may decide your minimum position size is $10,000, or $15,000. It is important to have a defined figure beyond which any smaller positions are not taken.

The sample trades on the chart in Figure 14.2 show two new positions in Sons of Gwalia during the mature stage of the trend. The first is at $7.86 and is trade 7. The objective is to reduce position size in a way consistent with our understanding of where the trend is placed in relation to its overall development. When the trend is young, we add positions of the same size. When the trend becomes robust, we reduce trading risk by reducing position size by one half.

As the trend moves toward maturity, there is increased likelihood of trend failure and the rate of return slows. We still want to be part of the action, but not with the same level of risk. The risk/reward ratio must balance the return against the increased risk of trend failure.

We add two new positions at one-third the size of the original trades, as shown in Figure 14.5. This summarizes the heart of the Grow_Up strategy. As trend risk grows, our capital at risk slows.

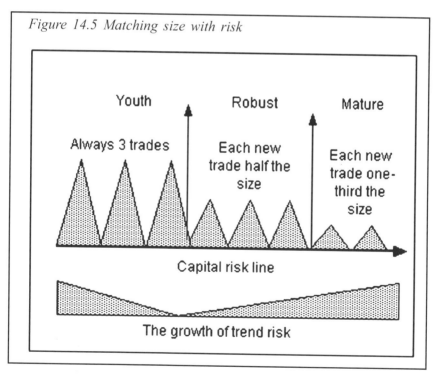

Figure 14.5 Matching size with risk

We spend $3,000 on each of these two trades. The trade 8 entry at $9.50 near the top of the trend is deliberately added to show the impact of losses at this late stage. There is no good technical reason for adding the trade at this price level.

In this example, we get an exit signal when prices close below $9.00. We close the eight open trades in Sons of Gwalia at this level. The last trade is a loser and we want to examine the impact of this on portfolio risk.

The spreadsheet extract in Figure 14.6 shows the profit position with Sons of Gwalia based on the highest high of $9.97. Profit growth for trades 7 and 8 is slow in dollar terms, but better in percentage terms. Trade 7 shows a 26.84% return on capital. Trade 8 has a 4.95% return. Trader Novice spurns such low dollar returns. Trader Success understands that the market is best measured by the return on capital.

Figure 14.6 Mature trend — two trades at one-third size

Trade 7		Trade 8	
price	$ 7.86	price	$ 9.50
number	382	number	316
Cost	$ 3,002.52	Cost	$ 3,002.00
Current value	$ 3,808.54	Current value	$ 3,150.52
Open profit	$806.02	Open profit	$148.52

Total trade capital	$ 46,520.67
Current value	$ 87,676.18
Total open profits	$41,155.51
%% Return	88.47

Trader Success and Trader Superstar look for one figure: the percentage return on capital employed. For an expenditure of $46,520.67, this series of trades delivers an 88.47% return on capital. This is not as good as the

125% return available for Trader Lucky, who purchased stock at $4.30 and still holds it at $9.70. However, this 88.47% return has grown steadily, while trading risk has declined just as steadily.

THE GROW_UP STRATEGY

Like a multi-stage rocket, this total Grow_Up strategy is loaded heavily in stage 1 and lightly in the final stages. We bought 5,758 shares when the trend was young. We added another 2,331 in the robust trend period over three trades. As the trend matured, we collected another 698 shares for a total position size of 8,787 shares.

How does this protect us when the trade is closed? Our exit is not at the very high of the trend. It comes at $9.00 with a close below the count back trailing stop loss line. All eight Sons of Gwalia trades are closed at $9.00. The last trade added takes a small loss of $158. This is well within the 2% rule where our maximum risk on any single trade was limited to $2,000. With eight open positions, the potential cumulative risk is 16% of trading capital.

The practical risk is less than 2% because only the most recent trade is at risk. All other trades show profits. Based on the last entry price of $9.50, the average price of each share is $5.29. Prices could fall to $5.07 on this total position size before risk exceeds 2%.

A fall of this magnitude is possible, but most times traders have ample warning of a trend collapse. An exit at $9.00, shown by the full summary of all Grow_Up positions in Figure 14.7, represents a 70.13% return on the capital used in the trade.

In the final analysis, trading is about obtaining the most effective return on trading capital given the reality of the market. Returns are not risk free, and although the buy and hold strategy used by Trader Lucky looks successful, it carries an opportunity cost. Once the trend is firmly established, Trader Lucky has no opportunity to go back and add stock at his original entry prices.

Figure 14.7 Grow_Up strategy results

Stock	SGW							
current price	$	9.00						

Trade 1			Trade 2			Trade 3		
price	$	4.30	price	$	4.65	price	$	5.19
number		2,094	number		1,936	number		1,735
Cost	$	9,004.20	Cost	$	9,002.40	Cost	$	9,004.65
Current value	$	18,846.00	Current value	$	17,424.00	Current value	$	15,615.00
Open profit		**$9,841.80**	**Open profit**		**$8,421.60**	**Open profit**		**$6,610.35**
Trade 4			**Trade 5**			**Trade 6**		
price	$	5.28	price	$	5.92	price	$	6.27
number		853	number		760	number		718
Cost	$	4,503.84	Cost	$	4,499.20	Cost	$	4,501.86
Current value	$	7,677.00	Current value	$	6,840.00	Current value	$	6,462.00
Open profit		**$3,173.16**	**Open profit**		**$2,340.80**	**Open profit**		**$1,960.14**
Trade 7			**Trade8**			**Trade 9**		
price	$	7.86	price	$	9.50	price	$	-
number		382	number		316	number		-
Cost	$	3,002.52	Cost	$	3,002.00	Cost	$	-
Current value	$	3,438.00	Current value	$	2,844.00	Current value	$	-
Open profit		**$435.48**	**Open profit**		**-$158.00**	**Open profit**		**$0.00**

Total trade capital	$ 46,520.67
Current value	$ 79,146.00
Total open profits	$32,625.33
%% Return	70.13

The risk of adding positions to the growing trend is more effectively handled by reducing the dollar size as the trend progresses and matures, rather than using alternative pyramiding strategies. By using the same dollar size positions early in the trend, we take maximum advantage of our growing certainty about the direction and strength of the trend. Unlike other approaches, we do not destroy this success by maintaining the same dollar size for new positions at all points on the developing trend.

I choose to use the Guppy Multiple Moving Average to identify the strength and growth of the trend. I use the count back line as a stop loss trigger for new entry points as the trend develops. You may choose other techniques from a wide variety of technical and charting tools. What is important is to understand the way the final trading outcomes are significantly influenced by the way you add new positions in the developing trend.

The most successful strategy for adding to winning trades while controlling the risk of trend growth, and trend collapse, is the Grow_Up approach. This achieves our objective of matching position size with our understanding of the development of the trend and the risk of trend establishment, and later trend reversal. When we get a trade right, we want to be very, very right. By matching each new position size with the risk of trend failure and reversal, we have a better technique to grow — and keep — profits.

Correct analysis and profitability come together at the beginning of the trend. This is where we load up on our position. As the risk of trend failure increases, we reduce our position size. We are still exposed to potential increases in profit, but the reduced position size limits the risk should the trend collapse. If we lose all of our most recently added position, the dollar value is much less than the initial positions we took early in the trend. The impact on overall profits is reduced. This matching of position size with the risk of trend breakdown is a useful money management strategy in trending markets. It gives us the ability to maximize our profits when we are right and to reduce the impact when the trend fails.

COMPETING PYRAMIDS

The success of any trading strategy depends more on how the trader handles the exit than on how he makes his entry. We compound market risk by unthinkingly applying common pyramid solutions to developing successful trades. We manage market risk effectively when we use money management to ensure that position size reflects market risk.

The results in Figure 14.8 summarize the return on capital results from the Sons of Gwalia example using different money management strategies. We use exactly the same entry points for each of the eight trades, but we apply the standard pyramid approaches discussed in Chapter 12. Readers can use the Grow_Up spreadsheet in the Better Trading Excel template pak from www.guppytraders.com to replicate these results.

Figure 14.8 Return on capital — three strategies

Grow_Up strategy		Constant size pyramiding		Dollar cost averaging	
Total trade capital	$ 46,520.67	Total trade capital	$ 102,543.18	Total trade capital	$ 72,027.39
Current value	$ 79,146.00	Current value	$ 150,768.00	Current value	$ 112,680.00
Total open profits	$32,625.33	Total open profits	$48,224.82	Total open profits	$40,652.61
%% Return	70.13	%% Return	47.03	%% Return	56.44

All trades opened at $4.30 All include eight trades. All closed at $9.00

The dollar cost averaging approach returns 56.44% on capital. Each new trade costs $9,000. The trader needs a total of $72,027 to complete this strategy. Not only is this more expensive, but the return on capital is less than the Grow_Up strategy.

The constant position size approach takes eight trades, each with exactly 2,094 shares. The trader needs very deep pockets to employ this strategy. It calls for nearly twice as much capital as the Grow_Up strategy but generates only a little more than two-thirds of the return on capital. The comparative returns are shown in Figure 14.9.

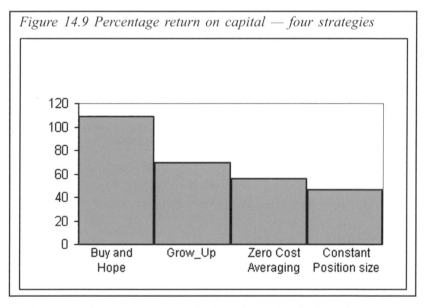

Figure 14.9 Percentage return on capital — four strategies

Despite using the same entry and exit points, the choice of money management makes a significant difference. Trader Lucky, with his buy and hope strategy, always outperforms the others, but his small capital commitment — just $9,000 in this example — means he does not maximize the impact of this successful trade on his total trading capital.

The relationship between the three pyramid strategies remains constant. The Grow_Up strategy is consistently the most successful of the strategies that add to winning positions. It uses the least amount of capital and generates the highest return on capital. Depending on choices, the returns from each of the pyramid strategies may be quite good, but the Grow_Up strategy is a consistent star performer.

This particular combination of money management and trading is a defensive approach to the market. Defensive trading would be unnecessary if we could predict the future. It is precisely because the future remains unproven and uncertain that these money management approaches play such a significant role in growing, or diminishing, our trading profits.

Trading is more than the application of charting and technical analysis tools. Without good money management, we cannot position ourselves to maximize our winning trades. Money management has a major impact on trading success. In these examples, we have used a particular range of entry and exit prices. Change these, even by just a few cents, and the outcomes change again. Getting your preferred entry and exit price has a significant impact on final profits. In the next chapter, we look at some methods to get the price you want.

FIFTEEN
ORDERING
PROFITS

Protecting profits in a winning trade, or capital in a losing trade, means getting our orders right. Money management is as important as good charting and technical analysis, but all our planning comes unstuck if our actual buy or sell order is unclear, inaccurate, or remains unfilled in the market. With correct instructions to our broker, electronic or otherwise, we buy stock at the best available price closest to our preferred entry point. Send the wrong instructions and our order sits unfilled while the opportunity we correctly identified develops just as we planned — but without our participation.

The trader who is fastest on the mouse is not necessarily the smartest. The exact management of entry and exit prices is important for traders. It is also significant for investors, although getting a price within just one tick of the preferred price is unlikely to have a major impact on the outcome of a long-term trade.

Good management of our orders enhances the opportunity for trading and money management strategies to work as planned. It is useful to understand the broad mechanics of the order system and the variations in order formats. This knowledge helps to protect capital when you buy a stock, and protects profits when you sell. We start this chapter with a general discussion and then examine how these strategies are implemented in U.S. and Asian markets in the following chapters.

STAND IN LINE

Before we launch into a more detailed discussion of specific order strategies, we take a moment to refresh our understanding of the way orders are processed and treated by different stock exchanges. Around the world, financial markets are divided into two quite distinct camps. Some, like the United States, are quote-driven markets. Others, such as Singapore and Australia, are order-driven markets. A few, including the United Kingdom, use a mixture of quote- and order-driven systems.

The quote-driven market uses market makers or specialists as middlemen. They quote prices at which they will buy or sell stock. It is not just traders who want to make money from the market. In quote-driven systems there are many others who take a cut from the trading traffic and this adds unexpected value to information about buyers and sellers. Quote-driven systems place a high value on this information and restrict access to it. In the next chapter, U.S. trader and author, Robert Deel takes readers through the steps required to carve a trading advantage from these processes.

Order-driven markets are built on trading transparency, so information is more freely available. An order-driven market matches buyers with sellers without the intervention of a middleman, so trades are automatically and instantaneously executed when prices are matched. The refresh time between filled and new orders is measured in fractions of a second. This theory is put into practice on the brokerage order screens created by the stock exchange or by an electronic communication network such as Archipelago or Island.

Malaysian dealer and trader, Sunny Low provides a perspective in Chapter 17 on Asian market operations and the way traders are able to manage their order placement. Trading success does not always require exact management of our order execution, but better management contributes to consistent profits. We start the discussion of these processes with an overview of trading screens and information from an order-driven system.

The level 1 screen shows the current bid and ask, and the last traded price. The bid is how much a buyer is prepared to pay for the stock. The ask is how much the seller wants to get for the stock. When buyer and seller are "matched," this is shown as the last traded price. The level 1 screen in Figure 15.1 is a quick guide to what is happening in the market for Pacifica Group. The last price was $3.33. The current "bid" shows a buyer willing to buy more stock at $3.33. The current "ask" shows a seller who wants $3.34 for his Pacifica Group stock.

Figure 15.1 *MarketCast live screen — level 1*

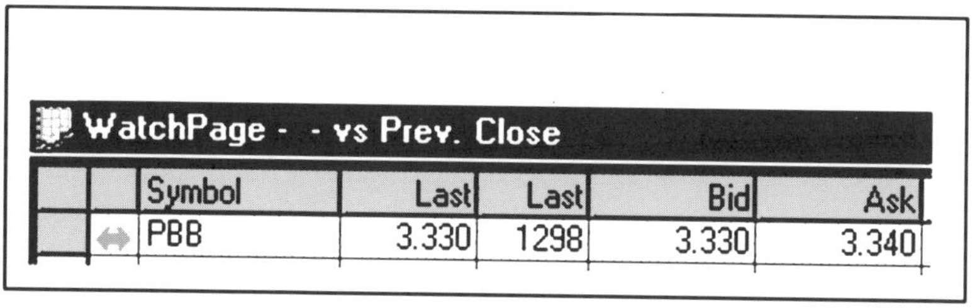

		Symbol	Last	Last	Bid	Ask
	↔	PBB	3.330	1298	3.330	3.340

WatchPage - - vs Prev. Close

The level 2 screen, or consolidated order screen, in Figure 15.2 is more useful. On the left-hand side we see a list of buyers, ranked in descending bid order. Those traders prepared to pay the highest price for the stock go to the top of the list, or line. This shows the total number of buy orders, or "bids," at $3.33. Not everyone is prepared to pay this much. Because the market is really an orderly continuous auction, we also see how much other buyers are prepared to pay. The second row in the order line shows a buyer who wants to pay $3.32. There are seven buyers who want stock at $3.30.

Every time a new buy order is placed with a broker, it is entered on the screen. We see the number of buyers wanting this stock. Their orders extend all the way down to $3.20 in this screen extract.

The same structure applies on the sell side of the screen. On the right-hand side the sell orders, or "asks," are arranged in ascending order, from lowest to highest. Traders who are prepared to sell at the lowest price go to the top of the list, or line.

When trades are completed, they start at the top of the list, matching buyers with sellers. These are the first orders filled. It is very useful to be at the top of the buy or sell line when it comes time to make a trading decision. Simply placing an order at the top buy price or the lowest sell price does not guarantee that your order will be filled. Just as orders are filled in strict price priority, they are also filled in strict time priority.

Figure 15.2 MarketCast live screen — level 2

MarketDepth - PBB - Second Level

Symbol	± $	± %	High	Low	Prev	Open	Tot Vol	
PBB	-0.020	-0.6	3.350	3.320	3.350	3.350	535994	1

	44 Bids			51 Asks			
Count	Buyers	Volume	Price	Price	Volume	Sellers	
1	2	12452	3.330	3.340	28069	2	
2	1	1000	3.320	3.350	58556	3	
3	2	2800	3.310	3.380	4000	1	
4	****7	20900	3.300	3.400	2873	2	
5	1	1000	3.290	3.420	1000	1	
6	3	44800	3.280	3.430	25000	1	
7	1	2590	3.270	3.450	1030	1	
8	2	2610	3.260	3.460	5500	1	
9	8	19500	3.250	3.480	2680	1	
10	1	400	3.230	3.490	500	1	
11	2	1400	3.210	3.550	1200	1	
12	3	1675	3.200	3.600	900	1	

In a quote-driven market the information shown in this level 2 screen may be restricted to the top five or 10 price levels. This also applies in some order-driven markets. In very transparent markets it is possible to drill down to a third screen level that shows the ranking and order line structure of individual orders. In quote-driven markets, this information is considered very price sensitive and access is restricted to brokers and dealers. The shift to decimalization in the United States had an unexpected side effect of causing share size to be less and lowering the amount of large block bids and offers at a specific price. To combat this problem, the NYSE tags a quote, which enables its institutional clients to have an idea of the size behind the price quote. This market depth indication is sometimes called the wholesale quote.

Some markets, such as Australia, routinely make this information available to traders, dealers, and brokers. To see this individual order line structured with time, we turn to the third depth of market screen, shown in Figure 15.3. This shows every order at every price level. Look at the detail of the order line-up for the seven buyers at $3.30 shown in the figure. The size of each order ranges from 300 to 10,000. Every order is treated equally, with priority position in the line based on the time the order was placed. Size does not matter.

Figure 15.3 MarketCast live screen — level 3

MarketDepth - PBB - Full Market

Symbol	± $	± %	High	Low	Prev	Open	Tot Vol
PBB	-0.020	-0.6	3.350	3.320	3.350	3.350	535994

	44 Bids				51 Asks		
Count	Buyers	Volume	Price	Price	Volume	Sellers
1	1	2452	3.330	3.340	15069	1
2	1	10000	3.330	3.340	13000	1
3	1	1000	3.320	3.350	18556	1
4	1	1800	3.310	3.350	25000	1
5	1	1000	3.310	3.350	15000	1
	1	600	3.300	3.380	4000	1
	1	5000	3.300	3.400	1773	1
Individual	1	1000	3.300	3.400	1100	1
orders at	1	2000	3.300	3.420	1000	1
$3.30	1	10000	3.300	3.430	25000	1
	1	300	3.300	3.450	1030	1
	1	2000	3.300	3.460	5500	1
13	1	1000	3.290	3.480	2680	1

The first buy order is for 600 shares. As soon as a seller offers stock for sale at $3.30, the first buy order is filled. If the sell order is for less than 600, then the buyer ends up with a partially filled order. The balance of his buy order remains at the head of the order line. If the sell order is for more than 600, then the first buy order is completely filled, and some of the second buy order in line for 5,000 is also filled. This is a key feature of an order-driven trading system. Orders are completed, or filled, based on the price and the time the order was placed. The time of order placement determines the position in the order line at each price level. In this example, the order for 600 was placed a few seconds or minutes before the order for 5,000 shares. Getting to the head of the order line plays a very important part in executing a trading strategy.

OPENING TICKS

Every market has different procedures for managing trading orders placed in the minutes before the market opens. Some exchanges randomize these orders. Others operate a matching procedure that rewards traders for their superior analysis. A randomized opening negates the advantage of better trade analysis because the entry price on open is not a result of the orderly balance of fear and greed between buyers and sellers.

The Australian Stock Exchange (ASX) provides one solution to this problem, and this in turn provides the opportunity for a specific set of strategies for traders who want to implement overnight analysis. In the pre-open period, traders set their preferred buy and sell orders. These may be well above or below the previous day's close. The spread between the pre-open bid and ask can be quite wide. The opening match process brings these trades together using a weighted average price and volume calculation.

If a stock before the open shows 7,400 shares wanted at $1.16 on the buy side and 3,500 at $0.95 on the sell side, then the ASX matching calculation looks like this:

- On the buy side: 7,400 x $1.16 = $7,584.
- On the sell side: 3,500 x $0.95 = $3,325.
- Add these together = $10,909.

Divide the dollar total of all orders — $10,909 — by the total number of shares in the order lines (7,400 + 3,500 = 10,900) to calculate the average opening price of $1.0008.

Those traders who first understood the process had an advantage because they used these rules to, effectively, buy the open in fast-moving stocks. As this knowledge became more widely available, the effectiveness of this strategy diminished. However, it is used to fine-tune the entry into a trade to get a price close to, or better than, the one used in our trading plan.

To see how this works, we look at the activity in the mining stock, Hardman Resources. Many traders wanted to buy Hardman Resources, as it showed signs of a strong rally. When they turned to the depth of market screen to place their order prior to the market open, they saw a substantial spread in the order line, as shown in Figure 15.4.

Figure 15.4 Pre-open order screen

BUY SIDE   **SELL SIDE**   Estimated opening match price

‖ MarketDepth - HDR - HARDMAN RESOURCES

Symbol	±%	BuyVol	SellVol	Estimate	Tot Vol	Trades
HDR	0.0	5007512	2239650	0.71	0	0

		188 Bids			140 Asks	
Count	Buyers	Volume	Price	Price	Volume	Sellers
1	1	3333	0.750	0.700	274123	20
2	1	5410	0.740	0.710	253870	15
3	4	106491	0.720	0.720	277552	16
4	7	157401	0.710	0.730	354542	14
Match cut-off	15	92524	0.700	0.740	189633	9
	8	144664	0.690	0.750	167150	11

The highest bid was $0.75, while the lowest seller wanted out at $0.70 — a spread of over 7%. When trading eventually opened, the first sale for Hardman Resources went through at $0.71. This was above the seller's ask, and below the buyer's bid.

If we particularly want to get shares in a stock at the opening price, then we use the ASX match procedures to calculate the estimated opening price. Real-time data services such as MarketCast provide an accurate, updated, estimated match price prior to the open. If we are prepared to pay this, we need to get to the top of the order line fast.

BUY SIDE

Using the information in Figure 15.4, we jump to the top of the line with a buy order at $0.76. Now we have the ability to be the first trade completed when the market opens and are able to take advantage of our overnight analysis. This means we get shares at the opening price. Jumping to the front of the order line by offering to buy at a higher price is a high-risk strategy. You should never bid more than you are actually prepared to pay for the shares. Astute sellers may pull out the cheaper sell order just on the open, leaving you to pay full price for the shares. This is good if the price continues to go up, but not so good if the price then falls.

We know in advance what the match price is going to be at that precise point in time. This may change in just a few seconds, so the calculated match price is used with some caution. If the match price is within our planned trading range, we join the order line at $0.76 and get shares at our preferred price.

Alternatively, if our buy order is already in place and is above the estimated match price of $0.71, then it is filled. In this example, the order at $0.70 is not filled on the open because by the time the orders above it are filled, the match price conditions have been satisfied.

SINGAPORE PRE-OPEN

The Singapore Stock Exchange uses a slightly different approach to match pre-open orders. The market starts trading at 9:00 am, and at 8:30 am it moves into a pre-open stage. Traders are able to place, amend, and remove orders for the next 29 minutes. In the last minute before the market opens, all current pre-open orders are frozen. No changes can be made in this non-cancel period.

The Singapore Stock Exchange trading system calculates the equilibrium, or match price, on the assumption that a buy order may be executed at a lower price and a sell order at a higher price. The cumulative buy volume at any price is the buy quantity at that price, plus the sum of the buy quantities at all higher prices. The cumulative sell volume at any price is the sell quantity at that price, plus the sum of the sell quantities at all lower prices.

Selling pressure occurs when the cumulative sell volume exceeds the buy volume at a particular price. The equilibrium is the price range within the price overlap where sell pressure changes to buy pressure.

The equilibrium price may be the price within the equilibrium that has the largest trade volume, or the average of all prices within the equilibrium with the maximum trade volume. The average may be rounded to the next multiple of the minimum price multiple for this stock in the same direction as trading on the previous day.

The details are different to the methods used by the Australian Stock Exchange, but traders are still able to bid higher and move to the top of the order line to ensure they collect stock at the opening price.

ORDER STRUCTURE AND E-TRADING

A visitor who asks a butcher for a chuck steak in the United States is in for a surprise. The cut of meat he gets is different from the cut he receives from his butcher in Singapore, the U.K., or Hong Kong. Both cuts come from a beast, but the results are quite different. When traders place a buy or sell order with a broker, we expect the same terms to mean the same no matter which broker we use. Unfortunately, this is not always the case. This is made even more complicated when we deal with Internet brokerages. Some of them have structured their internal order process quite differently and imposed their own rules for particular orders which are at odds with the order process used by the stock exchange. You do not always get what you expect.

Different names for the same cuts of meat is not a major problem for the weekly grocery order. When you are trading, it *is* an issue. The best way to approach the problem is to define what you want your order to do. This usually involves one of five choices:

1. Buy the stock at a set price.
2. Buy the stock up to a specified figure.

3. Buy the stock for the current market price, meeting the current asking price.

4. Buy the stock at the best price available during the day to get an average price.

5. Buy the open, or sell the close.

Not all brokerages accept all of these order variations, but they reflect the types of orders we want to place as traders.

When we talk to a broker to place an order, it is useful to translate what we want to do into a typical order instruction. These order instructions vary from broker to broker, but the structure I use with my live broker has these equivalents:

- Buy at $10.50. The buy order stays in the order line until it is filled, or until the order is canceled. If prices fall below $10.50, any outstanding part of my buy order is filled at lower prices.

- The limit order, usually given as "Chase the market up to $10.50." Any sell orders below $10.50 are immediately purchased, up to and including those at $10.50. If my order is not filled completely, no more purchases are made until prices fall back to $10.50 or lower.

- The buy-at-market order. The order execution usually starts with the current ask, say $10.50, and continues at whatever price becomes available until the entire order is completed. This is different from a limit order because there is no roof on how far the broker chases prices to fill the order.

- The buy-at-best order. The broker is given an order volume to fill and it is his responsibility to complete it at the best possible price during the day. Traders rely on their broker to manage the order through the market and to get the best "average" price during the day. This is the way institutions handle their buy and sell orders. They reward brokerages that deliver the best average price during the day.

- Buy-the-open or buy-the-close orders are difficult with full-service brokerages. If your account is large enough, your broker may be willing to explore off-market matching opportunities.

Internet trading changes the way we place orders in the market. The differences between the old order structures and the new interpretations — introduced to facilitate electronic trading — cause some confusion. They also offer some potential for making better use of old terms to get the price you want. Old terms are now applied in some slightly different ways. Some order instructions have disappeared, while other new ones have surfaced.

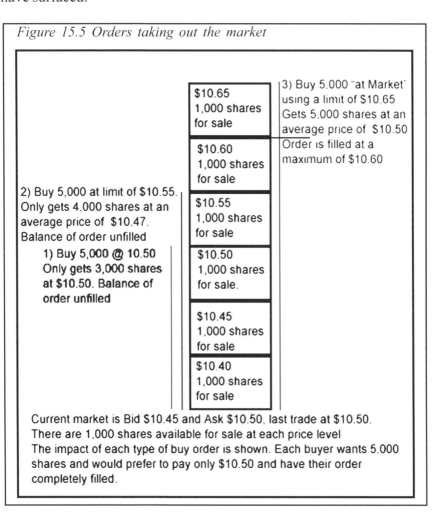

Figure 15.5 Orders taking out the market

| | $10.65
1,000 shares
for sale | 3) Buy 5.000 "at Market"
using a limit of $10.65
Gets 5.000 shares at an
average price of $10.50 |

3) Buy 5.000 "at Market' using a limit of $10.65 Gets 5.000 shares at an average price of $10.50 Order is filled at a maximum of $10.60

$10.65
1,000 shares
for sale

$10.60
1,000 shares
for sale

2) Buy 5,000 at limit of $10.55. Only gets 4,000 shares at an average price of $10.47. Balance of order unfilled

$10.55
1,000 shares
for sale

1) Buy 5,000 @ 10.50 Only gets 3,000 shares at $10.50. Balance of order unfilled

$10.50
1,000 shares
for sale.

$10.45
1,000 shares
for sale

$10.40
1,000 shares
for sale

Current market is Bid $10.45 and Ask $10.50, last trade at $10.50.
There are 1,000 shares available for sale at each price level
The impact of each type of buy order is shown. Each buyer wants 5.000 shares and would prefer to pay only $10.50 and have their order completely filled.

If you are clear on what you want your order to do, then make sure you select the most appropriate order format for electronic order placement.

The main option available is usually a limit order. This single order is manipulated to achieve these five outcomes. The impact is summarized in Figure 15.5 and is as follows:

- Buy at $10.50. Electronically this remains the same and the order is filled in the same way as with the traditional brokerage.

- Limit order. This has the same impact as in traditional brokerage. By setting a limit, you chase prices up to the price maximum and no further. Be aware that the order is completed instantaneously if there are sufficient sell orders available. Your order is filled from the lowest price available, and continues to be filled at successively higher prices up to the price limit until it is completed.

  With a limit order for 20,000 at $10.50, you might get 10,000 shares initially, perhaps from $10.40 to $10.50. The balance of the order, 10,000 at $10.50, now sits at the top of the buying line and only a fool sells to you at a lower price. An unfilled limit order signals your intentions to the market. Of course, when a buyer comes in at $10.51, then your order slips back in the execution line.

- The traditional broker's at-market order is gone in electronic order execution. Instead, it becomes a variation on the limit order. Normally, an at-market order means "Fill my order at whatever price you can" by chasing the market up. We complete the electronic equivalent of this by placing a limit order with the limit set well above the current asking price. This means the order is filled instantaneously, taking out all sell orders at $10.45, $10.50, $10.52, $10.54, etc. until the order is filled. Our intention is to fill the order completely with whatever stock is available for sale at this very moment.

  Just because you put your limit order at $12.00 does not mean you get it filled at $12.00. Instead, you collect the lowest-priced stock on offer, followed by the next lowest, etc. until your volume limit is reached. You effectively judge the upper price by using the depth of market volume.

- The buy-at-best order is difficult to duplicate electronically. A high limit order looks the same, but is executed as soon as it is placed. The only electronic equivalent is to place a low-level limit order at, for example, $12.30. When it is filled, place another low-level limit order at $12.32. When it is filled, place another low-level limit order at

$12.29, depending on how the market is moving. In this way, you get an average price for the day without revealing the full size of your order. This duplicates the at-best endeavors of a full-service brokerage. The main difference is you pay a brokerage fee for each trade instead of a single brokerage fee for the group of at-best trades.

- Buy-the-open uses the limit order to get to the top of the buying line before the market opens. The key difference here is that the market is not trading when the order is placed. Other traders have the time and the opportunity to see where your order is placed, and they could easily outbid you. In this situation, getting the timing right is difficult and critical.

When placing an order, work out what you want to do, then structure your order consistent with the way your brokerage executes those orders to achieve your objectives.

For some of the trading methods I use, it is important to set an advance sell order so that it is first in line at the target price.

Correct order structure and placement enhances our ability to effectively implement our trading plan and money management strategies. It is important for your brokerage to stand beside you and assist in this process. Brokerages with internal house rules that hinder your ability to trade the way you have planned, by slow or inaccurate execution, should be abandoned. Cheap brokerage is always poor compensation for the losses accumulating from poor or restricted order execution.

We protect profits by selecting appropriate money management strategies. We improve protection when our trading orders are executed with precision. Applied across all our trades, these methods protect our portfolios. In the next chapter, Robert Deel details how U.S. traders effectively navigate a quote-driven market to turn analysis into profitably executed trades. In Chapter 17, we then examine the nuances of order placement and execution in the order-driven Malaysian market to highlight the need for traders to work closely with their brokers and market order system to get the best possible order execution.

SIXTEEN
ORDERING U.S. PROFITS

Contributing author:
Robert Deel*

CEO,Tradingschool.com

Markets change, and increasingly the structure of the market order system is also changing as markets move toward greater transparency in their order lines and greater speed in trade execution. The globalization of markets means that administrative changes in one market have an impact on the way we trade in another. The shift to decimalization in the U.S. market has changed the trading landscape, making some order execution strategies ineffective and opening an edge for a different approach. Robert Deel is an internationally recognized trading expert, author of *The Strategic Electronic Day Trader* and CEO of Tradingschool.com. In this chapter he discusses recent changes and shows how all traders can now more effectively manage their order execution in U.S. markets to achieve the best results possible from each trade.

A consistently profitable trader will always trade with a fundamental knowledge of market statistics and time. For example, in most cases the months of September and October tend to be bearish months in the

---

* Robert Deel is an internationally recognized trading expert, author, and CEO of Tradingschool.com. Tradingschool.com trains traders and aggressive investors from all over the world in the disciplines of state-of-the-art trading tactics and technology. Robert Deel is one of the top traders in the United States. He trains not only the public, but institutional traders as well. He acts as a consultant to international corporations, funds, and offshore trading companies. He is the author of *The Strategic Electronic Day Trader* and *Trading the Plan*.

world markets. This is typically followed by three months of bullish trend in November, December, and January. There are specific days of the week that have more probability of success than others. If you are trading stocks that would be represented by the S&P 500, then Monday, Wednesday, and Friday represent the days that exhibit the best trend. If you are trading stocks that are represented by the NASDAQ, or technology stocks, then you need to focus on Wednesday, Thursday, and Friday. The Pacific Rim economies are directly connected to the U.S. NASDAQ market. Therefore, as a practical matter, it is a good idea to know if the NASDAQ ended its trading day with a bullish or bearish trend. In the very near future, 24-hour trading will be a global reality. Traders from all over the world will have access to all markets. Right now you can trade most major stock markets worldwide from your home or office. Almost anyone anywhere can afford the technology.

It is no accident that the U.S. markets went to decimalization and now have extended their trading hours. This is simply another prelude to 24-hour trading and the implementation of electronic execution of orders. Decimalization has narrowed the spread between the bid and the offer, which is positive unless you are a scalper who trades for 1/16th or 1/8th of a point. Decimalization had an unexpected side effect of causing share size to be less and lowering the amount of large block bids and offers at a specific price. This is much more evident currently on the NASDAQ than the NYSE. To combat this problem the NYSE tags a quote, which enables its institutional clients to have an idea of the size behind the price quote. This market depth indication, sometimes called the wholesale quote, has seemingly addressed the problem. Reuters and Bloomberg provide depth information as well to professional traders.

INTERNATIONAL EXCHANGE TRADED FUNDS

As a trader who trades on a global basis, I have found one very profound disadvantage that we do not experience in U.S. markets. This is the ability to trade a stock by selling it short. Most foreign markets outside the United States do not have a large number of stocks to short, or do not allow you to short stocks at all. I have an answer to this that almost anyone in any country can use to short an individual country's market and profit as that market declines. This is also an excellent way to hedge a long position in an individual stock or a portfolio of stocks. In general, stocks and markets fall 67% to 80% faster than they rise. This creates an opportunity to make money without the use of leverage by taking advantage of the implosion factor. Stocks and markets tend to fall rapidly. Money compounds faster by trading the short side, rather than by buying and hoping the stock will go up.

Using International Exchange Traded Funds (IETFs) also gives you the ability to hedge your long position in a foreign market. IETFs are an excellent way for anyone to trade globally with liquidly at very low commissions. Markets do not go up all the time, and this is a way to make money when they go down. IETFs also enable individuals to begin to trade outside their own country with confidence. A professional trader will go wherever the opportunity presents itself. Money has no national boundary or political ideology. I have no problem trading stocks in Australia, Europe, or Canada. Just make sure you don't miss an opportunity through focusing on just your own market. The world is a big place and it is getting smaller all the time. Two of the great equalizers making global trading possible are direct access technology and electronic communication networks (ECNs).

DIRECT ACCESS TECHNOLOGY AND ECNS

Direct access is often confused with level II trading. Direct access gives the trader a way to route his orders to various markets using several routing alternatives. A trading account needs to be opened with a direct access broker. Not all brokers can give you this technology. Using special software, the trader can engage in direct access trading which is far beyond the capability of browser-based online brokers. I will explain level II trading later in this section. For now, know that unless you have direct access capabilities, you are trading at a distinct technological disadvantage to someone who is using direct access.

ECNs are creating a global trading opportunity for anyone with a little capital, knowledge, and vision. Europe, Asia, Canada, Australia, and the United States can and do use this technology to trade globally. ECNs not only offer liquidity, but also make order executions possible within seconds. The driving popularity of the ECNs is simple. Your orders are matched with orders from other individuals without the involvement of a market maker. In the United States, decimalization and ECNs have led to a narrowing of the spread on bid and ask to US$0.01 on NASDAQ and NYSE stocks. Archipelago, another ECN, has replaced the need for a regional exchange, the Pacific Stock Exchange in Los Angeles. In France the Electronic French Futures Exchange replaced floor brokers in a matter of months. ECNs and direct access technology have made more changes in the trading world in the last five years than in the last century. The world is demanding 24-hour trading, and in most cases the ECN is a low-cost way of bringing this about. The most popular ECN is Island (ISLD). Specifically designed for U.S. NASDAQ stocks, it is now providing liquidity for many stocks traded on the NYSE, as well as for stocks all over the world.

SUPERDOT AND NYSEDIRECT

Currently the NYSE uses the SuperDOT system, which allows traders to send market and limit orders directly to the specialist at the trading post. SuperDOT is used for trades trading under 100,000 shares and gives priority to orders of 2,100 or less. Direct access trading software gives the individual access to the electronic system by a member firm. The SuperDOT system accounts for 50% to 75% of the small orders on the NYSE. Anyone in the world with direct access technology can place trades to the NYSE at minimal cost. The commissions are typically $9.95 to $14.95 per trade.

The NYSE is getting ready for a 24-hour traded market by creating its own answer to 24-hour worldwide demand. It is estimated that trading volume will be in the range of four to eight billion shares a day in a 24-hour trading environment. New technology and different approaches must be applied to meet this demand. One such innovation is NYSeDirect. This system will allow more liquidity at faster speeds of execution per trade. The system sends the order out, and in general, within two to six seconds, the order is filled. This system is a powerful tool for the small trader. It is a fully automatic executable order against the NYSE bids and offers. The size requirement is currently up to 1,099 shares, making this an excellent platform for the small trader. NYSeDirect is the NYSE's answer to ECNs, but with liquidity improvement. This added liquidity comes from a pool of customer limit orders, specialist interest, and floor orders left with the specialist. To access this system, you must find out if your trading firm subscribes to its use.

NYSE OPEN BOOK — NO, YOU ARE NOT DREAMING

No, I am not kidding. The NYSE plans to open up the specialist book to the public for a fee. This is the equivalent of the screen showing the third order level shown in the previous chapter. The specialist book will show all stock, all prices, aggregate volume, and will update every 10 seconds. This, in my opinion, will change the incentive of a specialist. In the future I believe that the specialist will be an employee of the NYSE and will be stationed at an electronic post, stepping in to maintain order and market balance when necessary. This new addition will be available in the very near future. Another factor is that specialists will no longer charge commissions for electronically entered orders that are transacted within five minutes. Yet another reason not to lie in bed at night dreaming of being a specialist on the floor of the NYSE. In today's high-technology world, the individual trader has advantages that traders in the past did not have. In some cases, you, as an individual trader, have advantages over the floor trader. In fact, many former floor traders and specialists are now trading for their own accounts. In many cases, they are making more money than they did when they were on the floor.

LEVEL II IS NOT WHAT IT ONCE WAS

Level II information is found in what is called a trade information box, or market maker box. Perhaps the best way to describe it is to first describe level I information. Most traders worldwide are familiar with the bid and ask price of stock and volume information. This is known in the U.S. as the National Best Bid or Offer (NBBO), which is simply the best price for those bidding for stock and the best price for those offering stock for sale. Most people only see these two prices. Level II shows not only the NBBO, but the underlying market as well. It shows, for example, that Merrill Lynch (MLCO) is bidding for x number of shares on the bid and is selling x number on the ask. This information also includes the price and size. All of this is under the NBBO. Level II provides more information, making the market a little more transparent.

When level II first came out, it was the ultimate information. Traders could see the directional movement of the market and position themselves accordingly. Today, everyone in the U.S. that is a serious trader uses level II information. This fact, along with decimalization, has all but ended the advantage of using level II information in the way it was used in the past. All direct access technology has level II information, but today it is used in a different manner. The main reason for using direct access is to route your orders and have them executed by the market in seconds. To do this successfully, you need to know if a market maker or an ECN is on the NBBO and that they are showing the right size or number of shares that you are willing to buy or sell. Level II shows this information. In Figure 16.1 you see a trade information box that includes NASDAQ level II information.

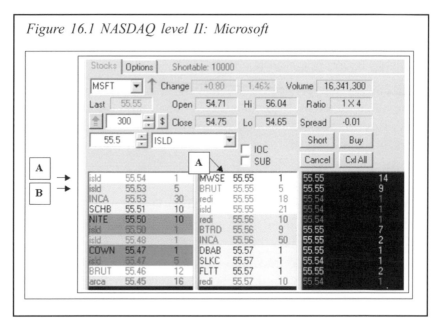

Figure 16.1 NASDAQ level II: Microsoft

Point A shows the current NBBO. On the bid side, Island — an ECN — is bidding 100 shares at $55.54. On the ask or offer side, you see one market maker — MWSE — offering 100 shares at $55.55 and three ECNs offering stock: BRUT 500, REDI 1,800, and Island 2,100. At point B below the NBBO, you see two ECNs: Island — ISLD — at $55.53 showing 500, and Instinet — INCA — at $55.53 showing 3,000. Charles Schwab —

SCHB — is showing 1,000 shares at $55.51. On the ask or offer side below the NBBO, three ECNs are currently showing interest: REDI at $55.56 showing 1,000, Bloomberg — BTRD — at the same price showing 900, and Instinet — INCA — showing 5,000.

This is a good example of how level II information is displayed. The information is also color-coded to better see the depth of the market. Orders at each new price level are grouped in a different color.

The stock in Figure 16.2 is traded on the NYSE and shows NYSE level II information. Note that on the bid side the NYSE — NYS — is bidding stock at 129.57 and is asking 129.61. This is the NBBO. This means that the best bid and offer for this stock are currently on the NYSE. In the undermarket, you can see various different regional exchanges and ECNs bidding and offering different prices and sizes. In B, you will note that Chicago — CSE — and Boston — BSE — appear on both the bid and ask orders just under the NBBO. Note that the ECNs Island — ISLD — and Archipelago — ARCA — are available to place orders. This represents a major change for the NYSE in routing orders to the exchange. This is another step toward better global access and 24-hour trading.

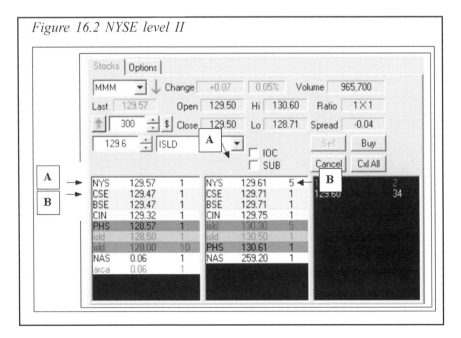

Figure 16.2 NYSE level II

ROUTING ORDERS

In Figure 16.3, point C shows the routing set to send a buy order to Island — ISLD. The price is $55.60. In this case, the trader is attempting to buy the stock on the bid. Note that ISLD is showing 1,500 shares of stock on the bid. Only direct access technology enables you to buy stock on the bid and offer it out on the ask. Currently, this is much more difficult than it was in the past.

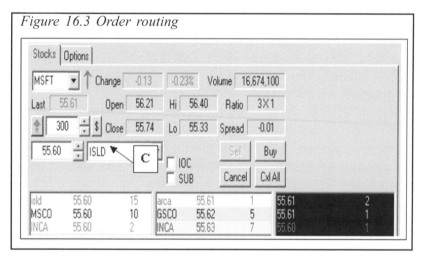

Figure 16.3 Order routing

In Figure 16.4, point D shows the route set to send a buy order to SOES. In this case, the order is a SOES limit order for a price of $55.60.

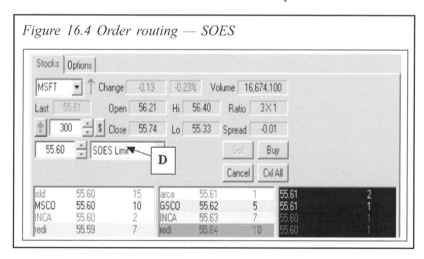

Figure 16.4 Order routing — SOES

From the order routing box it is possible to set up numerous different order routes. Remember that this technology is available for anyone in the world to trade. For simplicity, I would like to discuss two routing alternatives, Island and SSOES.

ISLAND

The electronic communications network Island — ISLD — came into existence in 1997. It has since become one of the most popular and most liquid of the ECNs. Today, Island accounts for a large percentage of the total NASDAQ market volume. One out of every four trades on the NASDAQ comes through Island. At the time of writing, Island makes up 34.8% of the volume trading the QQQ, which represents the NASDAQ. Known as the "Qs" or "cubes," they are identified by the symbol QQQ. Island also represents 16.5% of the trading in the S&P "spiders" (symbol SPY).

The future for this ECN, and for electronic trading, will continue to grow at an exponential rate. Once traders have experienced trading a stock with low commission rates at speeds of execution of two to six seconds, they will never want a browser-based online account again. The genie is out of the bottle and there is no going back. Some countries and companies may be resistant to this change, but change is a fact of life. If you do not adapt, or if you resist change, evolution has proven you will become extinct.

SSOES

In 1985 the Small Order Execution System (SOES) was first created in the United States. This allowed traders to trade against the market makers and was very effective. In fact, it was too successful for the traders using it. As a result, through political manipulation by the market makers, SOES had a set of very restrictive rules placed on its use. By 1996, when Island came into existence, millions of traders were willing to use a less restrictive order routing system. So, they began to use other ECNs as well as Island — until July 30, 2001, the date that launched SuperSOES (SSOES). Unlike its predecessor, SSOES allows a new flexibility and has put an end to many of the past restrictions.

Let us examine the new SuperSOES and address some of the specific improvements.

- The past small size requirements have been eliminated. Currently, using SSOES you can trade a maximum size of 999,999. This is a definite improvement over the previous 1,000 shares.

- One of the most restrictive rules of the old SOES system was what was known as the five-minute rule. This rule allowed you to buy, for example, 1,000 shares, but you could not buy again until five minutes had passed. In my book *The Strategic Electronic Day Trader*, I pointed out that this rule was, in my opinion, the largest limitation of the SOES system. SuperSOES has eliminated the rule.

- SSOES is much faster. In the old SOES system the market maker had 17 seconds to refresh his order. With SSOES the time is now between 0.5 and 0.8 seconds, making Island and SSOES the fastest order routing pathways to the markets for your order.

- You can cancel your SSOES order if you change your mind. This allows you to be more flexible in reacting to current market conditions. If your trade has not been filled, you hit the cancel button. The reply for your canceled order shows up on your screen in seconds.

- All market makers are required to post their tier size. This is the amount of stock that is available for the SSOES trader to trade against. A new addition to this is, if an order is not filled, the SSOES trader is now allowed to dip into market makers' stock reserves. This makes the odds better that the SSOES trader will fill her total size requirement.

The new SSOES gives the trader greater liquidity, faster order routing, and the ability to hit market makers' stock reserves; most importantly, it also removes the five-minute rule.

WORLD IMPACT

For years, traders have been taught that trading a consolidation breakout is a proper trading decision. This is no longer the case. Today, consolidation breakouts fail more often than they work. Chart patterns today in many cases don't work like they did in the past. One of the biggest mistakes a trader can make is not studying the market. Despite what you may have been told, what worked in the past won't necessarily work in today's trading environment. Markets typically change about every two-and-a-half years. From 1998 to 2000 the world markets experienced large high–low price-range compression. This simply means that on a given day, from the low to the high during that time frame, you would have seen $5 to $6 moves in the U.S. markets. Today, that is not the case in the U.S. or in other world markets. The range compression is now $1.00 to $1.50.

What this means is you can't use the same tactics or time frame as you did in the past and expect a profitable outcome. In my opinion, for the next 10 years we will be locked in bullish and bearish trading ranges. They will have trend, but not like they had in the past. This means that the average trader is going to have to be much more selective and have a time frame of no more than three to five days. The trader will also have to know how to day trade effectively.

Another reason for this will be 24-hour trading. This will cause investing in, or buying and holding, stocks to become as extinct as the dinosaur. In a 24-hour worldwide trading environment, no institutional money manager will hold stock over more than five days. In this kind of trading environment the risk of buying and holding stock is simply not acceptable on a risk-adjusted basis. This will change, by necessity, the old rules, especially those relating to pension plans. The rules of ERSA will be amended to allow the use of shorting and put options to protect and hedge a trading portfolio. Currently in the U.S., major pension plans, banks, mutual funds, and so on, are slowly laying off the old guard and replacing them with a new breed of trader — money managers. Banks are currently spending millions worldwide to address real-time settlement associated with real-time international 24-hour trading. Knowing this will give those who are ready an advantage. This environment favors the trader who has the knowledge and technology to take advantage of it.

***

I first met Robert Deel a few years ago in Australia when the two of us were speaking at a trading conference. Over the years, Robert has earned the respect of Wall Street traders with his insightful market and equity projections. Failure to listen to his counsel has taught many traders an expensive and painful lesson. As the saying goes, "When Robert speaks, Wall Street listens."

Traders come to Tradingschool.com to improve their skills. Regardless of whether you are a beginner or an experienced professional trader, Tradingschool.com's hands-on training can assist you in your quest for knowledge and experience. Traders from all over the world come to Tradingschool.com to become the highest probability traders possible. You will learn state-of-the art technology, strategy, and techniques used by world-class professionals. Don't let geography deter you from one of the finest trading educations in the world. More information is available from Info@tradingschool.com, tel: 1-626-599-8385.

SEVENTEEN
ASIAN PROFITS ON ORDER

Contributing author:
Sunny Low*

W e can spend our days reading and learning about trading, technical analysis, money management, and the psychology of trading. We spend many hours of hard work sifting through chart after chart, analyzing with all the indicators and methods we know, and still continue planning our trades. Yet, without knowing how to communicate and place our orders properly, no amount of reading and planning is going to be fruitful. Proper communication with your broker is essential. It allows you to effectively use your broker to better manage order flow and placement so that you can be ahead of the crowd.

One of Asia's most forward-looking and interesting places to trade in is the Kuala Lumpur Stock Exchange (KLSE). Compared to other markets in the region it has a high ratio of retail investor participation. To trade profitably on the KLSE requires a good understanding of the structure of the market system so that we can give the right kind of orders and instructions to our brokers. This will invariably give us a definite edge in the marketplace.

---

*   Sunny Low, AIBM (Sr), DipTA (ATAA) is a licensed dealer's representative of the Kuala Lumpur Stock Exchange with TA Securities Bhd, a major stockbroking company in Kuala Lumpur. He also holds a futures broker representative license with the Malaysian Derivatives Exchange. He is a Senior Associate of the Institute of Bankers, Malaysia and also a member of the Australian Technical Analysts Association.

The KLSE operates on a fully computerized order-driven trading system, eliminating the need for an open outcry trading floor. This automated trading system provides a single point for real-time price dissemination delivered by the SCORE system, which is the central computer responsible for the matching of all orders.

Stockbrokers use the WinScore system front-end trading screen for order and trade routing, as well as for confirmation. The WinScore system enables the broker to know the order status and market information on a real-time basis. Trade settlement and delivery is done electronically without the need for paper certificates. The buyer's account is credited and the seller's account is debited with the number of shares for each transaction.

ORDER ENTRY

Traders can only purchase or sell shares through a licensed broker, namely a dealer's representative. A dealer may be a paid dealer or a commissioned dealer, more commonly known as a remisier. Orders are entered directly into the WinScore computer terminals. These orders may be entered half an hour before the beginning of each trading session. This is not a continuous market, and this has a significant impact on the way traders manage their orders. The morning session trades from 9:00 am to 12:30 pm and the afternoon session from 2:30 pm to 5:00 pm.

All orders entered in the half-hour prior to the opening of each session are randomized for matching purposes. The SCORE computer system will decide on the sequence of the queue based on a randomized algorithm for these inputs. Hence, for orders put in before the actual trading starts at 9:00 am or 2:30 pm, traders may sometimes notice that even though an order was put in early, it may not be the first to get filled or matched.

This means the order line entry tactics discussed in Chapter 15 are not applicable in this market. However, once trading opens, all orders are matched on price and time priority. At the time of writing, the exchange is conducting a survey to determine whether the unmatched orders from the first trading session should be automatically carried forward into the second trading session. No decision has been made as yet.

Order size is usually set to a maximum of 500 lots. However, each individual stockbroking company may vary the maximum number of lots per order as a control measure. Lower limits set may be done by the reduced number of lots or by the monetary value of each order.

ORDER MATCHING AND TARGET PRICES

KLSE traders are no different from traders in other markets when it comes to the psychology of trading. So often, when our order is matched, some of us are filled with a sense of regret and disappointment, thinking "Oh, no, my order is done" or "I'm hit." Fear creeps into our heart the minute our broker confirms our order has been filled. We fear prices may move drastically higher after we have just sold or, worse still, sink even lower from our buying price.

We have a choice of order instruction. The first is a limit order. This order is executed at the price entered into the system, or better. Preference is given to the highest bid price and the lowest asking price. The second type of order instruction is a market order. This order is executed at a matching price within the upper and lower limit prices. Here, matching price means the price used to execute the next trade. For securities above RM1.00, the upper and lower limit is 30% higher or 30% lower than the previous session's closing price. Securities below RM1.00 have their upper and lower limits at 60 bids equivalent to 30 sen rounded to the lower bid.

Although pre-open orders are randomized, the market reverts to a first come, first matched process once the first trades in each session are completed. Orders are matched automatically during the trading session by time preference and price preference. Market orders have priority over limit orders in the matching priority.

When a buy order is quoted at the same price, preference is always given to the earliest buyer in the queue. The buyer that comes in first in line with the same price is the first to get his order filled.

Traders implement their overnight analysis more effectively by holding off their order execution until just after the market opens, because there is no clear advantage in participating in the randomized open.

Effective order management during the day is achieved by using the Target Price warning function available on the WinScore terminals. Not everyone is able to sit in front of the price terminals throughout the whole day's trading sessions, so brokers become the eyes and ears of their clients in the marketplace, executing trades at client-determined target prices and communicating with them.

Traders inform their broker of their intention to purchase or to sell at a particular price level. The broker keys in the client's name as a reminder to activate this contingency order once the price target is reached. The screen display in Figure 17.1 shows the counter Star as an example of setting price targets.

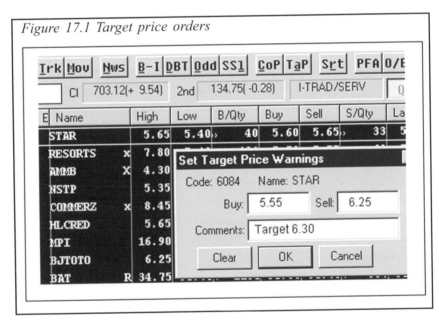

Figure 17.1 Target price orders

Once a buy or a sell target price has been keyed into this field, your broker's screen will flash a warning when the target price is reached. You may leave instructions for automatic execution, but many traders prefer their broker to contact them for further order instructions.

BEST BUY AND BEST SELL

Understanding the order screens makes it easier to execute trades at the most favorable prices. The screen in Figure 17.2 shows an example of price quotes sorted by highest volume traded. This represents the most actively traded stocks during the day. Day traders love this screen because of the high liquidity and concentration of activity involved. To be in the center of this action thrills many hearts.

Figure 17.2 Volume ranking

Name		High	Low	B/Qty	Buy	Sell	S/Qty	Last	Chg	Vol
AMMB	X	4.30	4.00	643	4.24	4.26	1491	4.24	0.280	46910
AMCORP		0.910	0.870	142	0.885	0.895	240	0.890	0.025	21406
COMMERZ-WA		0.510	0.435	172	0.495	0.500	28	0.500	0.060	11935
INTRIA		1.16	1.10	137	1.13	1.14	3	1.14	0.040	9275
CSM		1.11	0.860	328	1.09	1.10	21	1.09	0.245	8336
MAYBANK	X	8.70	8.55	2233	8.55	8.60	1324	8.60	0.000	7193
METPLEX	x	0.295	0.280	245	0.280	0.285	43	0.285	0.005	7013
MAGNUM	x	2.41	2.32	349	2.39	2.40	191	2.39	0.070	5219
GENTING	X	12.50	11.90	1008	12.40	12.50	1910	12.40	0.800	5179
TRI	x	3.34	3.18	213	3.22	3.24	1	3.24	0.040	5067

The numbers of buyers and sellers are also constantly changing in actively traded stocks. In Figure 17.2, Genting, marked with the arrow, was trading at RM12.40/12.50. It had 1,008 buyers and 1,910 sellers. Eight minutes later the number of buyers swelled to 1,284 and sellers to 2,001, as shown in Figure 17.3. This shows the best three buy and sell prices to help in your decision-making in purchasing or selling. There is a high concentration of both buyers and sellers at the current Genting price. Drawing away from the crowd at the price of RM12.40/12.50, we notice that fewer players are interested.

The constantly changing number of buyers and sellers on both sides largely influences the behavior and emotions of the traders. A trader who has made up his mind to get out of his position quickly will not waste time queuing behind the 2,001 sellers. Instead, he meets the buyer straight away, selling at RM12.40 to square his position.

Figure 17.3 Best buy or sell — Genting

E	Name		High	Low	B/Qty	Buy	Sell	S/Qty	L
	GENTING	X	12.50	11.90,	1284	12.40	12.50,	2001	1
	RESORTS	x	7.80	7.40,	417	7.70	7.75,	59	
	STAR	5							
	AMMB	X 4							
	NSTP	5							
	HLCRED	5							
	MPI	16							
	ADVPKG	3							
	BAT	R 34							
	COMMERZ	x 8							

Best Buy/Sell (GENTING) [X]

B/Qty	Buy	Sell	S/Qty
1284	12.400	12.500	2001
387	12.300	12.600	279
161	12.200	12.700	285
0	0.000	0.000	0
0	0.000	0.000	0

The best buy/sell screen provides important additional information about the status of the last traded price. The trade screen for MAA in Figure 17.4 at first glance looks like a tough resistance level to break at RM5.90 with 23 sellers lined up against five buyers at RM5.85. Price looks set to take a dip from this level. However, a quick click on the mouse shows the best buy/sell price has 53 buyers at RM5.80. The resistance barrier of 23 sellers at RM5.90 seems to fade away as compared to 60 sellers at the RM6.00 barrier. A seller may decide not to sell at RM5.85 after taking a look at the best three prices. In fact, he may even be tempted to join the queue with the rest of the sellers at RM6.00.

On this particular day, MAA closed at RM5.90, up 20 sen from the previous day's closing. On the following trading day it added another 15 sen to close at RM6.05. It pays to check the best prices.

CONTRA TRADING

One of the most exhilarating experiences, but also potentially the most fatal, is a trading method usually called contra trading. It is exhilarating because money is being made very quickly and seemingly easily on these trades, without the need to come up with trading capital. The trade is settled before payment is due. Contra trading is where traders take advantage of the delay in settlement. This is three days after the trade is completed, or T+3. Contra trading gives a unique character to the Malaysian and Singaporean markets.

Figure 17.4 Best buy or sell — MAA

Code	A	E	Name	High	Low	B/Qty	Buy	Sell	S/Qty	L
1198	*		MAA	6.05	5.80	5	5.85	5.90	23	
6084	*		STAR	5.75	5.60	21	5.70	5.80	141	
1562	*		BJTOTO	6						
2119			AHTIN	1						
8915	*		TCORP	2						
7552			EVERHAS	4						
5819	*		CHLBANK x	4						
7015A			GENSOIL-OA	2						
5215	*		ECONS	1						
2445	*		CKLK x	5						

Best Buy/Sell (MAA   )

B/Qty	Buy	Sell	S/Qty
5	5.850	5.900	23
53	5.800	5.950	26
34	5.750	6.000	60
0	0.000	0.000	0
0	0.000	0.000	0

The trader also knows that, come the due date to make full payment for his purchases, he probably does not have sufficient cash in his bank account to pay for his trade. Here, the time factor is the trader's constraint. He hopes to make a killing in the market within four days — T to T+3 — and he prays he will not be killed by the trade instead. If the trade is proven correct, he just needs to exit the trade by selling off his position. He makes a clean profit without having to come up with any capital. This is a very profitable strategy in Malaysia, where capital gains and profits made from the market are not subject to tax.

Die-hard contra traders usually rationalize this activity by thinking that although they may not have enough to pay in full for their purchase contracts, they do have sufficient cash to settle any contra losses incurred if the trade turns bad. This is done easily by exiting their position within the four days. Moreover, they are constantly watching the stock.

This strategy is similar to trading a very short-dated option. The settlement time factor may be a trader's friend or his enemy. The temptation to collect a clean profit within such a short time without having to come up with any capital is almost irresistible. However, if the trade turns bad, the trader is forced to liquidate his open position on the due date and settle the losses incurred.

Though profits have been made in contra trades, especially during an initial market upturn, many more traders have been severely hurt financially.

Your broker's assistance is crucial in trading contra transactions. Disciplined traders get their broker to help in setting exit price targets and to act on stop loss levels, as mentioned earlier in this chapter. Traders working with contra transactions monitor their position closely.

Contra trading is not a right of the client but, rather, a privilege accorded by the broker to its clients. In some situations, brokers require a deposit before executing such trades in order to reduce the substantially high risk involved. This strategy suits traders who are able to ride profits, but cut their losses fast.

SELLING TO THE BUY-IN BOARD

Trading mistakes happen where the seller accidentally oversells a stock. All verbal orders given by clients are treated as genuine and are keyed-in with speed and urgency. Sometimes the trader sells more than what he thinks he has in his trading account, or a stock that he mistakenly assumes he has in his account. This triggers a stock exchange process and provides an opportunity for other traders.

When a seller has oversold a stock, the KLSE institutes an automatic buy-in against him on day T+3 following the day of contract. The buy-in ensures that delivery is made in time to the purchaser. The purchaser receives his stock on the third day after the trade is executed.

The penalty imposed by the exchange on the defaulting seller is 10 bids above the T+2 day's closing price. The minimum bid varies from one half sen to 50 sen per bid, depending on the stock price. The higher the closing price of the stock, the more expensive each bid cost for the defaulting seller. Ten bids at RM1.00 would be RM1.10, but 10 bids at RM10.00 would be RM11.00. These are expensive mistakes for the defaulting seller and an opportunity for others.

The penalty levied on the defaulting seller is a gain and joy to other traders who have stock in hand. Selling on the buy-in board provides the opportunity to collect a windfall profit.

The trader instructs his broker before the opening of the morning trading session to sell to the buy-in board. The 10-bid spread is a market windfall, so the broker faces fierce competition from many others to place the entry at 8:30 am sharp. The fastest order to reach the SCORE matching center is filled first — a split second in time ahead of the rest.

Not all who try will win, but he who wins is handsomely rewarded. The reward comes in the form of repurchasing the stock that was sold earlier. If the trader manages to sell to the buy-in board, he can then instruct his broker to repurchase the same stock at the previous closing price or better. If the order is filled, the trader has in effect profited by the 10 bids, which may vary from five sen to RM5.00 per share, depending on the stock price.

The screen extract in Figure 17.5 shows an example of a buy-in done on Tenaga. Notice that the previous day's close was at RM10.10 and the subsequent buy-in price was RM11.10.

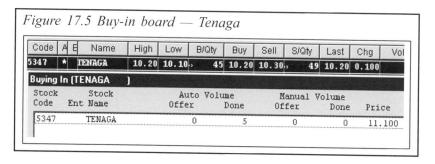

Figure 17.5 Buy-in board — Tenaga

Code	A	E	Name	High	Low	B/Qty	Buy	Sell	S/Qty	Last	Chg	Vol
5347		★	TENAGA	10.20	10.10	45	10.20	10.30	49	10.20	0.100	

Buying In (TENAGA)

Stock Code	Stock Ent Name	Auto Volume Offer	Done	Manual Volume Offer	Done	Price
5347	TENAGA	0	5	0	0	11.100

Each day on the buy-in board, there are various stocks that have been oversold. Some consist of a few lots, while others may run into hundreds. Surely on the buy-in board, the earliest and swiftest bird catches the worm.

ODD LOTS

The KLSE trades in board lots of 1,000 units or shares. The exchange also allows trading of board lots of 200 units for larger companies such as Maybank, AMMB, Genting, and Matsushita, so these higher-priced stocks are more affordable to the public.

Any amount that is less than a board lot is called an odd lot. Odd lots usually arise from the declaration of bonuses or rights issues by companies. Patience is the hallmark of a trader who intends to trade with odd lots. A lot of time and effort is required to be profitable in these sorts of trades. You may stretch your broker's patience as well.

Odd lots are traded on a different board, shown with Maybank in Figure 17.6. Access to this market and quotes is still through the broker's WinScore computer terminal. Genuine sellers usually do not mind disposing of odd lots at a slightly lower price than the current market price, so the buyer has a slight advantage. He quotes a few bids below the market price, hoping for a desperate seller who wants to get rid of his stock at that price. The buyer's objective is to collect sufficient odd lots to make up a standard board lot for the stock he is trading. Once he has enough to make a standard lot, he sells it at the current market price. In a way, he is also arbitraging these trades.

Figure 17.6 Odd lots — Maybank

Code	A	B	Name	High	Low	B/Qty	Buy	Sell	S/Qty	Last	Chg
0010	*		IRIS	0.415	0.405	0	0.000	0.000	0	0.405	-0.01
1155	*		MAYBANK	9.10	9.05	0	0.000	0.000	0	9.10	0.10

Odd Lot [MAYBANK   ]

Stock Code	Stock Name	Ref. Code	Buy Price/Vol	Sell Price/Vol	Last Price/Vol
1155	MAYBANK	349	8.950/100	0.000/0	0.000/0
1155	MAYBANK	358	8.950/100	0.000/0	0.000/0
1155	MAYBANK	361	8.800/80	0.000/0	0.000/0
1155	MAYBANK	402	8.850/140	0.000/0	0.000/0
1155	MAYBANK	408	0.000/0	0.000/0	8.800/50
1155	MAYBANK	468	8.800/110	0.000/0	0.000/0
1155	MAYBANK	471	8.850/175	0.000/0	0.000/0

There is no price limit as to how low the buyer could quote, so invariably, some buyers put in ridiculously low bidding prices. These are called fishing quotes.

A buyer collecting odd lots is exposed to the risk that he may not be able to collect enough to make it into a board lot to be sold later. Worse still, if the price reacts downwards, he is stuck with the odd lots. This risk is compensated for by quoting a lower buying price.

In 2002 the MESDAQ (Malaysian Exchange of Securities Dealing and Automated Quotation Berhad) was merged with the KLSE to create a single Malaysian Exchange. The MESDAQ was set up to bring together growth companies and investors. It is an equivalent of the NADSAQ in the United States.

Trading of MESDAQ counters is now similar to trading of any counter on the KLSE. MESDAQ counters are highlighted on the screen with a different color for easy identification. MESDAQ trades with a board lot of 100 units of shares each. Traders must use extra caution and give clear instructions when trading these counters.

We protect profits by selecting appropriate money management strategies. We improve protection when our trading orders are executed with precision by making the best use of the market order conditions. No two exchange trading systems are the same, so Trader Success makes sure he understands the most effective way to get his order executed at his preferred price.

Part 4

Protect Portfolios

EIGHTEEN
MADE TO
MEASURE

How does your money grow? Left to its own devices it usually shrinks, withers, and eventually dies under the pressure of everyday living expenses. We all want our money and the value of our portfolio to grow. As better traders and investors, we want ours to grow faster than ordinary. Fortunately, we have a readily accessible benchmark against which to measure our performance.

The benchmark is supplied by the general market performance and is traditionally captured by an index. These include the Dow Jones, S&P 500, Hang Seng, FTSE, and Straits Times indices. Should we use the index for our market as a target or as a starting point? We consider our answers below.

It is important to select a benchmark for comparison and to apply it consistently. We don't need to be distracted by the mechanics of index construction, or the merits of a broad market index compared to a sector index such as Media or Retail. As better traders, our objective is to beat our chosen market by superior stock selection, better trade management, and aggressive money management. We should do better than the broader market because, as private traders, we work in areas the institutional traders and fund managers avoid.

The consistent growth area in the market is among the mid-caps and smaller stocks. In many markets, trading volume in individual stocks is measured up to several million dollars a day. This pool is too shallow for the fund managers who want to trade consistently in large dollar amounts.

They cannot get in and out of the trade without creating a significant impact on the price.

Trading value of several million dollars a day in a single stock leaves ample room for the private trader to frolic. Our order for $6,000, or $50,000, or even $100,000, is not large enough to swamp the market. Our smaller size allows us to effectively trade in areas where capital growth is the highest. This is our advantage and we turn it into better portfolio performance when we move beyond the boundaries set by market benchmarks.

MEASURING RETURNS

To assess any portfolio management strategy, be it a trading portfolio or a longer-term investment-style approach, we establish an additional set of benchmarks. While the gross performance of the portfolio is important, the absolute performance is most significant.

A quick look at advertising by fund managers shows how this concept is poorly understood, yet it forms the basis of any accurate assessment of a trading or investment strategy. This approach also forms the basis of hedge fund management, although the techniques they choose to use are quite different from ours.

In *Share Trading*, I wrote that we must assess the returns from our trading capital against the returns available from fixed-rate interest markets. These returns are readily available from at-call term deposits and cash management funds. These cash returns are generally referred to as "risk free" even though they all involve some small level of risk. For our purposes, we accept that holding cash in the bank on interest-bearing short-term deposits is risk free. Unless our trading generates more than this risk-free rate of return, then we are not making effective use of our capital. The chart in Figure 18.1 shows a generous 5% risk-free return on funds invested.

The second column shows the market performance in 1999. We select this period because it was a time of excellent market returns. This is a high benchmark and it exaggerates the performance comparisons between fund managers and traders. The same relationships exist when the market performs less spectacularly. If we use these periods, the differences in performance are narrowed and may seem less significant, particularly as many investors happily accept that funds will deliver sub-par performance in difficult market conditions. In 2001, many diversified funds returned less than 1%. Even the average return was just 4% to 6%. This high-performance period in our example highlights the differences we need to consider when establishing the relevant portfolio performance benchmarks

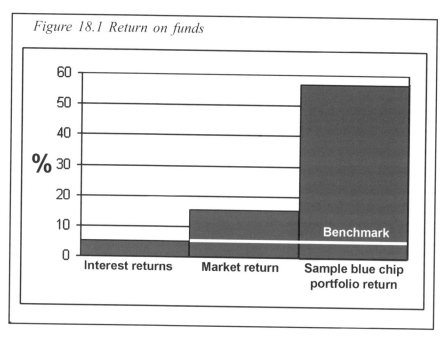

Figure 18.1 Return on funds

The third column shows the performance of a sample blue chip Swiss Roll portfolio included in our weekly Internet newsletter in 1999 and traded in real time. It applies a Swiss Roll strategy, discussed later in Chapter 20, to combine the trader's risk control strategies with longer-term investment strategies. The portfolio samples were designed to model the impact of excellent trading discipline and risk control. The returns also reflect the advantages available to all private traders — smaller trading size and greater trading agility than the institutions.

FUN WITH FUNDS

This interest rate benchmark is a way of assessing our performance. The next most important benchmark is the performance of the general market, as measured by a selected market index. Like it or not, this is the most commonly accepted measure and we should use it. In tracking the performance of our own selection of stocks, we may find it convenient to create a Private Index. This is done manually, as shown in *Share Trading*, or automatically using tools supplied by data suppliers such as JustData. The purpose of the Private Index is to track the performance of the stock you have selected. Ideally, the selection method you use should result in a group of stocks performing better than the selected benchmark market index.

A Private Index is not a market index. It is designed to tell the trader if his trade selection process is returning better results than a comparable market index. It is used to track trader performance.

In any market, we should do about as well as the general market. In the bull market of the last six months of 1999, it was very difficult to lose money. Some traders did succeed in this, but generally we look for returns to at least mirror the general market returns. This applies in any market condition.

Much of the funds management industry is set up to duplicate the general market returns. These are index tracking funds. Other specialist funds, sometimes called mutual funds, are established to capture growth in the market. In all cases, their annual results are reported in percentage terms. This is generally not helpful because it tells the investor very little. A fund return of 15.5% sounds quite good when compared to the interest rate return of 5.0%, as shown in Figure 18.2.

This is how many investors typically read these results. They want their capital, either in their own trading or in their pension 401K or superannuation funds, to do better than alternative risk-free uses, such as fixed-term deposits. The frequently published charts showing various investment classes — cash, property, and stocks — all use the risk-free interest rates as a comparison point. The comparisons look less successful when we add the current market return, shown in Figure 18.3. This shows a combination of interest rates, market performance, and returns from the best and the worst index tracking and growth funds performers in the period.

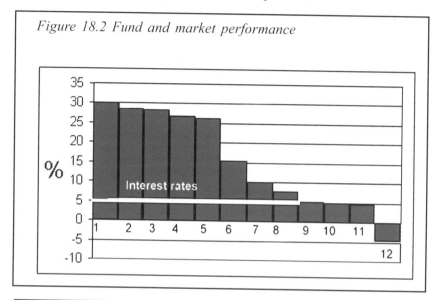

Figure 18.2 Fund and market performance

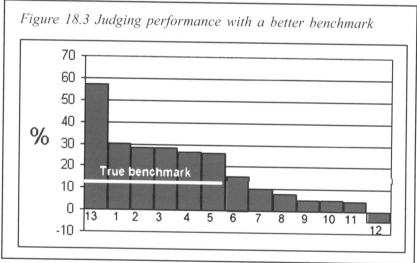

Figure 18.3 Judging performance with a better benchmark

We have not named these funds or their home market, because our purpose is to understand how benchmarks are applied more effectively. Simply selecting the best fund by name is not a long-term solution to growing capital. The top fund today may be a poorly performing fund over a five-year period.

Many readers quickly select Fund 12 as the worst performer for the period. In a strong bull market, this fund produced negative returns. Investors did better if they left their cash hidden under a mattress.

Other readers are worried about the performance of Funds 9, 10, and 11. These delivered returns just equal to the cash rate, or interest rate. Investors in these funds stepped into the world of market risk and got a return equal to their funds on deposit with a bank.

When asked to select the best-performing funds, many people tend to select all those on the chart where the return is above the risk-free rate of 5% available from the banks. This attitude is supported and encouraged by the financial press, who rank funds according to interest rate returns.

Interest rate benchmarks are misleading and this is where the hedge funds are relevant. When markets boom, new money pours in because the return on capital is greater than the returns available from interest rates. This disparity helps many people who are new to the market overcome their fear that the market is a risky place to be. As the boom goes sonic, even more people surrender their inhibitions, and their cash.

The funds management industry thrives on this flow of new money. In recent years this flow turned to a flood as tax regulations changed. Many citizens became part of a nation of shareholders by default. How do we know if our nest egg is being ably managed? The common answer is to compare fund performance with the risk-free cash rate. The real answer is to compare performance with the market index benchmark.

Apply this benchmark and only the top five funds pass. Funds 1, 2, 3, 4, and 5 all do better than the market return for the same period. Unfortunately, this performance is difficult to maintain. The top five funds in 1999 are not necessarily the top five funds in 2001 and they do not necessarily outperform the market. The advertising disclaimers always tell us historical performance should not be taken as a guide to future performance. This is very true with the index tracking fund management industry, because they try only to broadly match the market performance.

Our intention is to pursue superior portfolio returns as measured against the market performance. Figure 18.3 shows what is possible with Fund 13, our blue chip Swiss Roll strategy.

HEDGING RETURNS

Enter the hedge funds. These specialist funds were originally developed in the United States to service high-net-worth clients. Their aim is first to match and then to outperform the market by using a variety of trading tools and by trading a wide range of securities and financial instruments, including stocks, futures, currencies, and options.

The term "hedge fund" is now debased to include currency hedging by exporters, currency speculation by global funds, and fund managers who "hedge" their funds using overseas stocks. None of these activities is a true hedge fund activity.

Classic hedge funds have a common philosophy. Their performance measures, and their commission fees, start where the market finishes. If the market returns 15.5% in 12 months, then the hedge funds do not start reporting returns until they exceed 15.5%. The hedge fund managers believe that just by being in the market, they should be able to duplicate the rate of return generated by the market.

The hedge funds market their skill as finance professionals rather than just as money minders who thrive on fees. They believe that matching market returns is the bare minimum standard for professional money management. They do not charge their customers for gains made on the back of a generally rising market. The hedge funds employ a wide range of strategies to actively manage their funds so that they outperform the market.

Outperformance is a must, because the classic hedge fund survives by earning a commission. Traditionally, they are paid only for the performance over and above the market. Hedge funds do not make their money from management fees levied irrespective of the performance, or underperformance, of the fund.

This is in stark contrast to the activity of many new fund managers. For some equity managers, a 14.6% return in a roaring bull market returning 15.5% is considered good. It is also in stark contrast to the fledgling hedge funds industry that seeks to tap the interest of the broader investment market. Some of these new funds use the cash rate of interest as the benchmark for their performance! The relationship between hedge funds and other funds is shown in Figure 18.4.

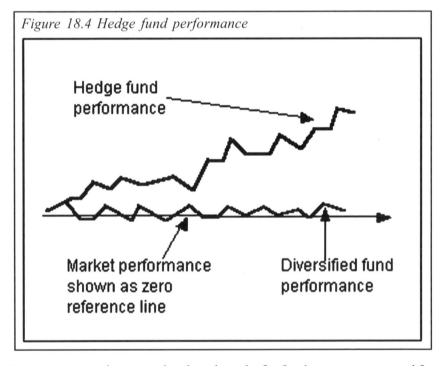

Figure 18.4 Hedge fund performance

Interest rates are inappropriate benchmarks for funds management and for the performance of our own portfolios, let alone for those claiming to be hedge funds. Figure 18.3 is the most appropriate way to understand and evaluate fund performance. Funds failing to reach this benchmark do not deserve our capital. When we assess portfolio performance, we aim for returns to outperform the market by 10%, 15%, or more.

Our objective is to use a variety of money management strategies to protect our personal portfolio. We do this realistically if we apply an appropriate standard to judge the level of required performance.

We can take out cheap property insurance premiums if we undervalue a property. This is easy on the pocket until it comes time to call on the insurance policy. We find we are underinsured and the damage to our personal finances is much greater than we expected. Apply the cash interest rate as a benchmark and it is the same as underinsuring a property.

The market involves a higher level of risk, and our rewards — our portfolio returns — need to be commensurate with that risk. Barely beating the interest rate from fixed-term deposits is not an adequate compensation for market risk. It is a poor reflection on our ability to manage our market exposure. It provides a good starting benchmark for traders who are just venturing into the market. Their levels of skill and experience are low, so survival is a bonus.

If we are serious about using the market as a more effective way of making our money grow, we should move quickly beyond the lowest benchmark and aim to match market performance. At this stage we aim to match the performance profile of many of the fund managers — better than cash, and about as good as general market returns. For many traders this benchmark is as high as they wish to aim.

The professional fund management industry has a vested interest in convincing you that achieving these benchmarks is beyond the skills of the average person. They claim that the big advantage of managed funds is that they are managed by professionals and the element of luck is minimized. There is more than a dash of self-interest in their assertion that they do better than an individual. Their assertions would be more acceptable if their income was based on performance, rather than on fees irrespective of performance.

Meeting these performance benchmarks is difficult for many private traders, but it is not impossible. Two keys unlock this potential.

The first is trading discipline coupled with appropriate risk control. By this stage of the book, I trust that readers understand the powerful impact of money management for protecting both capital and profits. These skills and techniques are not beyond the private trader or investor. These methods leverage success and reduce the impact of failure.

The second key is the size of our trading capital. Private traders and investors do not usually move millions of dollars, or even hundreds of thousands of dollars, in a single trade or investment. Size does matter. We are smaller and more agile than the fund managers. This agility provides very important advantages. The later chapters on the Swiss Roll and active investing approaches to portfolio protection show how these advantages are used.

Many traders and investors are satisfied when they generate returns matching market performance. To get there, they need to apply some of the techniques and methods discussed in previous chapters. They may well use other approaches.

Matching the market return is like breaching the jogger's pain barrier. The first five kilometers are agony, but the last five kilometers seem very easy. Once the investor consistently matches market returns, it is much easier to move beyond these and into hedge fund territory. It is easier because the hard work of developing trading discipline and appropriate risk control and money management strategies has been done. Without these skills, it is difficult to consistently match market returns. With these skills, it is much easier to move to higher performance levels.

The blue chip Swiss Roll portfolio performance, shown in Figure 18.5 as Fund 13, builds on the skills used to match market performance. The results outstrip the nearest fund management return. It is achieved using a handful of trades, each committing around $10,000. These are hedge fund-style returns and, in the long run, as our skills develop, these are the returns we aim for. Portfolio returns measured against our ability to match, and beat, market performance are a more accurate measure of our success.

When we assess the performance of our longer-term portfolio management strategies, we delude ourselves if we look at just the gross figures. A successful portfolio strategy must take the market performance as a starting point and report returns in relative terms. Achieving hedge fund-quality returns without using fancy trading strategies or complex derivatives, and without spending all day in front of a trading screen, is a challenge. The challenge is answered by portfolio allocation strategies, by money management techniques applied to portfolio equity curves, and by using a variety of investment strategies modified by the trader's close attention to risk.

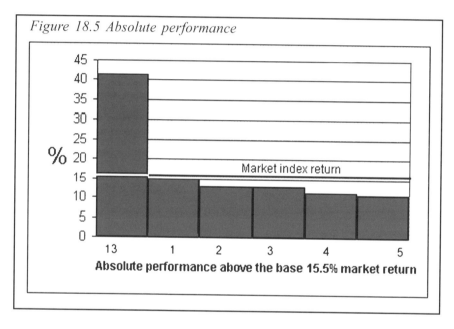

Figure 18.5 Absolute performance

Portfolio performance is made to measure. Equipped with better measuring tools, we now investigate these strategies.

NINETEEN
RISK AND
DIVERSITY

Quick, what falls the fastest — a shipping container of lead or a shipping container filled with feather pillows? The answer is simple. They both fall at the same rate. Here's another question. Which portfolio has inherently greater risk, a portfolio including speculative stocks or a portfolio of blue chips? The answer is, "Neither." The answer has less to do with the class of stock in the portfolio and more to do with the diversity of risk.

Portfolio allocation has a core question: "How much money should I allocate to a speculative stock compared to a blue chip stock?" The answer is not a simple one, and depends very much on your stage of trading. The solution for Trader Average is different to that for Trader Success. Trading is used to generate income and also to build wealth. Wealth-building strategies do not mean tying up capital in the market for generations. They involve money management strategies which deliver "paid for" assets protected from capital loss. These strategies are separate from the problem of portfolio allocation, and were covered in earlier chapters.

Trader Novice believes the market is risky and he is encouraged to believe that quality stocks protect him against risk. This belief costs dearly, as Nortel, WorldCom, Enron, HIH Insurance, and other blue chip stockholders know. Some have stopped trading and others have been reduced to penny stock status, trading at just a few cents. The market offers a variety of different levels of risk and this provides the starting point for portfolio allocation. Portfolio risk is managed by selecting diversity based on the different classes of volatility.

We start this discussion with the sensible idea that diversity offers some protection against risk. This investment approach is designed to take good performance with the bad, and we hope the good stocks perform much more effectively than the bad stocks. There is, however, a flaw in this belief, because a 10% loss cannot be made up by a 10% gain. This recovery calls for a return of more than 11% just to claw back to the original level of capital. In Chapter 1 we examined the impact of even a few losses on annual portfolio profits.

Diversity is at the core of modern portfolio management theory and is too complex to discuss in detail here. In summary, the theory accepts that in any portfolio some stocks will be up and some will be down. It is difficult to tell what will be up and what will be down at any particular time, but, on average, the return from the up stocks should balance out the losses from down stocks, so, on average, the return should be about the same as the general market. Because the result is about the same as the general market, we balance out the volatility — the up and down risk — of the individual stocks held in the portfolio. The result is shown in Figure 19.1.

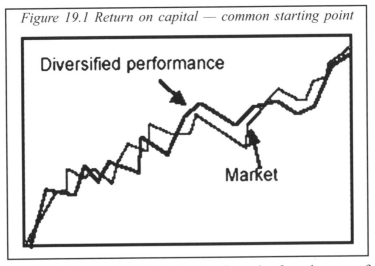

Figure 19.1 Return on capital — common starting point

Stripped of the jargon, this is the basis of much of modern portfolio management theory. It has its ultimate application when the broker or advisor suggests you need at least $50,000 to start in the market to get bare minimum diversification. Don't have $50,000? Well, they will sell you a fund where, for just a few dollars, you let the fund manager combine your money, less fees, with money from other investors, and together you all get the benefits of diversification.

Diversity does minimize risk, but somewhere the real meaning has been lost in the translation from the original theory to the fund manager's advertising. For Trader Novice, diversity has come to mean a collection of five or more blue chip stocks, usually spread across different sectors of the economy. Typically, these stocks have about the same level of annual volatility.

If our objective is to build a portfolio that performs better than the broad market, then we need the diversity that comes from a collection of stocks showing different levels of volatility, or different levels of return for the same degree of volatility.

VOLATILITY

All this sounds like a long detour from the question of portfolio allocation, yet our understanding of these concepts has a significant impact on the way we structure our holdings. I use a trader's perspective of the market. My understanding of risk and volatility is different from an investor's perspective. I actively and aggressively manage risk, and this determines the allocation of stocks in my portfolio.

Consider charts A and B in Figure 19.2. They both show a year of price action. The price scale could be $0.05 to $0.10, or $5.00 to $10.00, or $50 to $100. It makes little difference. Both show equal historical volatility, and both range between five and 10 over a one-year period. The question is: which one carries the greater risk, and why? The answer determines which stock is added to our portfolio. The investor and the trader look at the same charts and reach different conclusions.

THE INVESTOR

The investor believes that chart B is a high-risk stock. With many moves between five and 10, the investor is exposed to significant volatility. The price moves up and down with equal ease. The value of the portfolio changes dramatically as prices range between the upper and lower levels. Closer inspection suggests that changes are spread over many weeks and months, rather than just a few days. The investor believes the volatility is a bad feature, even though the return is equal to or better than the return in chart A.

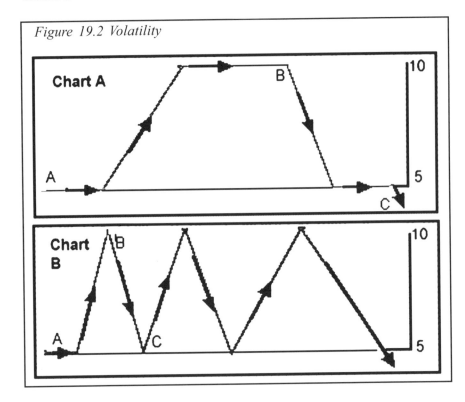

Figure 19.2 Volatility

The investor believes that chart A offers a more stable environment, partly because there is only one up and down movement for the year. The change in value between five and 10 is much slower than in chart B. This is a stable stock suitable for a stable portfolio. The risk of loss is not great. Unlike chart B, the values do not change rapidly. Any falls are likely to be gradual and, because they are slow, the investor believes they are more easily balanced against better performers in a stable, diversified portfolio. An exit is signaled on the downside when prices move below five.

The ultimate risk in both stocks is the same. A price rise from five to 10 delivers the same level of profits for both chart A and chart B. A fall from 10 to five delivers the same level of loss in both cases. The frequency of the rise and fall challenges us to better management. It does not distinguish an investment-grade stock from other stocks.

THE TRADER

For Trader Success, the high-risk stock is chart A. It is high risk because capital is tied up for an extended period. Buy at point A and she waits a month for the stock to move. Sell at point B and her cash has been tied up for eight months. The unskilled Trader Novice might hold on as prices fall from 10 toward five. A sell signal is generated by a drop below five at point C. He loses trading capital, and it takes a year to happen. His trading capital is tied up, unavailable for other opportunities, for a full year. The price activity in chart A carries a very high opportunity cost for all traders.

For Trader Success, the stock in chart B has less risk because of the frequency of its moves. Three trading opportunities exist between the lower and upper bands. This is about one opportunity every four months. In contrast with chart A, at any time during the year there is a high probability of a price move from five to 10. This calls for more active monitoring and management, but it also represents a much more effective use of trading capital.

Assume that both chart A and chart B are stocks with deep and liquid markets. An order to buy or sell $20,000 worth of stock is easily filled where average turnover is $2 million a day or more.

If we alter the scale on these two displays so that chart A is measured from $50 and $100 and chart B from $5.00 and $10.00, does it change our assessment of the risk?

It alters our intuitive assessment, even though there is no change in the risk profile of these two displays. The value of the underlying stock, $50 or $5.00, has little impact on the risk profile — providing trading liquidity remains the same. This is a counter-intuitive concept because we are accustomed to thinking that lower-priced speculative stocks are high risk. We confuse the execution risk — the ability to get in and out of the trade — with the volatility risk.

When we accept that the volatility risk profile is the same for both stocks, then we more effectively concentrate on managing the risk and achieving a better balance in our portfolio allocation.

WHEN THE CHIPS ARE DOWN

In *Share Trading*, I used a short-cut notation of blue chip, mid-cap, and speculative to describe levels of volatility. This created some confusion, because many readers construct these categories on the basis of capitalization. In this view, Enron is a blue chip just like Microsoft, because they are both well capitalized. Even a quick glance at a chart shows that General Electric, with its steady trend behavior, has an entirely different character from Merck, which has regular volatility-driven moves of 30% or more. We stay with the terms used in *Share Trading*, and examine them from a volatility perspective because many defensive trading strategies suggest that blue chips are safe. The strategy implies low volatility.

A blue chip stock has a low probability of returning 100% in a trade over a year. Exceptions are possible, but in most cases we look for a 10% to 20% return from a trade in a blue chip stock on a regular basis. What makes it a blue chip is the low level of return and the low volatility, or frequency, of these changes, as shown in Figure 19.3.

Blue chips typically offer these returns around twice a year. In a bull market, this may happen three times a year and in a bear market perhaps just once.

We expose ourselves to unexpected risk if we accept common classifications of quality for any stock without first understanding its volatility. Not all blue chips have low volatility.

With the U.S. retailer Wal-Mart, it was reasonably possible to take several trades with a 20% return in the 10 months of trading shown in Figure 19.3. The easiest way to determine this is to take the cluster of lows for the 12-month period, calculate the price equal to a 20% return, and draw this as a line on the chart. Then count the number of possible trades during the year with this level of return.

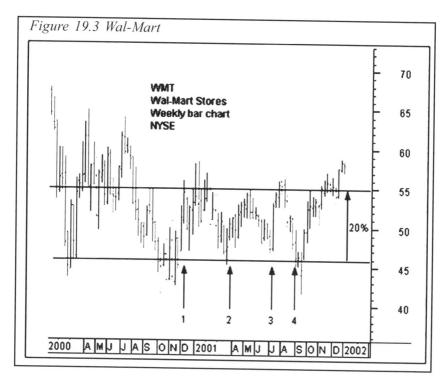

Figure 19.3 Wal-Mart

WMT
Wal-Mart Stores
Weekly bar chart
NYSE

Wal-Mart shows four trades between these points, starting at $46. Certainly, we could fine-tune trading strategies and perhaps make several more successful trades with 20% returns, but broadly speaking we are most likely to make just these four trades. Because it is a blue chip in terms of volatility, we normally expect to make only several of these trades every year, unless we are in an extremely strong bull market.

This sets our trading strategy. When trading these types of stocks, we look for lower returns over a longer period. This does not automatically qualify them as investment-grade stocks. If we are satisfied with performing at about the same rate as the broad market, then this return is acceptable. If we want better performance, then these stocks are unlikely to deliver it if we pursue the traditional buy, hold, and hope strategy.

It is not the price you pay that determines the nature of the stock. It is the behavior of price that determines both the nature of the stock and the risk it poses to your portfolio. This is one of the most important considerations for portfolio allocation strategies. Risk also depends on price behavior.

A mid-cap stock is expected to deliver returns of between 30% and 50%. This increase in volatility also suggests that these returns should be available more frequently, perhaps three to five times a year. In a bull market, we shoot for the higher 50% return.

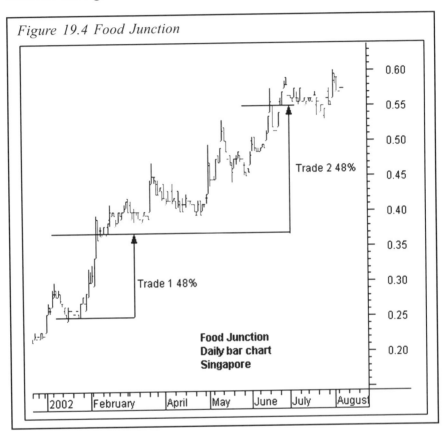

Figure 19.4 Food Junction

Using a daily chart of the Singapore stock, Food Junction, we start the calculations at the January low of $0.25, shown in Figure 19.4. This provides two trading opportunities where 48% returns are possible. They are shown as trades 1 and 2 on the chart. The character of this mid-cap stock tells us to expect several trading opportunities, each with a reasonable probability of a 50% return. Other opportunities for returns of 30% or more are found as prices move from support to resistance points. In developing a trading strategy for stocks with mid-cap volatility, we factor in both the level of return and the frequency of trading.

When we turn to speculative stocks, we expect a much greater reward for the risk we take. In a bull market, this reward is calculated at return levels of over 50% or 100%, and even more. This may happen several times a year in a bull market. In slower markets, these 100% returns are available two to four times a year. This is what makes the speculative end of the market so attractive in bear markets and sideways markets. No other type of stock has the capacity to increase capital so rapidly. These speculative stocks are traded with reduced execution risk by using good risk control based on the 2% rule.

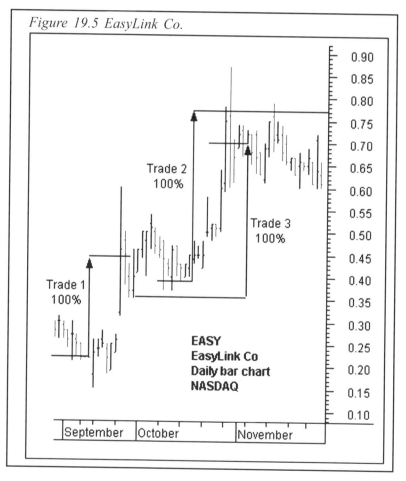

Figure 19.5 EasyLink Co.

The NASDAQ-listed EasyLink company chart spread over one year — Figure 19.5 — shows three readily achievable trades all returning 100%.

This is not an exceptional example, and an examination of many of the speculative stocks shows similar patterns. The trader reasonably expects a 100% return from a stock in this category. This is what makes it a speculative stock. It is not directly related to its capitalization.

Using this understanding of volatility, take a look at the stock in Figure 19.6. It has no price or time scale, yet you should be able to reach a decision about its volatility. It has consistently excellent trading volume, so trading liquidity is not a problem. Is this a blue chip, mid-cap, or speculative stock? Your decision determines how much you buy and how you manage the risk. The answer is in the next section. A summary of the characteristics of each volatility class is shown in Figure 19.7.

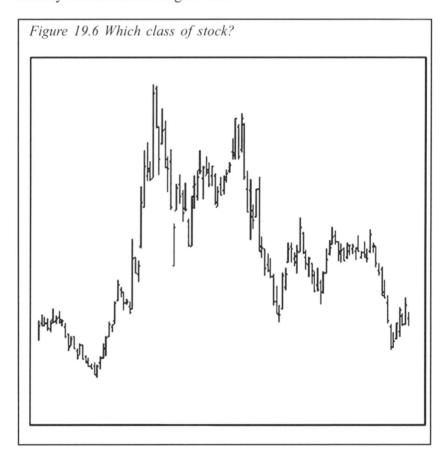

Figure 19.6 Which class of stock?

Category by volatility	Expected return per trade	Annual frequency of trading	Typical capitalisation	Typical liquidity
Blue chip	10% to 20%	1 - 2	Large	Deep
Mid Cap	30% to 50%	2 - 5	Mid range	Average
Speculative	50% to 100%+	2 - 4	Small	Low

Figure 19.7 Levels of volatility

Recognizing the type of stock we are dealing with, understanding its risk profile based on volatility, and knowing the probability of prices moving between these extremes are the first steps in deciding portfolio allocation.

DIVERSIFICATION AND ALLOCATION

The expected level of volatility, determined by price behavior, is the key to the distribution of cash within our portfolio.

In allocating cash to these three sectors of volatility, we work with an inverse relationship. We allocate a larger proportion of our capital to stocks with good trends and low volatility.

At the other extreme, stocks with high volatility and many trading opportunities are allocated a smaller proportion of our capital. Increased volatility carries increased risk. Although we intend to control the risk using tools such as the 2% rule, there is no guarantee that we will be able to apply this rule in practice. On average, we anticipate a 2% loss of trading capital across all losing positions. In practice, we may experience a string of trades where the portfolio loss is greater than 2%.

If we allocate our trading capital so that the greatest weighting goes to stocks with the highest volatility, then we increase the probability of destroying our trading capital quickly. If we hold a lot of drug maker Merck, financial provider Merrill Lynch, or Singapore's City Development because we believe it is a quality blue chip, then the volatility of this stock has the capacity to seriously destroy our capital.

Take another look at the chart in Figure 19.6. Did you decide this was a volatile stock based on the price moves?

The chart shows News Corp. If we added News Corp. to our portfolio, based on its status as a blue chip, then we take on unexpected volatility risk that is inconsistent with the capital allocation shown in Figure 19.8.

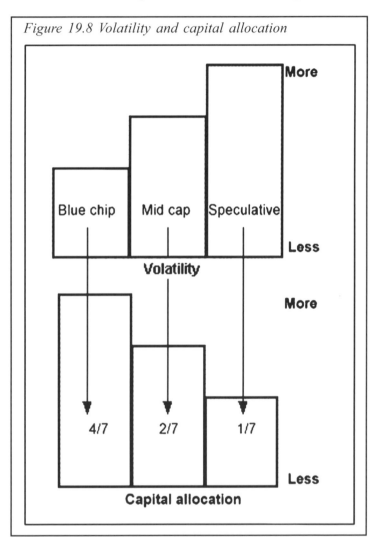

Figure 19.8 Volatility and capital allocation

The portfolio impact of a 10% loss of trading capital in a trade is the same regardless of whether the stock is a blue chip investment or a speculative trade such as News Corp.

In *Share Trading*, I suggested that 4/7 of a portfolio should be allocated to blue chip or trending low-volatility stocks, and 1/7 to fast-moving, high-volatility speculative stocks. The remaining 2/7 goes to the mid-cap stocks where the level of return and volatility is more stable than in speculative stocks.

The objective of this cash allocation is to protect our trading capital while taking advantage of volatility returns. It is not always possible to keep these exact proportions in place. Rather than absolute ratios, they are allocation levels we aim to achieve. Obviously, if we hold five stocks and four of these are speculative and only one of them is blue chip, then our capital is at much higher risk than if the ratio of exposure was reversed. Trading this portfolio mix successfully requires a higher level of discipline and trading skill, because we are called upon more frequently to make trading decisions.

Instead of controlling risk by diversification across a range of stocks so that failure in one sector is counterbalanced by the success of another sector, we find it more effective to diversify risk based on volatility. By matching capital allocation with volatility, we increase the opportunity to participate in reward while still containing risk in an effective way.

While this gives us a way of allocating levels of cash to each type of trading opportunity, it does not tell us how many positions we can have in each category.

CUMULATIVE RISK

We need to distinguish between the management of portfolio risk and the management of the risk in individual stocks. The risk in individual stocks is managed by applying the 2% rule. By applying this rule, we reduce the risk associated with faulty analysis. If we get the direction of the trend wrong, if price does not act as we believe it will, if the breakout does not develop, then the 2% rule protects us. It provides an exit strategy designed to limit damage to our trading capital.

While the risk in each individual trade is limited, on average, to 2% of trading capital, the cumulative risk may be much higher. With six open trades, or positions, the total risk is 12% of trading capital. This cumulative risk becomes an important factor if the systemic risk or the sector risk increases.

Systemic risk is the risk of the entire market falling. People worry that a general market fall will drag all stocks down, and fear that all their open positions — trades or investments — will have to be closed simultaneously. With six open trades, this means a 12% loss of trading capital, rather than a 2% loss. The same type of cumulative risk applies to stocks selected from a single market sector. When the price of gold falls, we expect most gold stocks to fall. If all of our trades are in the gold sector, then the risk becomes cumulative. It is likely that most, or all, of the trades in this sector will suffer a loss and trigger our exit conditions.

With a general market collapse, everybody with open trades is at risk. Only good stop loss discipline protects the trader, and even then, the loss is likely to be greater than originally anticipated. While a general market collapse is possible, it is also an unusual event. The only way to avoid it is by not being involved in the market. For all practical purposes, this risk is ignored unless there are sound market-wide indications of a significant drop in the market.

A sector collapse is a more likely event, and this should be factored into trading as part of portfolio risk. If all of our stocks fall into the blue chip volatility area, then we expect limited trading opportunities and limited returns. On the positive side, the reduced volatility also means that these sectors are unlikely to rapidly collapse. The probability of exiting at our individual 2% stop loss levels in any trade is quite high.

In contrast, if all of our open trades are at the speculative end and limited to a particular market sector, such as Internet stocks, then we expect to see many trading opportunities and significant returns. On the negative side, this increased sector volatility means that a collapse in the sector could be quite dramatic. It is likely that many of the trades would be closed at a loss greater than our planned 2%.

The relationship between volatility, returns, and risk is consistent and is summarized in Figure 19.9.

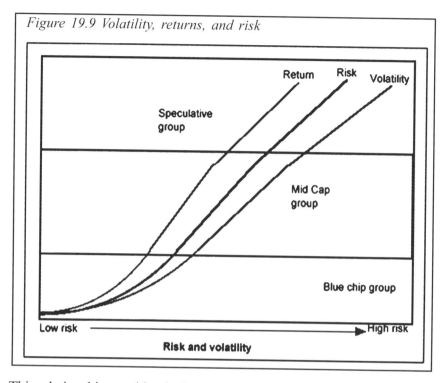

Figure 19.9 Volatility, returns, and risk

This relationship provides the basis of portfolio allocation across volatility groups as a means of limiting the potential risk to the portfolio. We overcome cumulative risk by the way we allocate capital to different sectors based on volatility. We add to cumulative risk if all our stocks show the same level of volatility, because gains are unlikely to overcome losses. By applying the 2% rule, we have a way to limit losses and maximize a variety of different gains based on a diverse mix of volatility.

The portfolio allocation ratios given in *Share Trading* are 4:7, 2:7, and 1:7. This provides diversity built on volatility. I have seen no reason to change these broad ratios since the book was written. You may decide on different ratios, but in general they should reflect a portfolio balance diversified in terms of capital allocation.

Some investment advisors suggest that people should allocate only money they are prepared to lose to the speculative end of the market. This is an excellent way to lose money, because people rarely take a careful interest in money they believe they can afford to lose.

In a general sense, the objective in managing portfolio risk is to allocate our capital consistent with the broad ratio based on expected volatility.

VOLATILITY FOR REAL

The tangle of fuzzy thinking about risk ties high risk to speculative stocks and low risk to blue chip stocks. This breaks the link between price behavior and volatility by inserting a mistaken notion that quality is equal to low volatility.

Speculative stocks are determined by their price behavior. Speculative stocks include those as diverse as Merck, News Corp., EasyLink Co., and Creative-T in Singapore. The list might include biotech stocks, gold stocks, Internet stocks, and oil stocks. What unites them is the level of volatility, not the industry group they are drawn from or their capitalization.

The broad sector ratios tell us how much trading capital we can afford to allocate to individual trades within each sector. In deciding whether to allocate $7,000 to a single trade or $3,500 to two separate trades within the same sector, the trader must make some realistic judgments about his trading skill.

While the 2% rule is designed to limit the risk on any one of these trades to just 2% of our total trading capital, we must also acknowledge that the greatest risk in any single trade is posed by our own analysis skills. Quite simply, Trader Novice is more likely to get it wrong than Trader Success. This is analysis risk. Some traders overcome it by seeking the best brokerage advice available, others by exploring how other experienced traders handle current market conditions. In our weekly newsletter, we aim to show readers how to better understand the use of charts and technical analysis. In all cases, the objective is to develop identification skills to allow us to pick the correct direction of price movements in trading opportunities with a better than 50:50 level of success.

We want to put the balance of probability on our side. Trader Novice aims for better than 50:50, while Trader Success works on a 70:30 ratio or better. This is an important factor in deciding just how much cash to allocate to an individual position.

When Trader Novice has a 50:50 success ratio, it does not mean he gets one trade right and one trade wrong. Over time this will happen, on average, but in reality he may face three or five or more losing trades in a row. While in theory it does not matter if all the trades happen simultaneously, in practice Trader Novice rarely has the skills to effectively manage multiple open positions. He improves his chances of success by taking just one trade at a time in each sector based on volatility. This gives him time to manage the trade and to analyze the reasons for its failure or success before moving into the next trade. By spreading the trades out, Trader Novice gives himself more time to learn, and to survive.

Trader Success has a 70:30 success rate. Her skill means that she has a better probability of managing multiple open positions in the one sector. It is appropriate for her to take several trading positions in each sector where volatility and risk are higher.

In trading less volatile sectors of the market — the blue chips in terms of reduced volatility — Trader Novice is able to take on additional positions. Once the decision is made to open a trade in a low-volatility stock, there is a reduced probability that he will be asked to close it quickly. There is more time for analysis of both entry and exit conditions.

If Trader Novice allocates all of his $7,000 allowable in the speculative sector to an individual stock, then the most he puts at risk is 2% of his total trading capital. His exit conditions get him out of the trade when 2% of his trading capital has been lost. This exit is irrespective of the size of the trade. This is a difficult concept to grasp if we persist in equating risk with the total amount of capital we have in a trade, rather than with the amount of capital we are prepared to lose.

It does not matter if the single position is worth $5,000, $7,000, or $15,000. If the maximum loss is limited to 2% of total trading capital, then the impact of analysis failure is limited. All traders improve their chances of survival and success by having just a few open trades and managing them carefully. It protects them against analysis risk.

It has been suggested that we also counter this by having two open positions, and limiting the risk to 1% of trading capital in each trade. The cumulative risk is still only 2%. Unfortunately, the analysis risk is doubled for Trader Novice.

As shown in Figure 19.10, by using these approaches Trader Novice may end up with a cumulative 12% of his trading capital at risk across a variety of market segments. By spreading his risk across different risk profiles, based on volatility, he effectively reduces the probability of all open trades being closed at the same time. This means that his effective diversified risk is less than the cumulative 12%, and not much greater than 2%.

Figure 19.10 Total risk

High Risk ↑	Speculative - high volatility	1 position	2% cumulative risk	2 positions	4% cumulative risk
	Mid cap - mid range volatility	2 positions	4% cumulative risk	4 positions	8% cumulative risk
Low Risk	Blue Chips - low volatility	3 positions	6% cumulative risk	4 positions	8% cumulative risk
		Trader Novice	Total risk for Trader Novice portolio 12%	Trader Success	Total risk for Trader Success portolio 20%

Trader Success, with multiple positions in each sector, may have a cumulative risk of 20%. Again, while the cumulative risk in individual sectors is likely to be greater than 2%, she also has a greater probability of being able to take an effective exit to successfully limit the risk in each individual trade.

The allocation of capital to each volatility sector — blue chip, mid-cap, and speculative — is a function of volatility. It is not a function of some vague notion of quality. The allocation of capital to individual trades within each sector is a function of trading experience and analysis skill. This requires realistic judgment by the trader and the ability to ignore other potentially good opportunities.

Once a trading record is established, Trader Novice should be able to determine when his analysis skills are improving. This is best judged after a series of winning and losing trades, rather than just a few winning trades. As analysis skill levels improve, the trader takes on multiple open trades within a selected volatility sector. His increased analysis skill weights the probability of success more in his favor and reduces the likelihood of having to exit the trade at a stop loss point as a result of poor analysis.

While we have no control over the market or the probability of a systemic or sector collapse, we do have control over our analysis skills. By matching trading exposure to our level of skill, we have an effective way of determining just how much capital should be allocated to individual positions within each sector of volatility. The performance profile developed in Part 1 helps match our developing skills with capital allocated to individual trades.

Portfolio allocation is part of risk management. It includes an understanding of volatility and of the risk imposed by our analysis skills, or lack of them. When volatility expands, we reduce risk by both the way we allocate cash within the portfolio and by the number of opportunities we provide for analysis failure. Which portfolio has inherently greater risk — a portfolio including speculative stocks or a portfolio of blue chips? It is the wrong question, because risk rests on volatility, rather than status.

Traders and investors reap the benefits of diversity by selecting stocks with a diverse range of volatility. Diversity is not a function of the number of stocks in our portfolio. It is a successful part of portfolio management when it covers a range of potential returns coming from selecting stocks with a range of volatility. We protect and enhance our portfolio performance by striking a diverse balance between blue chip, mid-cap, and speculative stocks based on their historical volatility rather than their reputation. Traders look for volatility because it provides their income. Investors can use volatility to grow long-term capital, and we examine a strategy for this in the next chapter. Used in this way, volatility is an investor's friend, rather than a portfolio enemy.

TWENTY
SLICING RISK

Many investors believe that volatility is the enemy of good portfolio management. High-volatility stocks are shunned because of the way they impact on portfolio performance. Traders look for high volatility because it provides the opportunity to generate income. Investors go to the other extreme, searching for low volatility and closing their eyes when volatility is greater than expected. Consider the investors in an initial public offering. They expect the stock to rise, and with many in new industry areas, they expect to join a long-term up trend by selecting the new Microsoft as it leaves the home garage and gains NASDAQ listing. Their response to the unexpected downtrend and volatility is to close their eyes because they are "in for the long term."

There are benefits in taking the trader's concept of risk management and applying it to longer-term trades intended to be investments. Good risk control in an investment protects capital. Good use of volatility helps to grow capital.

I held IPO stock in a privatized government business as part of an investment portfolio. My real desire is to trade, and had I acted on this, I would have captured profits. Instead, like other investors "in for the long term," I held on to them and had the pleasure of watching my capital diminish in the midst of a bull market. An investment portfolio is not supposed to be a hedge against wealth! Like many readers, I need a solution to the dilemma of running an investment portfolio and capturing the available capital gains.

One aspect of the dilemma is that these investment stocks still have considerable volatility in some market conditions. This contains the kernel of a solution.

The trader sees the instant solution to this volatility: buy near the beginning of the trend, and sell just before or just after the up trend starts to reverse. His concern is to extract trading profits. The investor is less certain of this, although the temptation remains. His objective is to deliver sound returns over an extended time. He argues that, because his time horizon is longer, he can afford to ride out the lows in favor of the highs to come. This reasoning is satisfactory only if the investor captures the profits on the highs. Merely holding on through a series of rises and dips does not capture any return or any loss. The dividend payments are rarely enough to compensate for the draw downs — the periods of loss of capital, or reduction in profits.

Additionally, there is a flawed assumption that prices will be on their highs when the investor wishes to turn the portfolio into cash. Real life suggests that when you really need to liquidate your portfolio, it is because times are hard and market prices low.

The solution to this dilemma lies in taking short-term profits on long-term investments on a rotational basis while strictly limiting losses. This is achieved by drawing on a diversified pool of potential investment stocks and rotating them in and out of the actual portfolio grouping in an aggressive manner. Dividend flow is important in this approach because it adds an additional cash flow to the portfolio. The pool of potential stocks could be selected on the basis of historical dividend performance.

When we use the term "trading" in this context, it is not the fast trading investors associate with traders. It is a willingness to monitor the stocks in the portfolio and to take action to protect capital and profits. This is normally a relatively infrequent process. We applied this strategy in real time and this means the examples in this chapter come from the Australian market. The National Australia Bank, shown in Figure 20.1, is an example of an investment-style blue chip stock. The chart shows that there are just five entry or exit points requiring action over 36 months. Hardly a short-term trading scenario.

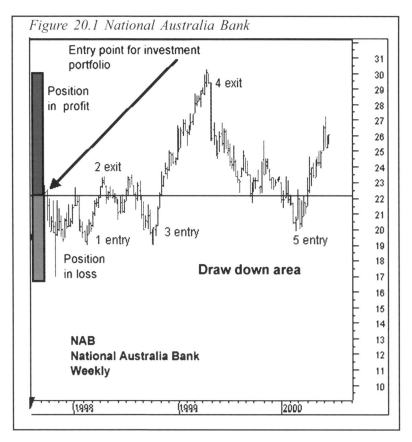

Figure 20.1 National Australia Bank

A SWISS ROLL STRATEGY

We call this combination of time, volatility, and active management a Swiss Roll approach, after the bakery treat. Jam, or jelly, is spread over a thin sponge cake, and then the cake is rolled up. The good bits, the jam, are twisted into a curve that repeats throughout the roll.

How do we slice the roll to collect the most jam? How much jam you get depends on where you cut. A vertical slice or cross-section of a Swiss Roll shows both desirable and undesirable sections. We get a lot of cake and a sprinkling of jam. Closing out a portfolio carries the same type of vertical risk. In a diversified portfolio in any market, some stocks will be good and some will be performing poorly. Any vertical cut in the diversified portfolio collects some "jam," but not a lot.

This vertical cut through time comes with the standard portfolio review and crystalizes losses on losers but fails to take profits on winners. This is shown in Figure 20.2.

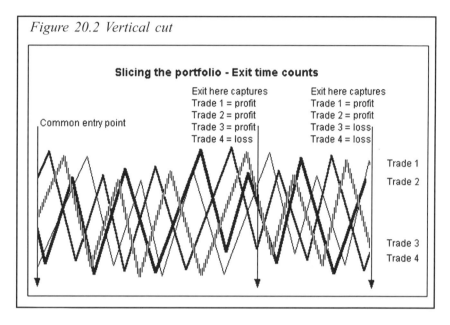

Figure 20.2 Vertical cut

This portfolio has four stocks. For this example, they are all purchased at the same time. A vertical cut exits all stocks at the same time. The result at point A is break-even, with two stocks in profit and two showing a loss. The "jam" is spread thinly.

If we shift the position of the vertical cut to point B, we do slightly better with three winners and one loser. The profitability of the portfolio depends on the timing of the cut. As shown in Chapter 4, we are all market timers.

A horizontal slice through the top of the Swiss Roll collects more jam. The jam is spread for the entire length of the cut. We get more jam out of the same pattern of rises and falls in the same portfolio if we slice it horizontally through the return horizon. Using careful cuts — investment exit and entry — we select slices with more jam than others.

This strategy demands more entry and exit points, as shown in Figure 20.3.

We have removed trade 2, the heavy dark line, for clarity. The Swiss Roll strategy is shown for just one of the stocks, trade 1. The time between each entry and exit may be months, or years.

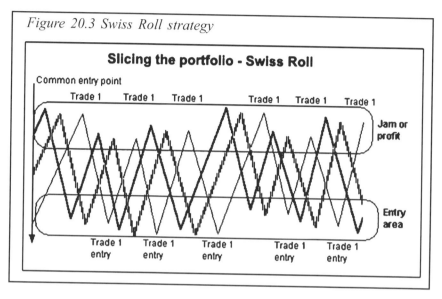

Figure 20.3 Swiss Roll strategy

The strategic advantage comes from the consistent collection of profits. This is not based on exact timing. In effectively managing an investment-style portfolio, the objective is to keep the integrity of the risk profile in the portfolio by selecting stocks with acceptable volatility while picking out the jam. This does not require exact timing as in trading, as shown in Figure 20.4. It does, however, require a willingness to act when necessary to capture the benefits of volatility.

This is the strategy we examine in this chapter. We start by looking at ways to build an effective pool of investment stocks. We consider a poor solution and a better one. We include both, because one is an intuitive solution and we need proof before we reject it as the best solution.

BUILDING THE POOL

In an investment-style portfolio, the search for suitable stocks includes four factors. They are:

- soundness, confirmed by membership of the top 100 stocks;
- high yield;
- price trending upward; and
- reasonable volatility to deliver capital gains.

Unlike some investment approaches, this strategy actively looks for volatility because it provides the trading part of the investment strategy. We start with size and reputation, so we limit our search to the top 100 stocks.

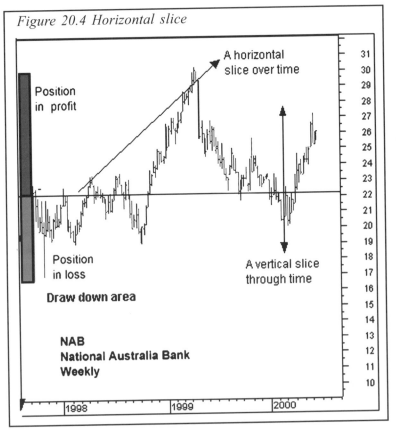

Figure 20.4 Horizontal slice

Next we select those stocks with the highest dividend yield. These figures are available from financial magazines and websites. We want a portfolio pool of around 10 stocks. They must be members of the top 100 and are selected in order of dividend yield. If we choose stocks purely on the basis of dividend yield, then only a few of the candidates also appear in the top 100 stocks.

This pool is the "jam" in the Swiss Roll. Because the list covers stocks from many areas, we achieve a diversification in terms of exposure to different sectors of the market. The high yields supplement any poor price performance.

These two factors — soundness and yield — form the base pool for portfolio candidates. Our objective is to have no more than five open positions at any one time. As one of the candidates fails to perform, it is dropped from the portfolio and replaced with the best performer from the remaining stocks in the pool. The total number of companies included in the pool remains constant, although the membership of the pool may change. The objective is to trade quality companies while having a reserve of quality companies to draw upon as replacements.

Selection for the Swiss Roll portfolio is based on trending activity and the volatility of the stock. We do not automatically select stocks in a strong up trend, as we need to determine the probability of this trend continuing. This decision is based on technical indicators such as the Guppy Multiple Moving Average and the ADX group of indicators. The best candidates are stocks where the trend is established, but still young.

The final selection filter for the five stocks in the pool is volatility. Instead of trying to reduce volatility, we recognize that trends do not continue forever. The objective is to keep the portfolio exposed to "sound" stocks, but to take advantage of the normal highs and lows in the sub-trends in these stocks. We want stocks with a reasonable degree of price activity to provide a useful capital addition to the portfolio performance.

This portfolio structure captures dividend yield and locks-in capital gains so that the portfolio increases in real cash terms over the selected period. We want to turn potential profits into real profits, and reduce the theoretical draw downs. The value of the portfolio fluctuates so that we take a horizontal slice off the top of the rises, capture the profits, and put them to one side. It is a trading approach on a long-term basis using stocks normally considered as stable investment candidates.

TOP STOCKS WITH TOP YIELDS

We have two choices in selecting the trading pool. Logic suggests that stocks from the top 100 with the best dividend yields should be ideal candidates for our portfolio pool. Alternatively, we could select just the top 10 stocks by yield. The differences in performance are important. If we start with the wrong group, we handicap portfolio performance. We look at both approaches below. With each group, we consider the impact of a buy and hold strategy and the Swiss Roll strategy.

We use a list drawn from Australian stocks, and constructed in January 2000 near the top of the bull market. Our real-time test period covers the next six months, capturing the tech wreck week in April and the subsequent market shudders. This was not a good time for investors. It is a good time to test investment strategy performance.

The first pool of candidates is made up of 10 stocks selected on the basis of yield and their membership of the top 100 stocks. Flip through these 10 charts and a disturbing feature emerges. Most are in strong downtrends, or extended sideways patterns. Dividends are not enough to compensate for the erosion of capital in these stocks.

This feature underlines the failure of the standard investment advice about looking for sound companies with real profits and steady dividends. It is often called a "flight to quality." The rate of capital loss in these stocks is so great that it takes much greater dividends than those paid to compensate for the steady, and at times, dramatic, erosion of capital. Long-term success depends on prices trending upward and not just on "quality."

Only four stocks, as marked in Figure 20.5, are in good up trends. All the others are in downtrends and show little sign of recovery. We allocate around $5,000 to each of these four, creating a total portfolio of $19,997. This period starts with irrational exuberance, plummets to the depths of despair, and then recovers slowly and painfully.

Figure 20.5 Top 10 stocks

The selection pool from the top 100

	Yield	Franking	
BRY	9.1	0	
MAY	8.94	40	
PDP	8.38	0	
MIG	8.06	6	X
AMC	7.74	20	
GAN	7.49	0	X
NDY	7.23	42	
WFT	6.84	0	X
WAN	6.66	100	
MGR	6.54	32	X

We want an investment strategy to accommodate this market volatility and to produce acceptable returns. We have a choice of two — a vertical cut or a Swiss Roll. Using the same pool of stocks over the same period, we compare the results.

We start with the traditional buy, hold, and sell strategy summarized in Figure 20.6. We take a vertical slice on June 30, 2000, selling all stocks. This vertical slice captures a 7.5% return for the six-month period. These figures have been rounded up, but they represent a barely acceptable return for the risk involved. The market index change from the January low to the June high is 8.0%. This strategy fails to meet the market benchmark.

If the investor had been unlucky enough to select the four worst-performing stocks for the period, the loss would be substantial, even though these are quality, dividend-paying stocks selected from the top 100. Good investing means we should have mechanisms to avoid this type of capital reduction.

Figure 20.6 Buy and hold — vertical cut

	Entry	Value	Exit	Value	Profit/loss
MIG	$ 1.34	$ 5,000	$ 1.40	$ 5,223	$ 224
WFT	$ 2.89	$ 5,000	$ 3.26	$ 5,640	$ 640
MGR	$ 3.13	$ 4,999	$ 3.44	$ 5,494	$ 495
GAN	$ 1.07	$ 4,999	$ 1.10	$ 5,139	$ 140
Total		$ 19,997		$ 21,496	$ 1,499

Using this same selection of four stocks, the Swiss Roll strategy delivers better returns, as shown in Figure 20.7. Instead of taking a vertical slice of time, the Swiss Roll strategy takes a horizontal slice as performance declines. We use an arbitrary exit point based on the best achievable price after January 1. It is not realistic, but it provides a consistent way to compare the performance between different strategies.

Figure 20.7 Horizontal cut

	Entry	Value	Exit	Value	Profit/loss
MIG	$ 1.34	$ 5,000	$ 1.40	$ 5,223	$ 224
WFT	$ 2.89	$ 5,000	$ 3.28	$ 5,674	$ 675
MGR	$ 3.13	$ 4,999	$ 3.63	$ 5,797	$ 799
GAN	$ 1.07	$ 4,999	$ 1.14	$ 5,326	$ 327
		$ 19,997		$ 22,021	$ 2,024

Realized profits are 10.3%. This is substantially better than the buy and hold result for the same period. The result is still not outstanding, as it outperforms the market by only 2.3%. By managing risk more effectively, the investor has collected a better capital gain using the same four stocks used in the buy and hold strategy. The performance difference is summarized in Figure 20.8.

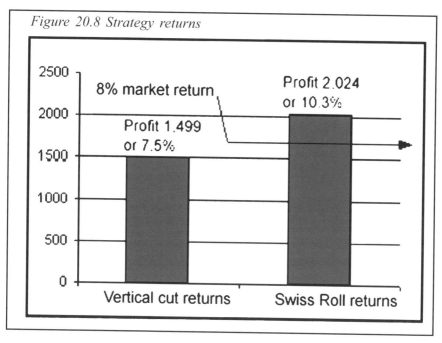

Figure 20.8 Strategy returns

BETTER YIELDS

We have two choices in selecting the trading pool. The second choice is more intuitive and selects the top 10 stocks by yield. We include this selection option because many investors believe that high-yield stocks contribute to outstanding portfolio performance. The reality is quite different.

The selection filters for this pool are:

* high yield — select the top 10;
* price trending upwards; and
* reasonable volatility to deliver capital gains.

We start the sample list in January 2000 near the top of the bull market. As with the first example, our real-time test period covers the next six months. Start with the top 10 stocks by yield shown in Figure 20.9 and bring up a chart of each stock. Most are a perfect hedge against capital growth, with prices dropping from the upper left-hand corner to the lower right-hand corner of the screen. Traders avoid these stocks, but investors seem quite happy to hold them because their dividend yield is so good.

Figure 20.9 Top 10 stocks by yield

	Yield	Franking	
NLY	34.48	100	X
MME	26.38	0	
BSO	16.45	0	X
PRX	15.48	0	
AGH	15	0	
PHT	14.41	0	X
VWD	14.08	100	X
MDC	13.91	50	
UCR	13.13	100	
APY	12.95	100	

Selecting the four best-performing stocks from this group is a matter of eliminating the worst performers. We use the same time period as we did with the first group, but now the rate of capital loss is catastrophic. These stocks all pay excellent dividends, but this does not compensate for a consistent fall in value among these stocks. It takes a lot to turn this collection of quality "dogs" into a profitable outcome.

Again, we allocate $5,000 to each of the best stocks for a total portfolio of $19,996. We start with the buy and hold strategy, ending with a vertical cut to close the portfolio on June 30, shown in Figure 20.10.

Figure 20.10 Buy and hold — vertical cut

	Entry	Value	Exit	Value	Profit/loss
NLY	$ 2.13	$ 4,999	$ 1.69	$ 3,966	-$ 1,033
BSO	$ 2.95	$ 4,997	$ 2.80	$ 4,743	-$ 254
PHT	$ 0.80	$ 5,000	$ 0.73	$ 4,563	-$ 438
VWD	$ 0.85	$ 5,000	$ 0.82	$ 4,823	-$ 176
Total		$ 19,996		$ 18,095	-$ 1,901

Taking this vertical slice on June 30 through this portfolio group shows a 9.5% capital loss! Remember that we have the advantage of hindsight and have selected only the best-performing stocks from this group of 10. These figures are rounded, but this portfolio struggles to reach the break-even point.

The vertical slice fails. How does the horizontal slice perform? The Swiss Roll strategy uses protect-profit strategies, rather than time, to manage risk. We use arbitrary exit points based on the best achievable price after January 1, shown in Figure 20.11.

Figure 20.11 Horizontal cut

	Entry	Value	Exit	Value	Profit/loss
NLY	$ 2.13	$ 4,999	$ 2.23	$ 5,234	$ 235
BSO	$ 2.95	$ 4,997	$ 3.40	$ 5,760	$ 762
PHT	$ 0.80	$ 5,000	$ 0.80	$ 5,000	$ -
VWD	$ 0.85	$ 5,000	$ 0.89	$ 5,235	$ 235
		$ 19,996		$ 21,228	$ 1,232

When profits are realized, the result is substantially better than the buy and hold result for the same period, as shown in Figure 20.12. The return is 6.16%. This is still a long way behind the market return of 8.0% and not as good as the 10.3% return from stocks selected from the top 100 based on dividend yield and managed with a Swiss Roll strategy.

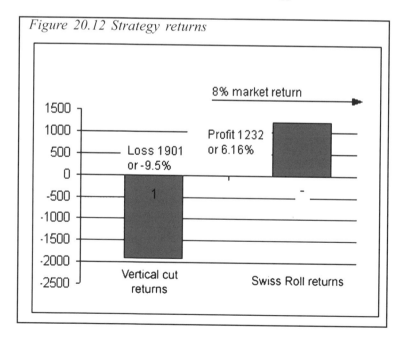

Figure 20.12 Strategy returns

BETTER POOL SELECTION

We develop a better pool of investment stocks if we focus on soundness and high yield. These are the first two of the four features discussed earlier in this chapter.

Better pool selection also includes prices that are in an up trend and reasonable volatility to deliver capital gains. We look at examples below. We use Mirvac Group, taken from the list in Figure 20.5. We do not automatically select stocks in a strong up trend, as we need to determine the probability of this trend continuing. We apply technical indicators such as the Guppy Multiple Moving Average and the ADX group of indicators to determine this. The best outcome is to select stocks where the trend is established, but still young.

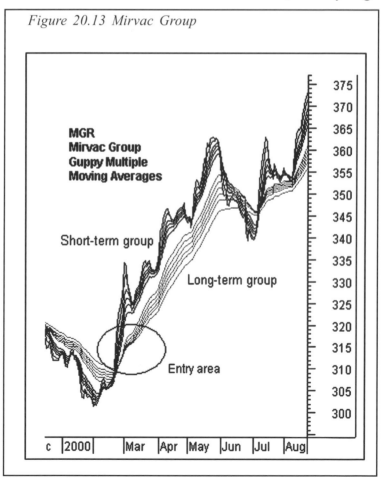

Figure 20.13 Mirvac Group

The chart of Mirvac Group in Figure 20.13 shows the preferred relationship. The multiple moving average display shows increasing support from long-term investors coupled with good trading activity and support from short-term traders. The entry area has the characteristics of the beginning of a new up trend. The price is trending upward. We do not try to capture the very start of the up trend. Instead, we look for proof that the up trend is in place. Traders hunt in the area where downtrends might turn to up trends, but this is not a suitable hunting area for investors. The risk of trend failure is greatest in this area.

The final selection criterion is volatility. The Swiss Roll portfolio treats volatility as a desirable feature. We do not want stocks that move rapidly up and down, but stocks with a reasonable degree of price activity provide a useful capital addition to the portfolio performance. Mirvac also has this characteristic with a sound up trend lasting three months, followed by a trend collapse, shown in Figure 20.14. These types of stocks are added to the Swiss Roll portfolio.

Figure 20.14 Mirvac Group — trends and volatility

As one of the candidates fails to perform, it is dropped from the portfolio and replaced with the most promising performer selected from those remaining in the pool. Mirvac is dropped in May. The total number of stocks included in the pool remains constant, although the membership of the pool may change. The objective is to trade quality stock while having a reserve of quality stocks to draw upon as replacements.

In this investment-style portfolio, the focus is on maintaining a stable risk profile developed from stock choice while capturing profits. This is counterbalanced by cutting losses quickly. This intention is to develop a long-term portfolio, so some investors do not expect to have to make an exit decision quickly to protect capital. This is a false expectation. Time is the least effective method of managing risk, as shown in Chapter 4. If a stock drops in price and meets our stop loss conditions, we sell it quickly. What we intended to do with it is less important than the damage to our capital right now.

GETTING THE MOST JAM

The percentage return results from each strategy and pool are compared in Figure 20.15. The most effective stock selection for an investment style of portfolio is based on the top-yielding stocks drawn from the top 100. A selection based on yield alone does not deliver capital appreciation with a vertical cut. When high-yielding stocks are caught in significant downtrends, their yield often falls in the next profit-reporting season. This leaves investors trapped in stocks with lower than expected yields and much lower than expected prices. This double whammy wreaks havoc on any portfolio, particularly if we start eliminating the worst performers based on a vertical cut annual portfolio review.

The Swiss Roll strategy for portfolio management is designed to capture returns from quality investment-style stocks while keeping the risk profile of the portfolio stable. This portfolio strategy captures dividend yield and locks-in capital gains so that the portfolio increases in real cash terms over the selected period. We want to turn potential profits into real profits and reduce the theoretical draw downs. When the value of the portfolio fluctuates, we take a horizontal slice off the top, capture these profits, and put them to one side.

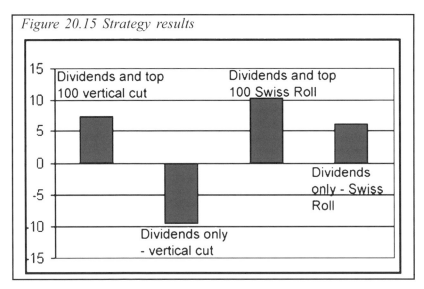

Figure 20.15 Strategy results

This approach introduces an aspect of timing into the management of the portfolio. Time is significant in two ways. The first is in the timing of the entry and exit conditions. The benefits of good portfolio selection are reduced when inappropriate exit strategies are used. In Chapter 4, we showed how we are all market timers. The sample portfolio selection in this chapter supports this conclusion. When a vertical cut is used to realize gains and losses in the portfolio, the timing of the cut has a critical impact on the results, shown in Figure 20.16.

Figure 20.16 Vertical cut timing

	Jan - Jun	Jan - Mar	Jan - Apr
Start	$ 19,997	$ 19,997	$ 19,997
End	$ 21,496	$ 20,624	$ 19,847
Profit	$ 1,499	$ 627	
%	7.5	3.14	

We use four stocks from the most successful top 10 by yield from the top 100 group. The return from an entry at the beginning of January and an exit at the end of June is a reasonable 7.50%. If a total portfolio exit is made on March 30, returns are reduced to 3.14%. An unfavorable exit on the lows in April provides a negative return of –0.75%.

It is easy to believe that we only exit in the most favorable conditions, but too often our exit is dictated by things other than the performance of the market. This is particularly true of investment portfolios used in 401K and other pension plans. A vertical exit from all stocks at a single point in time does not manage the volatility of the portfolio, nor does it lock-in returns while locking-out losses.

The second issue for Swiss Roll success is the timing of the exit in relation to dividend payment dates, because dividends provide an important addition to capital growth.

MAKING DIVIDENDS WORK

The portfolio candidates are drawn from a pool of stocks that pay dividends. The dividends provide a bonus to the earning capacity of the portfolio, but any dividend return needs to be balanced against the potential erosion in capital when the stock goes ex-dividend.

The objective is to capture the dividend and to keep the capital gains. Dividends are only a bonus if they add to capital in a continuing trend. They should never be used as compensation for the loss of capital as a trend slows or declines.

If we cannot capture the value of the dividend and retain at least an acceptable rate of capital gain, then the stock should be sold. We use the mining company Normandy Mining as an example of this problem in Figure 20.17.

This trade is managed with the long-term 30-day moving average setting the reference point for the trend. A close below this line is an exit signal. When Normandy Mining went ex-dividend, the value of the 30-day moving average was $1.01. Because we want to capture the dividend value, but also to avoid any sudden change in the trend direction, we add the dividend value to the existing stop loss. This brings the stop loss value up to $1.045, as the dividend is $0.035.

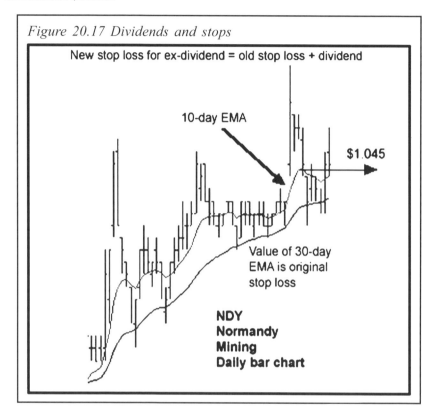

Figure 20.17 Dividends and stops

New stop loss for ex-dividend = old stop loss + dividend

10-day EMA

$1.045

Value of 30-day EMA is original stop loss

NDY
Normandy
Mining
Daily bar chart

By setting the exit at this level, we give the existing trend room to ratchet downwards by the value of the dividend and to continue in a way consistent with the previous trend. We only want to stay with the stock if it behaves in the expected theoretical fashion. Any lower price activity is inconsistent with a continuation of the trend and signals danger. A lower price eats away at our capital gain, and the dividend is not large enough to compensate for this loss.

We exit Normandy Mining on the day after the close below the new stop loss level at $1.045. It is coincidence that the new value is at the same level as the 10-day moving average. We capture the value of the dividend and protect profits. The later closes below this new trend line suggest that the bullishness of the trend was built around the dividend bonus, rather than a sound underlying trend. Closes below the new stop loss increase the probability the Normandy up trend is weakening.

With careful management we could get out of Normandy at higher prices, perhaps around $1.10. This is achieved with the benefit of hindsight. Without such hindsight, there is also a danger that we remain with Normandy as it moves steadily downward to $0.88 over the next three months.

How we decide to slice portfolio risk has a significant impact on portfolio performance. The Swiss Roll strategy combines the traders' understanding of risk with the investors' desire for capital growth and dividend yield. Managing this Swiss Roll portfolio calls for a portfolio-wide approach to equity curves and introduces an additional stop loss feature. We examine this in the next chapter.

TWENTY-ONE
SWISS CURVES

Traders and investors find it difficult to resist the temptation to count open profits. They are a measure of how well, or how poorly, we are doing. Do well, and the world knows about it. Do poorly, and few hear about it. Somewhere between euphoria and depression we slip from working out the value of the entire portfolio to calculating the value of the best-performing bits of it.

This deprives us of an important risk management tool. The value of our portfolio delivers independent signals over-riding the individual risk control strategies in any selected stock. In the last chapter, we examined how the Swiss Roll strategy is used to improve long-term trading and investment results. In Chapter 18, we included the 1999 real-time results for the Swiss Roll strategy as Fund 13. They are reprinted in Figure 21.1. Our intention was to show the importance of pursuing superior portfolio returns as measured against the market performance.

Fund 13 shows what is possible in a bull market. It starts with five stocks selected on the basis of yield and membership of the top 100 list. When some of these stocks are sold, a new stock is added from the pool of candidates. We allocated $50,000 to this portfolio and limited each trade to around $10,000. Profits were swept into a bank account and not used in new trades. A maximum of five open positions were held at any one time. This Swiss Roll portfolio was traded in real time in 1999, and tracked in our weekly newsletter.

Obtaining these results depends on two factors. The first group was discussed in the last chapter, but better stock selection and better entry and exit timing is only part of the solution. The final part of the solution comes from the way we transfer our understanding of equity curves, discussed in Chapter 5, to portfolio management. This is only possible if we always calculate the full value of our portfolio, even in bad times.

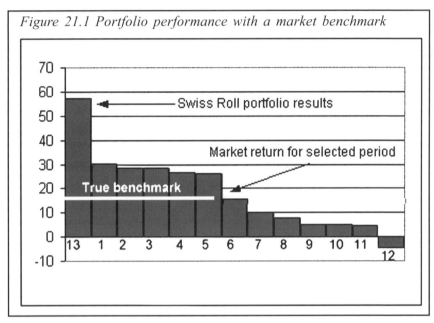

Figure 21.1 Portfolio performance with a market benchmark

Portfolio capital growth and dividend yield are calculated regularly, at least once a week. Understanding the financial status of the portfolio gives the investor a way to manage the portfolio as a whole, as well as managing individual stocks within the portfolio. There are times when decisions are required to eliminate a stock to protect the portfolio, even though no individual stock has generated an exit signal. This action protects the portfolio from the general decline in a market. It happens when many portfolio stocks have declined, dragging the portfolio value down by more than 2%. Knowing when to act depends on maintaining an accurate portfolio equity curve.

Diversity is just one aspect of protecting portfolios. The complex mathematics of modern portfolio management theory cannot conceal the true nature of this approach for small portfolios. As private investors and traders, we do not have enough cash to achieve the spread required to counter-balance the performance of individual stocks. These concepts are not scaleable in a downward direction.

We capture the benefits of diversity by selecting stocks with different levels of volatility. When this is combined with a Swiss Roll strategy, investors collect capital growth by applying the traders' risk control to make volatility work for them. Returns are boosted by taking the value of dividends. We manage the risk in the portfolio by our selection of stocks and by the application of broader financial risk management. These are based on the portfolio equity curve.

PORTFOLIO EQUITY CURVES

The portfolio equity curve tracks our total trading and investment performance on a weekly marked-to-market basis. The closing price of each stock is multiplied by the amount of stock we hold. The value of all open positions is totaled and compared to our starting capital. The calculation includes any dividends received. When we think of our portfolio, it is most likely about the same size as a single trade for a large institution. In overall market terms, our $100,000 or $500,000 or even $1 million portfolio is small. Accept this reality and we develop more appropriate ways to protect our portfolio as a unit.

By thinking of the portfolio as a single trade, or perhaps several large trades, we open the door linking risk control methods in individual trades with our portfolio performance. We are comfortable with the idea of risking no more than 2% of our trading capital in a single trade. We apply the same Profit Dollars at Risk approach to manage open profits. If we apply the same techniques to this single large trade — our portfolio — we have a means of managing our portfolio performance.

Portfolio management starts with a simple snapshot record of all trades. We take a snapshot once a week. You might choose to do this once a month or, at a stretch, once every quarter. We use the weekly snapshot because it helps to catch losses quickly, sometimes forcing an exit decision even though an individual stock has not delivered a complete exit signal. If you take this snapshot once every quarter, there is a danger that the portfolio has already slipped out of control. Half-yearly and annual reviews are suitable for lazy investors who hope that by not looking at the figures a poor performance will somehow turn into a good performance.

We show a summary of the sample Swiss Roll portfolio position in Figure 21.2. It is a snapshot taken at the end of a week.

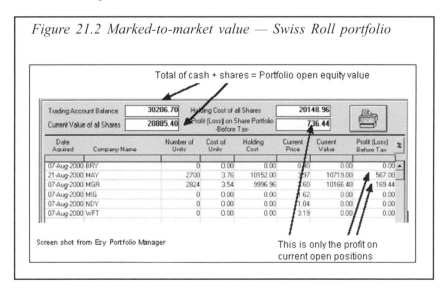

Figure 21.2 Marked-to-market value — Swiss Roll portfolio

This marked-to-market value is calculated by taking the trading account balance — cash available — and adding the current value of all stock. It includes:

- the current value of all open positions calculated using the closing price for the week;
- accumulated dividends held in the bank; and
- cash in the bank from previously closed positions.

With the open trades for MAY and MGR, the Friday close is shown on the screen display. The marked-to-market value of the portfolio is different from the portfolio-realized profit. The open profit figure is compared to the starting value of the portfolio of $50,000 and includes the value of dividends received. In an investment-style portfolio, the objective is to maintain a high level of open profits on a marked-to-market basis. The trader's equity curve makes greater use of realized profits from individual trades.

Each week this total is calculated and added to a spreadsheet. An Excel spreadsheet and chart template is available from www.guppytraders.com as part of the Better Trading spreadsheet pack.

Alternatively, we set up a synthetic stock data file. This is a blank data file suitable for MetaStock. Each week, enter the value of the Swiss Roll portfolio on the synthetic stock data file. Using your charting program, display this as a line chart just like any other stock. A simple line chart display is also constructed using the Excel charting facility embedded in the Portfolio Equity Curve spreadsheet template.

The result is a portfolio equity curve. It tells us how well, or poorly, our investment portfolio is doing. It also provides an important way to manage the risk in the total portfolio, but only if we understand the difference between our objectives as traders and as active investors. The curve in Figure 21.3 shows a snapshot of the performance of the Swiss Roll portfolio strategy in the first six months of 2000 and includes the tech wreck week. It is taken from real-time results with a total return of 17.8%. This compares favorably to the maximum 8.0% market return in the same period. It compares well with some negative fund returns for 2000.

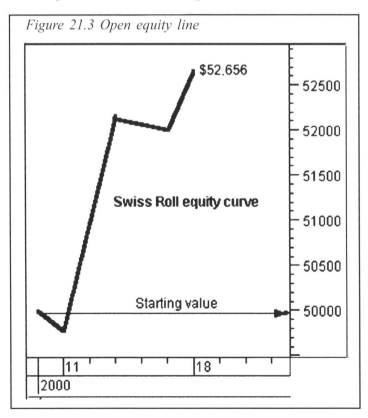

Figure 21.3 Open equity line

PORTFOLIO PROTECTION

The trader captures capital gain by closing a winning trade and adding the profits to his total of cash available for trading. From an effective Swiss Roll investment perspective, we aim to increase the portfolio value on a marked-to-market basis. We do this by cutting losers or underperforming stocks quickly and leaving the strong contributors to capital growth in place. The Swiss Roll strategy takes a horizontal cut through performance while maintaining a steady risk profile.

The objective of an individual trade is to capture profits. The objective of a group of portfolio trades is to collect profits and cut losses. The portfolio is more than just a collection of individual profits, and this is where the marked-to-market valuation becomes important. The open equity line shown in Figure 21.3 is a measure of the changing value of the portfolio, including cash waiting for allocation to new portfolio positions. Rather than reacting to individual trend changes in individual stocks, we use the open equity line to manage portfolio decisions that then translate into individual trading decisions.

The equity line moves up and down. We allow for this movement in the open equity line, but at the same time, we must decide when declines in value of the overall portfolio are unacceptable. We treat the equity line like a price chart. If the trend is up, we do nothing. If the trend starts to turn down, we brace for action. When the trend falters, we take action.

If the open value of equity — including cash on hand — drops below a defined level, it signals the need to close one or more poorly performing positions in the portfolio.

This is an extension of the protect-profit and Profit Dollars at Risk strategies discussed in Chapters 8 and 11. Here we apply it to the total value of a portfolio group. We set the trigger level for action at 2% of the current highest value of the equity line, shown in Figure 21.4.

This is how the trigger works. Each week the new portfolio value is calculated and added to the equity line. This is different from our total trading capital calculation used in Chapter 6. This calculation counts the value of open profits. We look for the most recent high point. From here, calculate the dollar value of 2% of portfolio equity. Plot this as a horizontal line on the chart. This trigger line alerts us to the need to take action to protect the portfolio. We expect the equity curve to move up and down. The trailing stop loss level puts a limit on the downside moves. Whenever a new equity high is reached, the 2% stop loss calculation is made again, and a new line plotted.

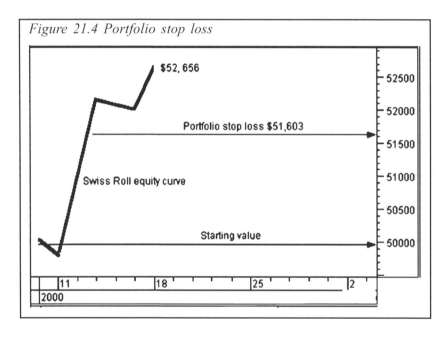

Figure 21.4 Portfolio stop loss

Some weeks the equity line drops as individual stocks take a market hit. This price stumble in an individual stock may be enough to trigger a trader's exit signal based on the Profit Dollars at Risk strategy. A price decline may trigger a trend exit based on a count back line, a trailing stop loss adjusted for dividends, or a Guppy Multiple Moving Average signal. Closing these trades is easy and consistent with our trading discipline.

Closing these trades may cause the equity line to dip below the stop loss value. This is not a problem, as the losing trade has already been closed.

The damage is limited.

If our selection of stocks based on sector and volatility diversity is successful, we expect that trading exit signals will not be grouped together. When one stock is performing poorly, we hope that diversity keeps the other stocks performing well. It is a sound risk management strategy.

MANAGING CUMULATIVE PORTFOLIO RISK

Practice is an altogether different beast from theory. There are times when many of the stocks in your portfolio are performing badly. No individual stock triggers a stop loss trade exit, but when the poor performance is combined, the impact on equity is substantial. When the marked-to-market calculations are made, it is possible for the equity value to fall below 2% of portfolio equity value. This is an early warning sign of portfolio trouble. Allowed to continue unchecked, it increases the probability of substantial portfolio loss.

A decline in portfolio value is a leading indicator of weakness in the market area you have selected. Often the general risk translates quickly into specific risk as individual losing trades signal exits in the next week. Although each individual exit is within 2% of risk, the cumulative risk of many exits exposes the portfolio to a higher level of cumulative risk.

The portfolio equity curve stop loss helps to short circuit the growth of cumulative risk in poorly performing, weak, and nervous markets. The dip below the stop loss line is our signal to examine each of the open trades. We need to identify the weakest of these open positions and sell it quickly, as shown in Figure 21.5.

This sale locks-in the capital and profits from the trade. It is a defensive measure designed to lift the portfolio equity line back above the stop loss limits. This capital is swept into a bank of reserve cash and not committed to any new trades. Most times a weak market initiates this action, and this is not a good time to add new trades. Better to preserve the capital until new trending opportunities arise.

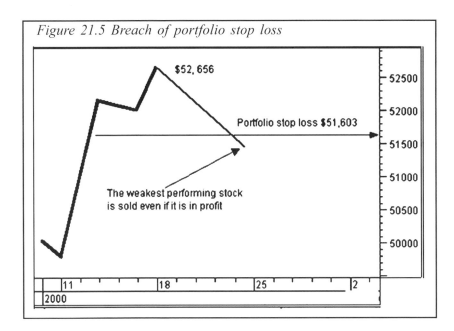

Figure 21.5 Breach of portfolio stop loss

If market weakness continues, and the next week the portfolio value falls below the equity line again, then the same defensive procedure is followed as shown in Figure 21.6, extracted from the Excel template spreadsheet display. The objective is to gradually move out of a nervous and weak market, rather than wait for cumulative risk to overwhelm the portfolio. These defensive exits free-up investment capital, collect available profits, and lower portfolio risk.

The objective in this portfolio management approach is to grow portfolio equity, and this may mean using changes in the portfolio value as an initiating signal for closing positions.

The trader turns his skill in risk management to the effective management of investment-style portfolios. This is a Swiss Roll strategy. Not all investors have the time or the ability to develop these traders' skills. Investors benefit from a greater understanding of the nature of risk in all open positions, whether they are designed as trades or longer-term investments.

We noted at the beginning of the book that this is a survey of techniques and not a definitive answer. Our intention is to show you the way we have applied money management to boost trading returns.

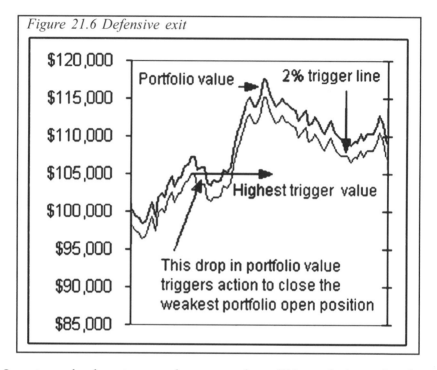

Figure 21.6 Defensive exit

Investors who do not want to become traders still have choices other than just the buy, hold, and hope strategy. This is active investing, and Alan Hull has contributed the next chapter by way of introduction to this approach. He uses different methods to reach similar objectives. He sees volatility as an undesirable feature, and this affects the way he selects stocks as investment candidates. His emphasis on the management and control of risk is consistent with the approaches already covered. We include the chapter as an example of how other traders approach and solve the same problems of risk management.

TWENTY-TWO
ACTIVE
INVESTING

Contributing author:
Alan Hull*

A ctive investing is a market approach that fills the gap between day-to-day trading and passive investing. While many "mom and pop" investors are loath to commit one to two hours per day to managing a portfolio of short-term trading positions, they are also frustrated by the ineffectiveness of fundamental analysis as a stand-alone market tactic. Active investing extends the conventional investment approach of buying and holding "quality" blue chip companies by employing testing and measuring procedures which facilitate "hands on" portfolio management. Testing and measuring also opens the door to modern risk management techniques, an area of neglect for most long-term investors.

We can break down active investing into two components: our market strategy, and ongoing portfolio management. Our market strategy is designed to shift the probability of selecting winning positions as far as possible in our favor, while our management techniques streamline execution, reduce indecision, and incorporate risk management.

---

* Alan Hull is an Australian trader and author. He developed the active investing strategy. Readers who want more detail on active investing will find information in *Active Investing — A Complete Answer,* by Alan Hull, or from www.alanhull.com. The book contains detailed information on indicator construction, including custom formulas for most popular charting programs.

DYNAMIC ANALYSIS

Our market strategy is centered on "dynamic analysis," which is a combination of fundamental and technical analysis. The diagram in Figure 22.1 illustrates the basic dynamic that drives stock prices either up or down. Factors that affect opinion generate positive or negative sentiment, which leads to rising or falling stock prices.

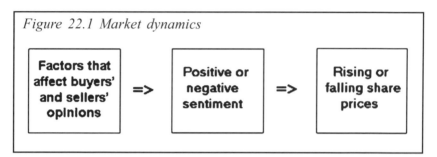

Figure 22.1 Market dynamics

| Factors that affect buyers' and sellers' opinions | => | Positive or negative sentiment | => | Rising or falling share prices |

Investors come at the market dynamic from the left-hand side of the diagram by employing fundamental analysis to find listed companies that are financially sound, and have solid management and good prospects. This market approach, although reliable, carries the caveat of time and requires patience.

The block diagram in Figure 22.2 reflects a fundamentalist's view of the market dynamic.

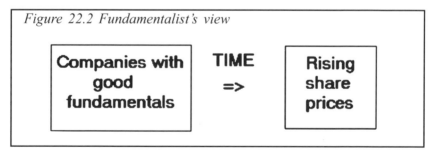

Figure 22.2 Fundamentalist's view

| Companies with good fundamentals | TIME => | Rising share prices |

Traders use technical analysis to observe price activity and buy stocks that are rising in price and sell stocks that are falling in price. Traders approach the market dynamic from the right-hand side, largely ignoring factors that affect opinion, but they are prepared to monitor price activity on a daily basis. Active investors test and measure the entire market dynamic by combining both fundamental and technical analysis. By employing "dynamic analysis," we can seek out fundamentally sound stocks that are currently rising in price, thus eliminating the "time" factor, as shown in Figure 22.3.

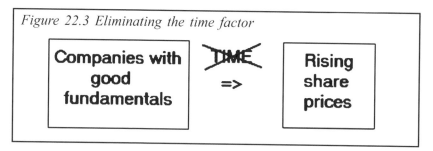

Figure 22.3 Eliminating the time factor

By testing and measuring the "flow-on" effect of good fundamentals, we can turbo charge our portfolio's performance. The block diagram in Figure 22.4 illustrates the market dynamic that we want to zero in on.

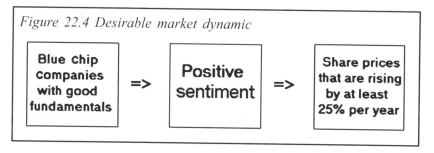

Figure 22.4 Desirable market dynamic

The benchmark of 25% per year isn't set in stone and can be adjusted to suit prevailing market conditions. If we need more candidates, we will lower our benchmark; if we are overwhelmed with possibilities in a bull market, then we will raise it. Dynamic analysis can pick the smallest opportunities out of the market in tough times and optimize portfolio performance during bull rallies. To put dynamic analysis into practice, we need to attack the market dynamic from both ends, with fundamental analysis forming the backdrop for our market search.

QUALITY STOCK

As active investors, we want to monitor our portfolio on a weekly basis and therefore we want to build a stock portfolio that is ponderous in nature and devoid of daily price volatility. Fundamentally sound, large capitalization stocks fit this bill and can be found through a variety of different sources. There are programs, books, websites, etc. that contain, in summarized form, the company research that we are after.

There are other sources, including the excellent software analysis program STOCKdoctor — www.lincolnindicators.com. This program uses fundamental criteria developed by Dr Merv Lincoln, a financial analyst, to sift out what the program refers to as Star Stocks. Screening is based on Dr. Lincoln's Ph.D. - researched methodology and uses key fundamental criteria to quickly and easily identify companies that meet our quality and financial health requirements. Star Stocks, given the financials of the underlying companies, are expected to outperform other, similar stocks. By filtering out Star Stocks that are in the top 500 companies by market capitalization, we have another list of approximately 100 possibilities. We can shop around for other products similar to these, or we can do the research ourselves if we are so inclined. At the end of the day, we should have at least 100 quality stocks to subject to further scrutiny.

RATE OF RETURN

From this pool of approximately 100 candidates we want to extract only those that have a rising stock price. To do this, we need to calculate the annual rate of return of a stock using its current stock price and its current rate of climb or fall.

To simplify this task, we can build a rate of return indicator, as shown in Figure 22.5 with the Lang Corporation chart. The MetaStock formula for this is included in Simon Sherwood's book, *MetaStock® in a Nutshell* and in the free formula pages on www.guppytraders.com.

Based on its price at the end of this period, Lang Corporation had an annual rate of return of 42%. Searches can be performed using the RoR indicator to sift out stocks that only have an annual rate of return higher than 25%. Once our search is completed, we should have narrowed down the number of possibilities to at least 30 quality stocks that are rising in price by at least 25% per annum.

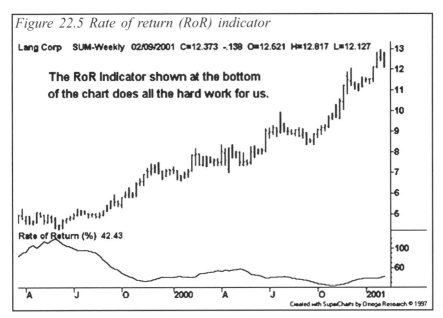

Figure 22.5 Rate of return (RoR) indicator

The final step in our search is to individually "eyeball" the weekly charts of these 30 or more stocks and seek out those that have the least amount of volatility. The stocks that pass this final test qualify to be in our portfolio and should resemble the examples in Figure 22.6. These stock prices are being driven up over the long term by good fundamentals.

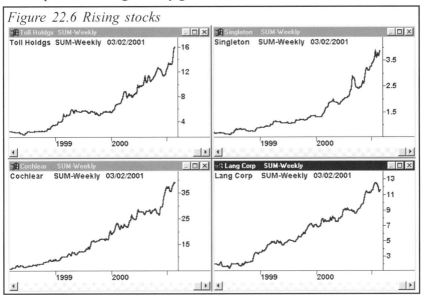

Figure 22.6 Rising stocks

As active investors, we are riding on the coattails of fundamentalists, who are sluggish and predictable in nature. Our strategy, while yielding annual portfolio returns well in excess of the broad market's performance, has all the attributes of a conventional investment approach.

RANGE INDICATOR

Once we have established our portfolio, we need to put in place a management system that will automate the task of active investing as much as possible, and enable us to quantitatively control our market risk. To avoid indecision, we need to establish an unambiguous set of rules that will govern when to buy, hold, and sell our stock. Our portfolio management needs to be simple and robust in design if it is to be decisive in execution and easy for us to implement. The solution to virtually all of our management problems can be found in a single indicator.

The range indicator provides us with a series of price ranges that tell us when to buy, sell, hold, or profit-take. Although simple in construction, it tells us when the price activity is pulling back, rallying up, or reversing. It is constructed around a line of linear regression that acts as a central cord, passing through the middle of price activity. A function called "average true range," which measures price volatility, is then used to create an envelope around the central cord. This envelope defines our tolerance toward price activity. We can reasonably expect that a quality stock being driven by its own fundamentals will stay within the boundaries of this envelope. The central cord, upper deviation, and lower deviation lines create four distinct price zones that tell us when to buy, hold, take profit, or sell.

The Aquarius Platinum chart in Figure 22.7 illustrates how the range indicator is used to set buy, hold, and sell zones.

When price trends either up or down, it moves in a sawtooth pattern and not a straight line. In an upward trend, this behavior is caused by the repetition of a rally/profit-take cycle. As long as the buying force behind the rallies is greater than the selling force behind the profit-taking, the trend will continue. Upward trends end when the buying force is exhausted, which is an inevitable occurrence. By employing the range indicator, we can identify pullbacks in price activity, trend reversals, or unacceptable levels of volatility; hence, we will know when to buy, hold, or sell.

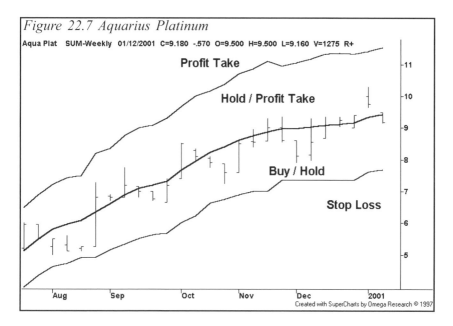

Figure 22.7 Aquarius Platinum

Aqua Plat   SUM-Weekly   01/12/2001   C=9.180 -.570 O=9.500 H=9.500 L=9.160 V=1275 R+

Profit Take

Hold / Profit Take

Buy / Hold

Stop Loss

Created with SuperCharts by Omega Research © 1997

MARKET ENTRY

Once we have found a quality stock with a good trend and an acceptable rate of return, we can fine-tune our entry. Although we want to jump on board a trend when the price is in a dip, we do not want to buy into the start of a trend reversal. We can reduce the chances of being run down by a trend reversal if we refrain from entering the market when the price activity is "gunning the stop loss." We need to wait for the direction of price activity to reverse and show evidence of buyer support. The green light is flashing after we have witnessed a rising week with a close higher than the previous week's close. When the green light is flashing, we can enter the market during the forthcoming week providing our purchase price is in the buy zone.

Occasionally we will miss opportunities because price activity has escaped back into the hold zone. This is where we must exercise discipline and be prepared to move on to the next opportunity rather than chase a running market. The chart in Figure 22.8 shows the points of entry into an upward trend in Aquarius Platinum.

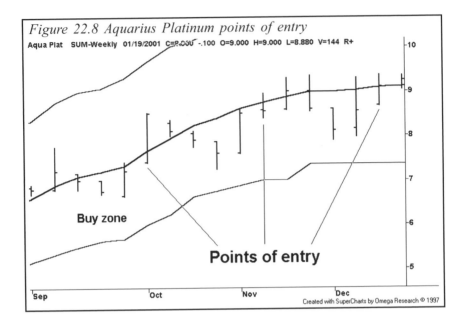

Figure 22.8 Aquarius Platinum points of entry

Aqua Plat SUM-Weekly 01/19/2001 C=9.000 -.100 O=9.000 H=9.000 L=8.880 V=144 R+

Buy zone

Points of entry

Created with SuperCharts by Omega Research © 1997

The following is a summary of our entry criteria:

- a rate of return equal to or greater than 25%;
- we have witnessed buyer support; and
- our purchase price is in the buy zone.

We will not be able to enter most of the stocks that we have selected for our portfolio immediately because they won't be in the buy zone. It is quite normal to spend several months buying into the market, catching each of our stocks as they dip down into the buy zone.

HOLDING AND TAKING A PROFIT

Market newcomers often believe that the most difficult aspect of buying and selling stocks is knowing which stocks to buy and when to buy them. But reality differs considerably from this perception, with holding and profit-taking being the most discretionary and, hence, the most difficult aspects of trading and investing. The range indicator, as shown in Figure 22.9, dictates, as much as possible, the boundaries for holding and profit-taking.

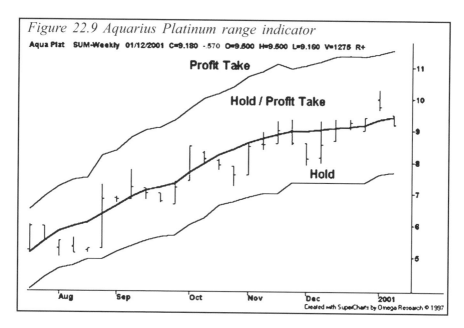

Figure 22.9 Aquarius Platinum range indicator

Active investing is a trend-following strategy and, providing price activity remains inside our envelope, there is no need to close a position. If, however, the price activity overheats and moves into the profit-take zone, then selling is highly recommended. The reason for selling when the price activity exceeds the upper line is because the next stop, on the balance of probability, is the stop loss zone. The volatility in the sawtooth action of price activity tends to build in amplitude with the passage of time and this rarely subsides. The fact that our price envelope has initially been breached to the upside is fortuitous, as we can make a timely and profitable exit.

We can also apply individual discretion when it comes to profit-taking in the upper part of the price range. While some of us will always hold, others will want to take quick profits if they are significant enough. My personal benchmark for voluntary profit-taking is "Am I up 10% per month or more on my original purchase price?" If I am in profit to the tune of at least 10% per month, then I am looking at an annualized profit of 120%. As an active investor I am aiming for a return of between 20% and 50% per annum. At 120% per annum I am well ahead of the curve and I consider it prudent to take profit at this point. A true cliché is: "You will never go broke by taking profit."

SELLING

Knowing when to sell is the most critical aspect of any market strategy, and the decision to sell must be mechanical and carried out with total discipline. The range indicator provides us with a clear and totally unambiguous stop loss condition. The chart of the Institute of Drug Technology in Figure 22.10 shows a definite break in the long-term weekly trend.

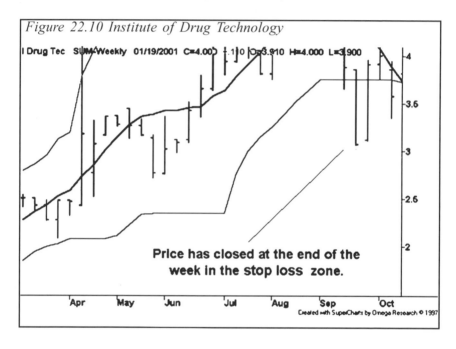

Figure 22.10 Institute of Drug Technology

I Drug Tec SUMA Weekly 01/19/2001 C=4.000 +.110 O=3.910 H=4.000 L=3.900

Price has closed at the end of the week in the stop loss zone.

Created with SuperCharts by Omega Research © 1997

Notice how the price activity bounced back up after breaching the stop loss. This "bounce back" is not uncommon and often leads market newcomers into ignoring their stop losses by rewarding their lack of discipline. However, our volatility-based stop loss is designed to tolerate normal pullbacks in price activity; if it is breached, then price activity is no longer behaving as we would expect it to. What's more, quantitative risk management is totally reliant on stop loss execution. If the trend does recover, then we can always wait for a re-entry signal and re-join the market. The following rules are set in stone:

• If price closes at the end of the week in the stop loss zone, then close the position.

• If the rate of return falls below 25% per annum, then close the position.

The rate of return indicator also provides us with an exit condition if it falls below 25%. By selling stocks that fall below this rate of return, we will ensure that our money is always hard at work. The range indicator is designed to work in harmony with the natural forces that drive stock price movements. It integrates several functions into the one indicator, reducing complexity and also the time it will take us to manage our open positions. Furthermore, we can employ range indicator values to perform our risk management calculations.

MANAGING RISK

The basic building block of any quantitative risk management strategy is position risk. As active investors, we have the advantage of having the range indicator, which gives us a predetermined stop loss price, for performing our position risk calculations. Using Figure 22.11, we will do the calculations using actual figures from the range indicator.

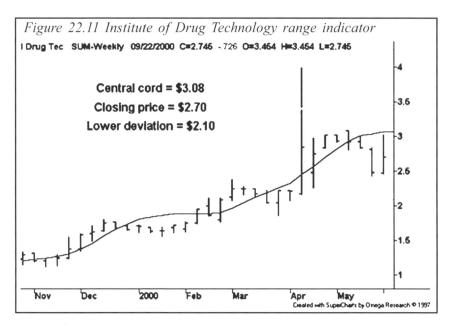

Figure 22.11 Institute of Drug Technology range indicator

I Drug Tec SUM-Weekly 09/22/2000 C=2.745 -.726 O=3.454 H=3.454 L=2.745

Central cord = $3.08

Closing price = $2.70

Lower deviation = $2.10

Created with SuperChart by Omega Research © 1997

Looking at the right-hand edge of the chart, we can see that the price activity has fallen into the buy zone and then closed up for one week, indicating the presence of buyer support. The green light is flashing for an entry and it is time to do our risk management. However, there are a couple of disadvantages with using the closing price as our entry price in the calculations.

The first problem is that the stock price could move higher when the market opens on Monday morning. We would then be forced to re-do our risk management calculations during the trading day. The second problem is that we have not allowed for our brokerage fees. So a quick and easy solution to both of these problems is to use the value of the central cord, rather than the closing price, for doing our sums. Using the central cord will always yield a more conservative result than the closing price, providing we always enter the market in the buy zone.

APPLYING THE 2% RISK RULE

If we have $50,000 total capital and we are using the 2% risk rule, this is how we would calculate our position size:

1. The central cord price is $3.08 and the lower deviation price is $2.10.

2. The potential loss per share is: $3.08 – $2.10 = $0.98.

3. 2% of $50,000 = $1,000, which is the amount of money we are prepared to lose.

4. Divide $1,000 by $0.98 to get the amount of stock we can buy — 1,020 shares.

5. Multiply 1,020 by the closing price of $2.70 to get the position size — $2,754.

On Monday morning I will ring my stockbroker and issue my instructions: "I want to purchase $2,750 worth of IDT and I will pay up to $3.08 per share." It is his job to work out the number of shares that need to be purchased and my job to monitor the stop loss on a weekly basis. In fact, monitoring my stop losses on a weekly basis is about the only task I have to perform once my portfolio is established. Shopping for new opportunities is only necessary when I am stopped out of the market or I have elected to take profit by closing one of my open positions.

DIVERSIFICATION

Portfolio risk is the sum total of our position risk and it is calculated by multiplying the number of positions we own by the position risk rule we are using. If we are using the 2% risk rule and we have seven different stocks in our portfolio, our portfolio risk is: 2% x 7 = 14%.

In a catastrophic event such as a stock market crash, our total exposure, based on the above example, is 14% of total capital. To limit our portfolio risk, we must minimize the total number of stocks that we own. What's more, a large number of positions not only means greater portfolio risk, but will also lead to a reduction in our portfolio's overall performance. This is because there are only a limited number of stocks that offer high rates of return. If we diversify our portfolio unnecessarily, then we will be doing ourselves more harm than good.

Looking at the rate of return pyramid in Figure 22.12, we can see that there are only a small number of stocks that give the highest possible rate of return. If I only own five stocks, then I can optimize the average performance of my portfolio by having most, if not all, of my holdings near the top of the pyramid.

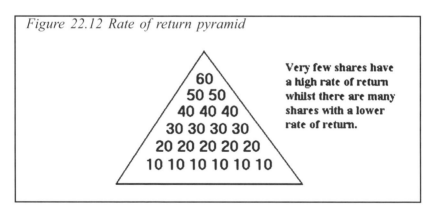

Figure 22.12 Rate of return pyramid

60
50 50
40 40 40
30 30 30 30
20 20 20 20 20
10 10 10 10 10 10

Very few shares have a high rate of return whilst there are many shares with a lower rate of return.

If we arbitrarily set the minimum number of positions that we own to 15, then we will be forced to accept a lower average rate of return from our portfolio. Under the 2% risk rule, the minimum portfolio risk, based on 15 positions, is 15 multiplied by 2%, which equals 30%. We would be better off owning just five stocks with an average rate of return of 40% to 50%

and a total portfolio risk of 10%, than 15 stocks with an average rate of return of 30% and a portfolio risk of 30%. Diversification is an unmanageable and "gooey" form of portfolio management. It is, in fact, the result of risk management.

Active investing can be viewed as a business model where the primary objective is "maximum return for minimum effort." Better business is about focusing on the business strategy and management techniques, not on the underlying product or service. Better trading is about focusing on the market strategy and management techniques we employ, not on the stocks we own.

TWENTY-THREE
NO SWEAT

Clichés develop because they encapsulate a relevant and pertinent point. They are slogans to remind people of deeper and more complex problems. They slip into common usage, and are quickly devalued. At best, the cliché provides a short-cut to exploring a solution.

How often have you stifled a groan when you heard the term "a level playing field"? Don't you just itch to tip the field to one side so that at least you can get a small advantage? When Trader Novice enters the market, he believes that skill will tip the playing field. This is real and necessary sweat work. It forms the foundation of all trading survival. Skill counts, but not as much as we hope.

The market provides a wide playing field. Anyone can participate. No teams are required, and the entry price starts at around $2,000. Spectators are encouraged to become players, partly because they provide the fuel necessary for the markets to continue. Some spectators continue to become successful traders, but they do this without tilting the playing field. It is the first step toward success.

Trader Success uses more than just the raw understanding and mastery of the technical and theoretical tools of trading. He combines this with an appreciation of how they reveal the balance of probability to highlight those results that are more likely than others. This gives him a trading edge. Even this is not enough to tilt the financial playing field in his direction.

Despite our best efforts, the playing field usually remains doggedly level.

Tipping the playing field is a wrong answer, because the question triggered by the cliché is wrong. It distracts us from the real basis of trading success.

There have been points in market development where the professionals seem to succeed in tilting the market field very much toward them. The clubbish atmosphere of the market, with its secret network of gentlemen's clubs with rules and insider conventions, that prevailed for much of the last century certainly ensured that the playing field was tipped toward the professionals.

The balance was altered in the 1960s. Ironically, the threat came from within the profession. Those with long memories may remember the "quants," or quantitative analysts, who harnessed the power of the computer to trawl through oceans of financial analysis. It gave them an edge, and shook up the closed information, "old boy" networks of the stockbroker clubs.

Eventually computers trickled down to our desktops at work, and then into our homes. This cheap computational power decisively tilted the playing field back to level. Try as we may, it is unlikely that we will successfully tilt the playing field decisively or consistently in our favor. At best, we aim to reduce the time lag between the development of new analytical processes and the time it takes for them to appear on our desktops as part of an affordable software package. The playing field is most likely to see-saw slightly, handing a permanent advantage to no single group.

However, the market playing field is now irrevocably as much ours — the private traders — as it is theirs — the professional financial and broking industry. We all feed off the same financial products. The predatory nature of market risk, the potential for financial injury, and the rules of the trading game are played on a relatively level playing field.

So, who wins and how?

If the playing field is level, what makes the star? In a modern team game, one player has the leadership skills and the inspirational ability to build on his skills and take a team to victory.

Unfortunately, the private trader does not work in a team. We play on the level playing field among much larger and more experienced teams. Having the skills is enough to gain admission into the arena, but it is not enough to ensure survival. Our competitors are tough, experienced, and have their eyes firmly focused on the object of the game.

It is money management that elevates us to star status. It is the penultimate decision before a trade is actually executed that decides how successful we will be. Before we reach into our bank account and electronically slap down the cash to buy a parcel of stock, we make a decision about how much we will spend.

Make one type of decision, and the small victories garnered from the financial markets are multiplied. Make another type of decision, and our small successes remain small in terms of reward.

Attaining the same level of skill does not mean that we have the same results. Trader Success and Trader Average use exactly the same toolkit, and their selected tools may be exactly the same. It is possible for Trader Average to reasonably aspire to develop the skills used by Trader Success. The difference in the knowledge about how charting, technical analysis, and fundamental analysis are applied to analyze a trade or an opportunity is not the gulf that it appears when Trader Novice first enters the trading game.

The difference in results comes most consistently from our understanding and application of money management techniques. They boost our returns. They leverage our skills irrespective of any slope on the playing field. We cannot reasonably expect to tilt the playing field. We cannot reasonably expect to play with large financial teams, and many private traders do not aspire to this. We can reasonably expect to be more than moderately successful.

We do not need to tilt the playing field. If we accept that it will remain level, then we find the solution to success in another modern cliché. We all know that we are supposed to work smarter, rather than harder. In most circumstances, this is easier said than done.

In the financial markets, we turn this cliché into reality by understanding and applying money management.

It is a no-sweat solution.

INDEX

R

S

DISCOUNT COUPON – TRADING WORKSHOPS

10% off the regular seminar fee – single and group rates
(These workshops are held in Asia, the USA and the UK.)

Trading looks easy, but it takes skill. How best to approach your market and survive is a skill that can be learned, and improved. Trading success means knowing how to GET IN by identifying a trade. It means knowing how to manage the trade so you GET OUT with an overall profit.

You can become a better trader by attending a half-day or full-day workshop because Daryl Guppy will teach you how to understand the market from a private trader's perspective, how to use those advantages, and how to manage a trade to lock in capital profits.

All traders – those considering entering the market and those who want to improve their trading – can benefit from these workshops.

Nobody can give you the ultimate trading secret, but Daryl Guppy will show you, using local examples selected by the audience on the day, how a private trader identifies and manages a trade. You will enter the market better informed than your competitors.

Daryl Guppy holds regular trading workshops. Dates and details are posted on *www.guppytraders.com* eight weeks before each workshop.

How to claim your workshop discount
When you book your seminar, mention that you own *Better Stock Trading* and get 10% off the advertised fee. Bring this book with you to confirm your discount. It can be autographed for you if you wish.

Some comments from workshop participants
The workshop covered all the essential building blocks of the trade better and more effectively than any book that I have come across.
                                                    – Equity analyst, Hong Kong.

In my seven years attending continuing education programs I have never found a session as useful and interesting as the one which you have conducted.
                                                    – Remisier, Singapore.

On the subject of the seminar, I must say that it was an inspiring night. Daryl was energetic, spontaneous and his comments were thought-provoking. Additionally, he was very generous with his time, staying back after the official closing time to discuss specific issues with us. I've not been to a trading seminar before where the examples used during the evening were drawn from the audience (not pre-planned).
                                                    – Stock and derivatives trader, Australia.